D0122903

INFILTRATED

INFILTRATED

How to Stop the Insiders and Activists
Who Are Exploiting the Financial Crisis
to Control Our Lives and Our Fortunes

JAY W. RICHARDS

New York   Chicago   San Francisco
Athens   London   Madrid
Mexico City   Milan   New Delhi
Singapore   Sydney   Toronto

1 2 3 4 5 6 7 8 9 0   DOC/DOC   1 9 8 7 6 5 4 3

ISBN   978-0-07-181695-3
MHID   0-07-181695-X

e-ISBN   978-0-07-181696-0
e-MHID   0-07-181696-8

McGraw-Hill Education books are available at special quantity discounts to use as premiums and sales promotions or for use in corporate training programs. To contact a representative, please visit the Contact Us pages at www.mhprofessional.com.

This book is printed on acid-free paper.

To my parents, Rusty Richards and Jo Richards

CONTENTS

INFILTRATED

THE ROAD
OF GOOD
INTENTIONS

Even if you haven't been paying close attention for the last five years, you know that the 2008 financial crisis led to the worst recession since the Great Depression, swelled the ranks of the unemployed, and saw multibillion-dollar companies disappear overnight and millions of people either lose their homes or walk away from their mortgage contracts. You likely have heard that the meltdown nearly crippled banks and other financial industries worldwide. You also hope that the new regulatory bodies and governmental bureaus created under the Dodd-Frank Wall Street Reform and Consumer Protection Act will help prevent a recurrence.

What actually caused the meltdown? This has been the subject of much speculation. We've all been told that it was largely the fault of greedy Wall Street bankers who got rich while impoverishing ordinary people and leaving the economy in a shambles. From the earliest days of the crisis, this was the seemingly unanimous conclusion of the media and commentators, and it stuck. But even the 10 members of the official government commission formed to study the crisis couldn't agree on its causes. How likely is it then that the politicians in Congress at the time of the crisis, or reporters for *Time*, *Newsweek*, and CNN, truly understood it? And if they did not understand it, how likely is it that the politicians' and reporters' favored remedies will actually cure the disease?

If you've studied the crisis beyond the first-blush impressions, you may be aware that a myriad of issues play a role in this story. But you probably don't know the intriguing details of how Washington insiders, joined by activists and philanthropists in the private sector, laid the foundation for the crisis that broke into full public view in the autumn of 2008. Or that they did so through a cluster of political efforts and policy decisions originally designed to help the poor and disenfranchised. Those policies ultimately had the curious effect not only of hurting the poor but also of lowering many middle-class Americans into the ranks of the poor—while further empowering both the special interest groups who pushed for the policies and the political class who enacted them.

Even less well known, and perhaps even more important to understand, is that many of the same insiders and activists responsible for creating the financial crisis are now claiming to have the solution—and using the crisis to infiltrate and seize control of large swaths of the American economy. To do so, they are using the apparatus of reform to make permanent the very causes of the meltdown. Aspects of this story have leaked out in dribs and drabs, but many important and disturbing elements of this tale are revealed here for the first time. Understanding them is the first step in recognizing what we can do to prevent a far more serious financial and political disaster.

BEING THERE

How I came to tell this story requires a little autobiographical background, since it's not obvious why a philosopher with an interest in economics would write about the financial industry. You see, I recognize many of the insiders, activists, and philanthropists I discuss in these pages because I thought just like them not so long ago. If you were to travel back to 1985, to a small liberal arts college near Austin, Texas, you'd find there an enthusiastic freshman listening with rapt attention to all the standard arguments against capitalism. The college was welcoming and stately, its buildings constructed with a white stone indigenous to South Texas. The school was in the process of shedding its religious roots in favor of a social gospel similar in origin, if not in presentation, to that of the Reverend Jeremiah Wright, President Obama's longtime pastor in Chicago. It was a liberal setting, encouraging political activism and appealing to bright young minds eager to absorb enough knowledge and wisdom to change the world.

During my freshman year, my political science professor assigned *The Communist Manifesto*, by Karl Marx and Friedrich Engels, along with a book by American socialist Michael Parenti called *Democracy for the Few*. I read voraciously, and it wasn't long until I was convinced that if I cared about the poor, if I cared about justice, I needed to oppose capitalism and to champion aggressive wealth redistribution schemes. I adopted these ideas in a scholastic setting imbued with Protestant Liberalism, with a belief that human beings, using their own intellects and abilities, can perfect themselves and society. In this atmosphere, I found it easy to soften the violent and atheistic edges of Marxist philosophy and repackage it in a more idealistic form that I imagined would elevate the poor.

Fortunately, I may have been an enthusiast for leftist sentiment, but I also identified with that older liberal aspiration to ponder seriously the arguments on all sides of an issue. So I read widely, often beyond my class assignments. I was lucky to have a textbook by economist Thomas Sowell assigned for a course on Marxism. Sowell's book was clear, descriptive, and neutral as far as I could tell, so I looked around for other books he had written. As it happens, elsewhere he made compelling arguments in favor of free markets and against what he called the "unconstrained vision" of socialism. In reading Sowell, I stumbled onto the conservative magazine *National Review*, and, like so many who've traveled the same intellectual journey, I eventually read *The Road to Serfdom*, by the great Austrian defender of the free economy, Friedrich Hayek. It took a few years, but slowly my views on economics changed. Eventually, they flipped 180 degrees.

I still thought of myself as a liberal, because I thought the word meant that you cared about the poor and the disadvantaged. That hadn't changed. I cared deeply—and still do. But I became aware that not just socialism but many of the liberal policies designed to help the poor really do the opposite. The rhetoric doesn't match the reality. By my senior year I had abandoned my youthful fascination with socialism and wealth redistribution and moved into a broader understanding of a free market economy. While not a utopia, a free economy was far better than the alternatives at doing what a healthy economy should do—distributing goods and services, allowing wealth to be created and poverty reduced, and freeing people to pursue their interests and develop their talents.

I came to see that a free market economy wasn't just a little better than the alternatives or an interesting philosophy to debate in graduate classes. It was really the only system that, historically, had allowed entire cultures—not just an elite few—to emerge from extreme poverty. It was the only approach that had actually worked to achieve, at least in some places, this lofty goal for humanity.

Once I saw it, I had trouble remembering how I had ever missed something so obvious. The evidence was in plain sight—South Korea versus North Korea, the United States versus the Soviet Union, Hong Kong versus Mainland China. Digging deeper, I found that the evidence went well beyond these comparisons and anecdotes and casual observations.

A compelling correlation exists between prosperity and economic freedom: the freer a country is economically, the more prosperous the average citizen in that country tends to be. Other variables are in play, of course, but the correlation is strong, broad, and persistent across regions and cultures. In free countries, even the poor tend to be better off than the middle class, such as there is, in closed economies. In the 2012 Index of Economic Freedom, vibrant and prosperous Hong Kong ranks first, and poor Stalinist

North Korea last.¹ Those two facts reveal a lot of economic truth, but there's more—much more.

There was another important distinction I had previously over-looked: when big business colludes with government to gain spe-cial favors and tilt the playing field away from entrepreneurs and competition, that isn't a free market but rather a subversion of it. Free markets and the interests of big business aren't the same thing. Moreover, I realized, it was when governments most manipulated markets that the problem of cronyism and collusion seemed to spread most aggressively. Cronyism is the antithesis of true, free market capitalism.

Still, I was bothered by a contradiction that became acute during my senior year. That year I took the ideal liberal arts course—a political science "capstone seminar" that started with Plato and Aristotle and dipped into Cicero, Machiavelli, Locke, de Tocqueville, Mill, Marx, and the American Founders. Besides these assigned readings, our professor let the students vote on a final author. A majority picked Ayn Rand. So, improbably, we read a collection of her essays. I went on to read *Atlas Shrugged*, a book that, despite its deficiencies, helped reveal more flaws in my earlier socialist point of view.

Rand immigrated to the United States from Russia in 1925. She despised the communism she experienced in her youth—with its poverty, despair, and misguided attempts to create perfect equal-ity—and her antipathy found its way into her writings. Early on, she worked as a scriptwriter in Hollywood. She was a moderately successful novelist, but it was *Atlas Shrugged*, published in 1957, that made her a national figure.

In her novels, Rand developed characters who expressed her philosophy "of man as a heroic being, with his own happiness as the moral purpose of his life, with productive achievement as his noblest activity, and reason as his only absolute."²

Unfortunately, her work fueled my worry that capitalism was, if not evil, then morally unsavory. As expressed in another Rand book title, *The Virtue of Selfishness*, she was a vicious critic of what she called altruism. "Capitalism and altruism are incompatible," she wrote. They "cannot coexist in the same man or in the same society."[3] Her vision of the entrepreneur as a heroic being was attractive, but the fact that this creature was utterly self-regarding was not only unattractive, it was disturbing.

She defined words like *selfishness* and *altruism* idiosyncratically, so what she meant did not necessarily carry the stark connotation that her words may have implied. Still, her defense of capitalism seemed to contradict what every decent mother teaches her children: Don't be selfish. Share. Treat others kindly. Help those who can't help themselves. As a result of Rand, for a couple of years, I thought that capitalism worked on an economic level but was nevertheless morally questionable.

Eventually, however, I came across two thinkers, George Gilder and Michael Novak, who both challenged Rand's account. Gilder argued that great entrepreneurs are altruistic, not in the sense that they visualize world peace, but because in a lawful free market they act imaginatively in response to the needs and wants of others. In a free market, great entrepreneurs serve the common good. They are, as Novak puts it, "other regarding." (Altruism comes from the Latin word *alter*, which means "other.")

Great entrepreneurs put their wealth at risk in pursuit of a vision to provide something that others will want. They may find a way to build a better mousetrap or to mass-produce cars so ordinary people can afford them, as Henry Ford did. Or they may imagine something before it even exists, such as a smartphone in 1995, that people would want if it were available. In that case, the entrepreneur doesn't just meet a market need. He or she creates a new market and hires the workers to produce its goods. Free economies are best at channeling the creative risk taking of entrepreneurs for the long-range benefit of everyone. Rand was right to lionize entrepreneurs. But she missed the subtleties of their virtues and their actions and of the system that best allows them to prosper.

Soon after my discovery of these thinkers, the Soviet Union collapsed, the Berlin Wall came down, and even the Democratic nominee for president, Bill Clinton, strongly defended free markets. Communism lost. Capitalism won. End of story.

Or so I thought. In the decade that followed, I found myself speaking on college campuses around the country, and I discovered to my dismay that the socialist story hadn't died the respectable death I'd imagined. All the confused economic ideas I had entertained in the 1980s were alive and well in the minds of a great many American college students. (This probably reflects the fact that, according to a 2006 study, college professors are far more skeptical of capitalism than are ordinary Americans.[4]) At first, I thought academia was in an intellectual bubble, an alternate universe where the failed socialist experiments of Europe and Asia had simply never happened. How else could they have missed the landmark events and living history lessons that marked our era? The more I looked, however, the more I realized that the bubble enveloped much more than college campuses; it covered the culture as a whole. We had celebrated with joyful tears the collapse of a flawed system but somehow had missed its all-important lesson.

The experience was so unnerving that I felt compelled to help mount a moral defense of free enterprise. Clearly, all the evidence and arguments I knew in its favor were not finding their way to ordinary Americans. I eventually distilled what I had learned into a book written for people who have never studied economics and don't much care to. I delivered the manuscript for that book, called *Money, Greed, and God: Why Capitalism Is the Solution and Not the Problem*, to the publisher on December 31, 2007.[5]

The book was what publishers call "evergreen." It didn't address a current event so much as answer philosophical questions that thoughtful people have asked for decades. Because of this, my publisher decided to wait to publish until after the 2008 presidential election so that it wouldn't get lost in the hullabaloo of books about secret love children, Vietnam, and missing birth certificates. It turned out to be the right choice, but the result was that *Money, Greed, and God*, an unapologetic defense of capitalism, landed in bookstores smack-dab in the middle of the worst financial crisis since the Great Depression. All the stock arguments against capitalism from the 1980s, and all the usual villains—greed, bank CEOs, and free enterprise—were being dusted off, spruced up, and put back into circulation.

To avoid embarrassing myself in interviews, I read every book and article about the financial crisis that I could get my hands on. I soon realized that many of the details—especially involving the culprits and causes—were not only complicated but pointed to a narrative quite different from the story that was already becoming settled opinion in the media and elsewhere. In fact, there seemed to be an orchestrated effort to covertly shift attention from the real causes.

Soon I found myself in radio and television interviews being challenged to defend my book and the free economy against arguments that consisted largely of variations of two phrases: "unfettered capitalism" and "greedy Wall Street bankers." I pointed out that the first term trades on a common confusion between the rule of law and the law of the jungle, and the second on the perennial prejudice against bankers. Greed, I noted, exists in every time and place. Were we really to believe that Wall Street bankers suddenly got greedier in the few years before 2008 and for some reason concentrated their greed in the markets for houses and mortgage-backed securities?

As I explored these issues, however, I discovered an altogether different story—a story that began long before the financial crisis and reaches far beyond it. It is the saga of a movement devoted to a fundamental transformation of the U.S. economy much like the transformation I myself once credulously sought as a young student at a small Texas college. This book reveals that story.

CHAPTER 1

THE EDGE OF
THE ECONOMY

In April of 2005, Jim and Annie Everhardt,* a couple in their midthirties with three kids, moved the almost 5,000 miles from Hawaii to North Carolina. A career marine, Jim was between tours of duty in Afghanistan and had been posted to Camp Lejeune in Jacksonville, North Carolina. The family had barely stepped down from the moving van when the vehicle suddenly caught fire and blew up in their driveway. It happened so fast, they could only stand and watch as everything they owned was consumed by flames.

In their extremity, they appealed to the military relief agency responsible for emergency loans. There, they learned that this wasn't actually an emergency since insurance would (eventually) cover the loss. The relief agent encouraged the Everhardts instead to apply for an installment loan, which a borrower repays in a fixed number of payments over a specific period of time. The military had long sanctioned these small loans for its members, not only for emergency stopgaps but also as a way to build good credit.[1]

Because they moved often to new military assignments, the Everhardts had been turned down previously for loans from ordi-

---

* I have changed their names to protect their identities.

nary banks. But in this case the installment lender took the time to gather all the information about their specific situation and determined that they were not a serious credit risk. With the loan approved and money in hand, the Everhardts were able to move into their new home. While they were waiting for the insurance money, they could quickly purchase furniture, clothes, and school-books for the kids.

Because of the fire, the Everhardts had suddenly been pushed perilously close to the edge of the economy. This is the critical border area between organized economic life and the streets. Experienced by millions of Americans every year, it is the transitional region between home and homelessness, between solvency and destitution, between work and welfare, between stable family relations and family break-down, and between children raised at home and children assigned to the often cold comforts of family court and foster care.

Though the welfare system can be bountiful for its qualified beneficiaries and long-term dependents (mostly unmarried and unemployed), its slow bureaucratic processes make it inept at deal-ing with sudden exigencies and crises of independent workers and families. With its mazes of rules, forms, and investigatory routines, government services simply cannot deal quickly with intact families facing a fire, flood, sickness, or other emergency.

For the Everhardts, welfare or even military relief was not an appropriate option. They did not want or need long-term support; Jim had a good job. They wanted emergency money, and they got it quickly and easily from a private installment lender. This type of loan is often the best form of credit available for those who need cash quickly and have maxed out credit cards or prefer not to use them.

Outside of North Carolina, a nonmilitary family in need of quick cash might have acquired the needed funds from a so-called payday lender at one of the neon-signed corner stores offer-ing advance funds in exchange for a fee and a postdated check. These short-term loans, totaling some $40 billion a year in the United States as of 2012, have proved a valuable backstop for mil-lions of families stricken by emergencies. A University of Chicago researcher, Adair Morse, conducted an elaborate statistical study of the payday loan phenomenon in California, which provided a kind of "natural experiment" of the effects of the availability versus the unavailability of emergency finance. California is a state with hundreds of mudslides, wildfires, and other natural disruptions. Morse found that different zip codes in the state showed drastic differences in the availability of payday loans. Comparing the incidence of death rates, drug and alcohol treatments, foreclosures, and petty larcenies in areas with and without these financial services—and correcting for an array of social indexes—she managed to separate the impact of loan availability from other factors that might differentiate the communities. She concluded that by all four measures the payday loans conferred significant benefits on their communities. For example, she notes that "natural disasters induce an increase in foreclosures by 72 percent, but the existence of payday lenders significantly offsets half of this increase, [preventing] 1.22 foreclosures per 1,000 homes." She found that natural disasters increase petty larcenies—such as shoplifting—by 13 percent. "Access to credit, however, mitigates 2.67 larcenies per 1,000 households, or 30 percent of the effect of the natural disaster."

Pointing out that roughly two-thirds of all payday loans are taken in emergencies, she wrote that her findings about communities could be extended to apply to individuals who experience a disaster in their personal lives, such as the Everhardts. While financial institutions other than payday lenders were beneficial to communities, she determined that banks and other institutional forms of credit were no substitute for payday loan products. Other established financial institutions failed to supply finance to individuals in distress as swiftly and reliably as payday lenders did.

Nonetheless, in 2006, payday loans were effectively banned in North Carolina after a "consumer advocate" group had led a series of campaigns to outlaw them for alleged usury (excessive interest rates) and allegedly preying on the poor. Fortunately for families like the Everhardts, small-dollar installment lenders had survived. Installment lenders had been in the state for decades, meeting qualified customers' need for small-dollar loans. With the Everhardts they had two more happy customers.

These small-dollar lending institutions, pejoratively labeled by some as "fringe finance," give loans to many middle-income people in all sorts of circumstances across the United States, but one of their most valuable contributions is to serve people in crises for whom bank loans are not an option. They are also an important stopgap to help keep some families from a life on welfare and the nightmare of family breakdown and dependency. Nimble specialists in "edge" loans, small-dollar lenders often shore up precarious families in trouble. They came through for the Everhardts. With the money from their installment loan, the family managed to make it through their bad stretch and within a short time had paid off the loan. They moved back several giant steps from the edge of the economy where financial catastrophe is a constant danger. Potential nightmare averted. This was a classic use of a traditional installment loan—to protect the household budget and a family's lifestyle while dealing with life's uncertainties.

But it turned out that the Everhardts' ordeal was not over. They would later find themselves in the crossfire of a national struggle over U.S. financial policy.

THE "FORBIDDEN" *SATURDAY NIGHT LIVE* BAILOUT PRESS CONFERENCE

More than three years passed. During this span, much of the nation's financial system plunged over the edge, and thousands of people needed emergency loans to carry them through the crisis. On October 3, 2008, the $700 million bank bailout called the Troubled Asset Relief Program (TARP) became law, and Wells Fargo bought North Carolina's leading bank, Wachovia, for pennies on the dollar. The next evening, *Saturday Night Live* ran a sketch titled "Bailout Press Conference." It not only offered a drastically different perspective on edge finance, but it also provoked responses that would play a part in a later bizarre turn in the Everhardt saga.

Taking over the "press conference" from George W. Bush in the *Saturday Night Live* skit, the Speaker of the House, Nancy Pelosi (played by comedienne Kristin Wiig), intones: "Behind every home foreclosure, there is a story of real suffering by real Americans. And, today, we'd like to introduce you to some of them." First up are a pair of rotund twenty-somethings. The white one ("Michael McCune, deadbeat" says the C-SPAN caption) explains his situation as the black one (whom the caption more cautiously identifies as "Jerome Gant, non-credit-worthy person") chimes in. "I still don't understand how this happened. I mean, I've got all the requirements for a subprime mortgage: no credit history (Gant: "Same here!"), no job ("Me, neither!"), minor criminal record ("Dit-to!"), dishonorable discharge from the army (Gant slaps his palm with a piece of paper: "Yeah, I got mine right here!"), drug problems ("Me, too!"), alcohol problems ("Guilty as charged!"), gambling addiction! ("Yeah!"), pregnant girlfriend—actually, *two* pregnant girlfriends! ("Just the one!" says Gant jovially.)

"You could say I'm a double victim, since I've never had a job, and now I don't have a home!" concludes McCune.

"Well, I'm a triple victim," chuckles Gant, "'cause I've also been charged with arson, for allegedly setting fire to the house they evicted me from."

Nancy Pelosi manages to interject, "You are both in our thoughts," as she brings the next pair to the microphone, a slim couple in their midthirties (the wife played by guest actress Anne Hathaway). As the screen identifies them as "Greg & Judy Phillips, Acquisitive Yuppies," they explain that they can't make their mortgage payment on their 12 timeshare condos "without selling the boat . . . or putting off essential cosmetic surgery."

The sketch, as it appeared on the NBC website in the first week in October, ends with Pelosi and Barney Frank (then the House Financial Services Committee leader) fawning over George Soros— "Multi-Billionaire Hedge Fund Manager and Owner, Democratic Party." Meanwhile, Soros bosses George W. Bush around in a measured, sonorous voice: "So, what became of that $700 billion?

Well, basically, it belongs to *me* now. And it's not even American dollars anymore, but Swiss francs, since I have taken a short position against the dollar."

As the show originally ran on October 4, 2008, however, another couple came to the microphone before "Soros": a business-suited husband with wire-rimmed glasses and gray hair, with his well-made-up wife dressed in a prim cardigan. Nancy Pelosi asks for their story.

> HERBERT SANDLER: My wife and I had a company which aggressively marketed subprime mortgages, and then bundled them as securities to sell to banks such as Wachovia. Today, our portfolio's worth almost nothing, though, at one point, it was worth close to $19 billion.

> NANCY PELOSI: My God, I am so sorry! Were you able to sell it for anything?

> HERBERT SANDLER: Yes! For $24 billion!

> [The C-SPAN caption pops up: "Herbert & Marion Sandler, People who should be shot."]

> NANCY PELOSI: I see. So, in that sense . . . you're not here to speak as actual victims?

> HERBERT SANDLER [chuckles]: No, no, no! That would be Wachovia Bank!

The Sandlers, as it turns out, are real people, who really did sell their company, with its time-bomb-like loans, to Wachovia at the height of the bubble. And—unlike the politicians or George Soros—they were litigiously hypersensitive to the confrontational clowning of *Saturday Night Live*. (The next year they would fight the *New York Times* tooth and nail over an article initially titled "Once Trusted Mortgage Pioneers, Now Pariahs.")

By Monday, NBC had pulled the "Bailout Press Conference" from its website, explaining that "upon review, we caught certain elements in the sketch that didn't meet our standards. We took it down and made some minor changes."[2] After *SNL* edited the skit to NBC's austere standards—which simply meant removing the Sandlers— they reposted the video. Later it disappeared into the digital abyss, along with the comments complaining that it had been yanked.

Before the Sandlers sold their company to Wachovia, and long before they achieved *SNL* stardom, they began their careers as philanthropists. One of the causes closest to their hearts was a nonprofit they had conceived and helped found in 2002. This organization forms a fascinating thread between activists agitating against small-dollar and mortgage lenders and the politicians at the heart of the postcrisis government financial regulatory apparatus.

Called the Center for Responsible Lending (CRL), this organization was a spearhead of the forces mobilizing to transform the U.S. financial system, root and branch, in the wake of the crisis. CRL's tendrils would even reach in an unexpected way into the lives and finances of Jim and Annie Everhardt.

In the spring of 2011, Jim was serving his third tour in Afghanistan. Annie, at home, was fighting a different battle— against breast cancer—while working part time and raising their three kids. She heard more and more stories in the press vilifying installment lenders, with talk of usury and "predatory lending." The same group of consumer advocates who had managed to get payday loans banned—led by the Sandler-backed Center for Responsible Lending—were marshaling their considerable firepower against installment loans.

After 28 years with no change in rates for these traditional loans, an upcoming bill had proposed a slight loosening of the rules in North Carolina. It proposed minor changes, including a modest late fee, which would encourage borrowers to repay their loans in a timely way. But the consumer advocates had transformed the public discussion over the bill into a forum on whether these installment loans should exist at all. An opponent of the bill, State

Representative Rick Glazier, had scheduled a press conference for April 28, 2011, at the pressroom of the Legislative Building in Raleigh. Annie Everhardt felt strongly enough about it that she decided to make the four-and-a-half-hour round trip to the capital from Camp Lejeune.

Little did she know that she was entering the path of a national political and philanthropic juggernaut. For this movement, consumer lending reforms were only a step on the way to an effective nationalization of the entire U.S. financial and banking systems—from the heart of the economy to its fingertips. Embodying this agenda was a massive hunk of legislation that had passed the previous July, called the Dodd-Frank Wall Street Reform and Consumer Protection Act, and the creation of a new federal bureaucracy named the Consumer Financial Protection Bureau.

Representing the movement at this press conference were people from the Center for Responsible Lending and the North Carolina Justice Center (with backup from the support command for the local marine bases). The spokesmen for the two centers, Chris Kukla and Al Ripley, had spent their careers trying, in their view, to defend people like the Everhardts from the temptations of "edge" finance. To Annie, this meant they wanted to stop her family from being able to get the type of loan that had helped them in a crisis.

On the surface, this bill—North Carolina House Bill 810— was an especially unlikely one to fire up the consumer advocates. Traditional installment lenders in North Carolina had been regulated to the point of suffocation for decades. The bill merely gave them a little more elbowroom. (For instance, it would have allowed them to increase their fees for a $1,500 loan by $1.37 per month.[3]) The Everhardts were among thousands of satisfied customers of installment lenders. The consumer advocates' argument against the bill was going to be hard to make.

So the trio of advocates who appeared at the press conference did what most people do when losing an argument: change the subject.

When representatives of the installment loan industry arrived at the April 28 press conference, they found an empty pressroom.

Combing the building, they eventually found a small group of reporters gathered around Al Ripley in the rotunda. Ripley glared at the arriving group as if they had crashed a private party and, in a sense, they had. The original press conference[4] had been abruptly canceled, and Ripley had seized the moment by arranging an impromptu substitute. Oddly, State Representative Rick Glazier was nowhere to be found. It appeared that the advocates were proceeding without the presence of a state representative, which was required for a press conference in the building.[5]

Also odd, it seemed that Ripley had told the military and local news stations that the press conference—and, by inference, the new bill—was about bringing the outlawed payday loans back to North Carolina. When a representative for the installment loan industry asked him to clarify, Ripley's hands started shaking. "Same as! Same as!" he exclaimed with a concussive blast.

The next question seemed to upset Ripley even more: Why had he orchestrated a press conference bait-and-switch? Skipping the usual pleasantries, he abruptly indicated that a military representative, Mike Archer, was there to speak to the press.

As the camera rolled, Archer began to read a statement that harkened back to the campaign against payday lending from a decade earlier. To onlookers, it appeared that, at the last minute, Archer had scratched out the title, "Payday Loans," on his yellow notepad and replaced *installment* for *payday* throughout. When asked who had told him the press conference was about payday loans, Archer pointed to Ripley. A television reporter from Charlotte's WRAL news channel said the same: he showed up because Ripley had implied that the press conference was about payday loans returning to North Carolina.

Ripley had effectively diverted attention away from the popular installment loans addressed by the House bill and onto the "short-term" loans that advocates had already maligned—payday loans. The resulting confusion might help to defeat the bill. This defeat could then be used in other states as a model for driving out all small-dollar lenders: demonize payday and then conflate it with installment lending.

A FEW GOOD MEN AND
ONE STRONG WOMAN

The TV reporter from Charlotte struck up a conversation with Annie Everhardt, and decided he'd like to interview her.

The idea didn't sit well with Al Ripley, who had planned quite a different form of testimony at his press conference. Turning toward Annie, and in front of onlookers, he began yelling in her face. "Why are you here?!" he bellowed. Annie explained that she had a personal story she wanted to share. "You have no *right* to be here!" Ripley spat out. Annie reached up, wiped her face, and continued as if nothing had happened. "I have every right to be here," she answered quietly. "I am a consumer and I want to share my story."

"You have no idea what you have gotten yourself into!" Ripley thundered. "No idea!"

A representative of the installment loan industry stepped in to ask that she be allowed to speak. The argument attracted a crowd. Soon people on the rotunda balcony were stopping to watch, and a Capitol worker called security. In the end, Annie was only able to get out bits and pieces of her story.

It was, in short, surely not what the North Carolina Justice Center—or anyone else—had planned. Why would Ripley, a "consumer advocate," be so angered by Annie, an actual consumer? She was part of the large but inconvenient group who were grateful to installment lenders. But worse, as the wife of a marine, her presence undercut Ripley's attempt to present the U.S. military as monolithically opposed to House Bill 810.

Ripley's bait-and-switch press conference was still a partial success. The evening news report did mention Annie but, in a muddled narrative, described the press conference as pitting the Department of Defense against a military wife mostly in the bogus context of a possible doubling of fees on short-term payday loans in North Carolina.

What happened to Annie two weeks later was not reported by the press. She received a rare surprise phone call from her husband in Afghanistan. Her heart raced as she wondered what could be prompting it. Jim told her that a superior officer had him contacted while he was in the field. The officer's message: your wife must cease and desist talking about your experience with the loan, or there will be consequences.

Annie was stunned. Some weeks earlier, the couple had volunteered to film an interview describing their experience with the installment loan company. With the Everhardts' approval, this had been posted on the Internet. Since the military looked favorably on these loans, Annie and Jim had thought they were doing a service by sharing their story.

But then came Jim's phone call relating the bizarre order from a superior officer. Suddenly Annie found herself being forced to choose between protecting her husband, who was in a war zone overseas, and speaking the truth. What could she do? Annie explained her position to the installment loan company. At her request, to protect the Everhardt family from reprisals, the video was removed from the Internet. I have changed their names for the same reason. Annie has not publicly spoken about the loan again.

So who cared so much about one small loan in North Carolina? Why had it mattered so much to Al Ripley? And even more curious and unsettling, who had the power and long arm to reach from an impromptu press conference in Raleigh, through the military chain of command, to a battlefield on the other side of the planet? One thing was clear: whatever was going on, it was bigger than either Al Ripley or an installment loan in North Carolina.

"You have no idea what you've gotten yourself into," Ripley told the marine's wife.

That day in Raleigh, no truer words were spoken.

THE NEW COP

That February, the "consumer financial protection" campaign had achieved a new triumph. A new .gov website devoted to consumer finance had appeared in cyberspace. It featured a YouTube video of

Elizabeth Warren, a law professor who, by her account, had become a Democrat in 1995 at age 46. Nineteen ninety-five had been a momentous, career-making year for her. She arrived in Washington to advise the National Bankruptcy Review Commission, and she became a full professor at Harvard Law School (where she was listed as "Native American," a family tale and possible affirmative action ploy that would later cause her trouble).

This website, and what it stood for, was her brainchild. In the video—titled, disarmingly, "Open for Suggestions"—Warren came across as equal parts professorial and parental as she explained with barely suppressed excitement, "For the first time in many years, we have the opportunity to create a brand-new consumer agency from the ground up."

Another video featured the voice of director Ron Howard nar-rating—in a Warren-like professorial-paternal style—"the story of a market that fell apart and a new consumer agency that's charged with putting it back together." Under a banner reading "Welcome to the Bureau" stood a shining policeman's badge emblazoned with what looked like four varsity letters: CFPB. This heroic acronym stood for the Consumer Financial Protection Bureau. A creation of Dodd-Frank, it would officially begin operation that July. Cheerful animation showed the CFPB badge shining a flashlight into dark company towers, putting out fires, and pulling over speed-ing bankers in sports cars.

Soon, YouTube videos of government staff sitting at their desks, reading carefully scripted responses to the suggestions it had been "open for," began to appear on the website. (The first few were vari-ations on the question, "Why do we need another bureau?" Answer: "We'll be a new cop on the beat.")

By the next January, in 2012, the bureau would have a direc-tor from among its YouTubing start-up ranks, Richard Cordray—a onetime high school quiz show champion who paid off his law school debt using the proceeds from his five *Jeopardy!* wins of 1987. (He and Elizabeth Warren may have bonded over this; she herself had been Oklahoma's top high school debater in the mid-1960s.)

The bureau moved into one of the more expensive locations in the country, a stone's throw from the West Wing of the White House: 1700 G Street. This was the just-emptied former home of the agency it was replacing, the Office of Thrift Supervision, which, 22 years earlier, had itself been the "new agency" formed in a crisis to replace a discredited old bureaucracy.

Upon arrival at these imperial quarters, the bureau had officially opened for business. The awkward-but-sincere Cordray even left 1700 G Street to hold "'field hearings' and town-hall meetings far outside the Beltway, listening to regular Americans' perceptions of the financial industry," as Nicole Gelinas reported in *City Journal* in the summer of 2012. "He has worked to fashion an anti-TSA: a government agency people trust and like."

With the former quiz champion taking the reins from the former debate champion, the "cop" rhetoric died down, and the bureau's acronym became humbly lowercase. Nonetheless, it started nabbing the bad guys with plenty of coplike vigor in the summer of 2012. One of these, a lawyer who had been ostensibly engaged in selling expensive, feckless mortgage assistance, described on his Facebook page how officials with a restraining order stormed into his office in a surprise raid, disconnecting the phones. Before they had any proof of wrongdoing, they had frozen the company's assets, including a 2004 Lamborghini Gallardo (perhaps essential for adjusting mortgages).[6] By December the CFPB had taken down two other companies accused of using a pseudo-government loan "help center" run by a woman with eight pseudonyms.[7]

More revealing of the CFPB's power and scope is that in the second half of 2012 the bureau also nabbed three of the top five credit card companies: Capital One, Discover, and American Express. Capital One and Discover had failed to make sure that their third-party vendors stuck to the script in selling credit card extras, and American Express had allegedly violated consumer protection laws "at every stage of the consumer experience, from marketing to enrollment to payment to debt collection."[8] The companies refunded over $400 million to their customers and paid over $100 million in fines, about a third of these to the CFPB itself.

How do these megaliths compare to the shady loan-abatement outfits? American Express, the original international credit card, and Capital One, the upstart data-crunching reinventor, are the only credit card companies that make Fortune's 2013 list of the hundred best companies to work for. (Capital One's CEO, who founded the company in 1988, has not taken any salary for himself since 1997.) And, just before the CFPB started its investigations, American Express and Discover had been named the best in "credit card customer satisfaction" in the J.D. Power & Associates study.[9]

No one from the CFPB stormed in to disconnect the megaliths' phones; instead, the company lawyers just received a "civil investigative demand"—a 20- or 30-page government subpoena requiring the company to produce, within two weeks, every conceivable document the bureau's lawyers might later require to understand and litigate the company. As Ronald Rubin, one of the earliest enforcement attorneys at the CFPB, explains: "Receiving one of these monster [subpoenas] is, simply stated, a nightmare for the unfortunate recipient,"[10] with legal expenses piling up from the moment it arrives. Rubin, who no longer works at the bureau, has called for the bureau to reassess this fabulously expensive and disruptive approach when it is dealing with companies whose best interests are manifestly to cooperate with the government investigation.

Rubin described training the CFPB's enforcement branch on "How to Conduct an Investigation" in June 2011: "I advised the attorneys to 'always see if it's possible to do things the easy way before doing things the hard way.' To my surprise . . . they argued that government investigators should almost always proceed formally"—hence their "one-size-fits-all, litigation-centric investigation process."[11]

The danger is not just that the Consumer Financial Protection Bureau will exercise too much power but that it will exercise unpredictable and arbitrary power based on the whims of its generals. Although the Congress and president created it, it is outside the funding and oversight of the U.S. Congress. The bureau gets its money from the Federal Reserve and from fines it imposes on financial institutions. The president can only remove the director for "good cause," such as gross negligence or criminality. (Policy disputes wouldn't qualify.) Neither the Federal Reserve chairman nor board can remove the director for any reason. Although the agency's budget comes from the Fed, the Fed chairman has limited control over it. In fact, the Fed has no control over any employee of the CFPB or over any rule that the CFPB implements. It is essentially a sovereign entity.

"The CFPB," argues legal scholar Michael Greve, "is an 'independent' agency (bureau? Whatever) of a form never before seen in 225 years of our history."[12]

By the end of 2012, this bureau had an annual budget of a half-billion dollars and some 1,300 employees. How had it used these substantial resources to further the welfare of the American citizenry? Busy regulating and nationalizing the financial sector of the economy from edge to center, the CFPB in its first year, according to estimates of a House oversight committee, "has increased the cost of consumer credit by a total of $17 billion and depressed job creation by about 150,000 jobs."[13]

This colossal price tag may be summed up as the cost of misguided good intentions.

CHAPTER 2

THINKING CLEARLY ABOUT USURY AND CONSUMER CREDIT

The moral struggle with debt is as American as apple pie. "Come into [debt] with the pace of a Tortoise," preached Puritan Cotton Mather in 1716, "and get out of it with the flight of an Eagle."[1] Two generations later, the American Founders were still preaching the dangers of debt. Benjamin Franklin depicted it as a despotic master. "Maintain your Independency," he warned. "Be frugal and free."[2] Many of us have been raised to believe that both lending and borrowing are vaguely unsavory. But debt's bad rap is hardly something American or something new. Human beings have been arguing about the morality of moneylending since money was first invented. Invariably, the lead character in these debates is the greedy banker. This stock stereotype has been kept alive, undoubtedly, by a steady supply of abusive moneylenders down through the centuries.

It has also been nourished, I suspect, by a centuries-long debate—and persistent confusion—about the concept of usury.

Judging from the nonscientific sample of people I've asked, most people don't actually know what the word *usury* means. If the state campaigns of the Center for Responsible Lending continue, however, a lot of folks will hear from the pulpit about what the Bible says about it. (More on that later.) Unfortunately, much of what they hear will be misleading.

These days, we think of usury as charging an astronomical interest rate on a loan, but for most of the last 2,000 years, usury did not refer to *high* interest rates but to *any* interest charged on a loan—that is, usury meant selling money.

Far from being a trivial moral peccadillo, usury was seen as a damnable offense. In his *Divine Comedy*, written in the early fourteenth century, Dante Alighieri describes a journey through hell, purgatory, and paradise. In the *Inferno* portion of the poem, the poet Virgil leads Dante down and down, ever deeper into the circles of hell. The deeper the circle, the worse the sin and consequent punishment. Noble heathens get off easy in the relatively pleasant, if wistful, first circle. Adulterers and gluttons find their eternal abode in the next. Farther down, murderers are confined to the outside ring of the seventh circle. And, in the inner ring of this tough neighborhood, Dante discovers usurers. For most modern readers, even for those who don't like bankers and banking, the usurer's punishment seems like overkill.

You might think Dante's harsh judgment against usury was simply the benighted prejudice of medieval Christians, but hatred of usury was not unique to Christianity. The Greek philosophers Plato and Aristotle—along with such Roman thinkers as Cicero, Seneca, and Cato—also disdained it, with the latter comparing it to murder.[3] It wasn't even just a Western hang-up. Buddha denounced it, and Islam still follows Muhammad in condemning it.

While Greek and Roman thinkers shaped Christians' view of usury throughout the Middle Ages, the other influence, of course, was the Bible; the Old Testament in particular seemed to prohibit charging interest on money loans.[4] In Leviticus,[5] for instance, God describes the rules that should apply after the Hebrews have entered the Promised Land:

> If any of your kind fall into difficulty and become dependent on you, you shall support them; they shall live with you as though resident aliens. Do not take interest in advance or otherwise make a profit from them, but fear your God; let them live with you. You shall not lend them your money at interest taken in advance, or provide them food at a profit.

But wait. If the Hebrew Bible condemns usury, how did Jews come to be associated with usury in the Middle Ages? The short answer is that the Old Testament allows Jews to charge interest to non-Jews.[6]

Christians, for their part, had to grapple with a passage from the New Testament book of Luke, where Jesus seems to condemn charging interest altogether:[7]

> And if you lend to those from whom you hope to receive, what credit is that to you? Even sinners lend to sinners, to receive as much again.
>
> But love your enemies, and do good, and lend, expecting nothing in return; and your reward will be great, and you will be sons of the Most High.

Because of these admonitions, for centuries Christians were officially forbidden from charging interest while Jews were free to make interest-bearing loans to Christians. Since Jews were often prohibited by laws and prejudice from pursuing other lines of work, many Jews ended up working as moneylenders to Christians. When these Jews became successful financiers, they often were vilified for appearing to exploit Christians. Hence the long-lived stereotype of the miserly Jewish banker, brought to life most famously in Shakespeare's *The Merchant of Venice* through the character Shylock.[8]

STERILE OR FERTILE?

Although profound developments in science and technology took place in the intervening 2,000 years, in terms of their economies, most classical and medieval Europeans were not all that different from the ancient Israelites. Most were subsistence farmers. Some fished for a living. A few worked at crafts such as carpentry and had regular access to basic goods in open city markets. But most people lived and worked in the country or in villages and traded mainly within their extended families, clans, or tribes. So the way they interacted economically was more informal and reciprocal than the typical market transaction of today.[9] By modern standards, almost everyone was dirt poor, and banks as we know them didn't exist. Moneylending, then, involved rich people lending to their poor neighbors, probably their kin or longtime employees, for a basic need such as food or winter clothing.

The early Christian world, like the Roman world before it, tended to see money as sterile, functioning only as a means of exchange but without value in itself. This was Aristotle's view, and in the Middle Ages the great theologian Thomas Aquinas, along with many others, adopted the philosopher's thinking on the subject.[10]

Money, they noted, doesn't wear out like clothing or a house. If somebody wears your clothes for a year, you can't get your original clothes back. At best, you'll get used clothes. So you can rightly charge rent for your clothes. When coins get too shabby-looking, however, they are simply removed from circulation and replaced with freshly minted coins of the same worth. Also, a borrowed sum of money can be repaid exactly, even if repaid with different coins or bills. So charging for money seems different from charging rent on, say, a horse and cart or a three-bedroom apartment with a carport.

These differences led most people to conclude that charging interest on money was more or less charging for *nothing*. So what changed their minds? In the West, scholars slowly realized that they hadn't really understood the changing nature of money. The growth of trade and banking exposed the problems. Around the twelfth century, trade began expanding throughout Europe, leading to a greater division of labor and higher productivity. This created several dilemmas. First, growth in trade led to a shortage of gold and silver coins—the common form of currency. Second, it's hard to make large exchanges of money over hundreds or thousands of miles when money is made of gold and silver and easily stolen by roadside bandits or lost in a shipwreck. Finally, the different coins used in Bruges, Milan, and Rome were often reminted and debased with less valuable metals, so the ordinary person could easily get ripped off by unscrupulous merchants or conniving kings.

Out of these exigencies, the bank as we know it was invented.[11] Moneychangers were crucial to the new system. They knew how to compare florins, guilders, and pounds, and to separate them from the counterfeits. Moneychangers also began keeping deposits for various clients so that when two clients made an exchange, all the moneychanger had to do was credit one account and subtract from the other. Simple arithmetic had replaced a risky and cumbersome movement of coins.

Eventually banks emerged with branches in different cities. This gave merchants a way to transfer payment safely over large distances, since bank notes now stood in for the money stored safely in a bank vault.[12]

This process became so common that not only merchants but also governments and even the Pope used bank notes to pay bills. In fact, some banks had such large deposits that they could lend money to kings. What was fit for a king was soon fit for the commoner. Individuals and firms with extra money began depositing their money in banks, to be withdrawn as needed. This could only happen once people were convinced that their money was safer in a bank than hidden in a mattress or a hole in the ground. Thus banking grew only as ties of trust grew beyond family and ethnic lines to connect larger and larger groups of people.

Eventually bankers realized that if they had enough depositors, they didn't need to keep all their deposits on hand to meet the day-to-day demand from depositors. They could safely lend some of it out, not literally by dispersing coins, but by circulating more bank notes than they held in reserves as coins and precious metals. Because they were now putting the money of their depositors at a slight risk, they started paying interest to the depositors. They were issuing credit. Over time, all sorts of credit forms developed for purchasing land, equipment, and other forms of capital.

Insurance was also invented in the Middle Ages, allowing investors who transported goods by ship to spread out the risk of a shipwreck. Everyone who owned cargo paid a little bit up front, just in case disaster struck. If the ship with its cargo went down, the insurer would pay out the benefit. The sharing of risk prevented any one investor from suffering catastrophic loss. This, in turn, attracted more investors into international trade.

So it was that, with these new modes of buying and selling risk—insurance and banking as we know them today—many new ventures and enterprises came to life.

Banks and insurers, of course, needed to earn a living, and so they charged for issuing loans and insurance policies. Usury was still condemned, however, so instead of talking about interest on money, they spoke of a fee for service. This fix fell short of a robust theological understanding and defense, but the result was that the use of business credit and insurance spread. Soon the surplus money of a privileged few was no longer hoarded and unproductive but set free for others to use creatively in launching new enterprises. People began to create more wealth than they consumed, and, with the accumulated wealth, banks could create yet more wealth by functioning as brokers between depositors and investors.[13]

Aristotle had argued that money, unlike monkeys and monkey trees, did not produce after its own kind. (The Greek word for usury, *tokos*, translates as "offspring.") Quarters do not sprout quarters, and if you plant a dollar in your garden, you won't get a money tree. What followed from this, Aristotle argued, was that while charging interest on money might enrich the banker, it is ill-gotten gain because it's based on a fact "contrary to nature."[14] It's treating something as fertile that is in fact sterile. The argument seemed plausible to Aristotle and many who followed him over the next two millennia. Certainly it would be wrong to trick someone into paying for something that had no value in itself. But in the Middle Ages and Renaissance, it slowly became clear that money, at least in certain settings, is indeed fertile, and has what economists call a "time value." As Ben Franklin said, "Time is money."[15] If I lend my neighbor $1,000 for a year, I forgo the opportunity to invest the money in some wealth-creating enterprise for a year. That's worth something.

Notice that charging interest for money was no longer likely to be a rich man bilking his destitute brother or cousin. Now banks were making *capital loans*, that is, loans that could be used to start or fund business ventures. When a bank lends money at interest, it isn't charging for nothing. Strictly speaking, it isn't charging for the money itself, as a butcher would charge for a ham that will be smoked and eaten. It's charging for the "opportunity cost" that the lender bears by not having the money for a while. To lend the money, the lender has to forgo all other uses he might have for the money. And for the borrower, getting the money now rather than a year from now is a benefit. It's no surprise, then, that people will pay a premium for that benefit, since it self-evidently has value to the borrower. That's why if you lend someone $1,000 today, he will be paying you *for something* if, a year from now, he repays you $1,000 plus interest. Whatever this is, it isn't usury as the ancients envisioned it.

Besides the time value of the money lent, there is also risk. A banker or insurer charges for the risk that he won't get his money back on time, or ever. So what is the just price to offset that risk? There's no one answer. The price to borrow money, just like the price of anything else, depends on the situation. If only one bank can lend, and lots of people want to borrow money, the bank can charge a relatively high interest rate, though it is still limited by what potential borrowers are willing to pay. But in a free market with lots of banks competing for customers, interest rates will be much lower as the rates reflect the underlying supply and demand for credit—along with the perceived riskiness of a given loan. A wealthy tech executive with a perfect credit rating can get a much lower interest rate than the guy who just graduated from college and has never had a checking account or a credit card.

THE BANKERS AND THE THEOLOGIANS

All of this seems pretty commonsensical once it's been worked out, but the historical debate among theologians over usury and interest has been anything but simple. For centuries everybody believed charging interest on money was immoral, and they tended to identify such acts as "usury." Slowly but surely, though, scholars found flaws in the arguments that charging interest was necessarily wrong. Catholic scholars worked out many of the details, and then in the sixteenth century, John Calvin abruptly dropped the ancient ban on interest, concluding that "it cannot be said that money does not engender money."[16] Martin Luther, the German priest who had sparked the Protestant Reformation, continued to rail against usury for all the traditional reasons, as did many Catholic thinkers.[17] Most Christians, though, eventually came to the same conclusion as Calvin. As it was said in debates at the time, "When the reasons for the law ceases, the law itself ceases."

These days, few Christians—whether Protestant, Catholic, or Orthodox—offer a blanket opposition to charging interest, and the Vatican participates in modern banking.[18]

It wasn't that they decided simply to ignore inconvenient biblical passages against usury. It was that once they had gotten rid of the false assumptions about the nature of money they had brought to such biblical passages, they could draw some key distinctions that had been overlooked.

In reading the Bible or any text, context is everything. Many scriptural ordinances are epigrammatic. Pithy and concise, they rely on a specific context and typically leave the exigencies, exceptions, and alternate circumstances to the side. Of the three passages[19] forbidding usury in the Hebrew Torah, two refer to the rich Israelite lending money to a poor "brother" in dire straits; the lender should not take advantage of the situation by charging interest. The third passage, in Deuteronomy, repeated this ban but allowed Jews to charge interest to people outside the community. So the practice must not have been seen as intrinsically evil. Ancient Jews were simply forbidden from confusing family relationships with commercial ones.

Look at the passage in the New Testament book of Luke, which I referred to earlier. "If you lend to those from whom you hope to receive," Jesus said, "what credit is that to you? Even sinners lend to sinners to receive as much again. But love your enemies, do good, and lend, expecting nothing in return."[20] Historically, many readers have thought that Jesus was prohibiting the charging of interest. But in context, things look quite different.

In the first part of this sermon, Jesus has given his famous "beatitudes," such as "Blessed are you who are poor" and "Woe to you who are laughing now, for you will mourn and weep." Then, he says, among other things: "If anyone takes away your coat, do not withhold even your shirt." Does Jesus mean we should hope for everyone to be poor, so that they can be blessed? Is he commanding us not to laugh? Are Christians not allowed to sell shirts and coats? Is Jesus forbidding society from enforcing laws against theft? Of course not.

Jesus is using a rhetorical device common in first-century Judaism: hyperbole. Even sinners lend money, he observes, and they expect to receive back the *same* amount. Jesus says nothing about interest. And Aristotle's argument is nowhere in sight. Instead, Jesus says we should lend *expecting nothing in return*. Jesus is encouraging his followers to be generous toward friends in need; he is not denouncing banks for charging interest on loans. Similarly, when Jesus drives the moneychangers out of the Temple, he also drives out everyone selling sheep, cattle, and doves. Nobody concludes from this that Jesus issued a blanket ban on livestock auctions. He did not denounce commerce or money-changing in general, but rather the misuse of a house of worship.[21]

Jesus also condemned hoarding and stinginess. "Do not store up for yourselves treasures on earth," he told his disciples, "where moth and rust consume and where thieves break in and steal; but store up for yourselves treasure in heaven."[22] Here he's reminding his disciples that their ultimate loyalty is not in wealth or possessions, but in God's kingdom. He's denouncing selfish hoarding, not pensions.

In the parable of the talents, Jesus even draws a distinction between the sterile hoarding of money on the one hand and, on the other hand, the interest-bearing savings of money placed in a bank; and he seems to approve the latter.[23] There a man calls three servants and entrusts each with huge sums of money. While the master is away, the first two double their capital while the third servant "went off and dug a hole in the ground and hid his master's money." When the master returns, he compliments and rewards the first two for their productive investments but castigates the third: "You wicked and slothful servant! You knew that I reap where I have not sowed, and gather where I have not winnowed? Then you ought to have invested my money with the bankers, and at my coming I should have received what was my own with interest." (Though modern banks did not exist yet, first-century people in the Near East were familiar with investing.)

The first two servants are rewarded for investing the money they were given—for putting it at risk, where it can bear fruit. The third servant is condemned for playing it so safe that he is rendered economically sterile. The master expected the servant to invest, to put the money at risk. *At the very least*, the master tells him, he should have put it in a bank where it could bear interest. Jesus isn't giving an economics lesson—the parable is about the kingdom of God—but he treats prudent risk, investment, *and* interest in a positive light, and trusts his listeners to do the same.

This overview is just a brief sketch of how scholars came to see that the Bible doesn't teach that charging interest on money is always and everywhere wrong.[24]

Wouldn't it have been better if all the cultures that condemned charging interest for money had understood this from the beginning? Perhaps. But John T. Noonan, in his distinguished study of usury, argues that the usury debate helped give rise to modern banking and economics by providing us with unique insights into the nature of money and commerce. "[T]he scholastic theory of usury is an embryonic theory of economics," he argues. "Indeed it is the first attempt at a science of economics known to the West."[25] The centuries-long debate over usury gave the West an economic head start.

CAPITAL AND CONSUMPTION

Credit and debt have been around even longer than money itself. When a shepherd first gave a goat to a farmer on the promise that the farmer would repay him with wheat at the next harvest, there was credit, and there was debt.

Seen from the twenty-first century, when Americans have racked up a trillion dollars in consumer debt and another trillion in student loan debt, we might view that long-ago exchange involving the wheat and the goat as an early step down the road to financial perdition. But such acts of trust, when rewarded with a trustworthy response, are the seeds from which widespread prosperity grows. This is because large markets and large wealth-creating enterprises can never get off the ground until trust spreads beyond tribe and kin.

But even after Westerners came to accept charging interest on money, they still made sharp distinctions—between lending and partnering, and between money lent as investment capital and money lent for consumption. These distinctions are useful but not as clear-cut as they seem at first glance.

In the 1990s, a young, energetic guy approached an older, established venture capitalist at a dinner party in the Seattle suburb of Medina and pitched him on the idea of an online bookstore. It seemed a bit farfetched at first: how was a website going to compete with multibillion-dollar bookstore chains like Barnes & Noble, where customers could see, feel, and smell the books, and even sit and read them in lounge chairs while sipping a latte? Despite these obvious objections, this venture capitalist was a risk taker, and so he offered the impetuous young entrepreneur $100,000 in start-up money. The entrepreneur's name was Jeff Bezos, the founder of Amazon.com. The venture capitalist's return on that investment was about $20 million after five years.[26] He had allocated his capital extremely well.

Here we have the quintessential capital loan: an investor risks his own money in support of a venture that may, or may not, pay off. If we thought of the $100,000 as a bank loan, the interest rate on the amount repaid at the end of the five years would be vastly higher than any small-dollar loan from the most avaricious loan shark in history. We're talking about an annualized interest rate of something like 4,000 percent! Still, few people find that morally troubling, even though when we hear about credit cards that charge, say, 36 percent annual interest, we consider it an outrage. Why is that? It may be because we don't understand what is involved. But it may also be because we view credit card loans as consumption loans rather than capital loans. Of course capital loans should yield interest, we think, since the whole venture is about creating more wealth. But where's the good in charging interest for people to go out and buy things for their daily consumption?

For instance, imagine that my wife and I have always wanted to drink a bottle of Dom Pérignon in elegant surroundings and, blast it, we're tired of waiting, so we go to Canlis, one of the most elegant and expensive restaurants in Seattle. Along with our Kobe steak dinners, we enjoy a bottle of the famous champagne. Unfortunately, the bill is so high—the champagne alone costs $300—that I have to charge it on my Visa card and then pay it back over several months with interest. And the extra expense means I can't afford to take my two daughters to the dentist for a year.

That, my friends, is the quintessential dumb-as-a-sack-of-hair consumption loan—paying a wheelbarrow full of interest on a luxury item consumed instantly, that I don't need and can't afford, and that wipes out my ability to make another important expenditure. We have to eat, of course, so we fulfill a legitimate need in eating the dinner. But we could have eaten burgers, fries, and shakes at Dick's for about $13.

I've given two extreme examples—a clever venture capitalist versus a profligate purchaser of pricy Champagne—to illustrate the value judgment hanging over practically every conversation about credit for the last 200 years: "Capital loans are good; consumption loans are bad." At one time or other, everything from mortgages to remodeling loans to car loans and credit card payments have suffered bad branding as "consumer loans." Adam Smith and other classical economists approved of "productive" loans but disparaged loans for "immediate consumption."[27] Capital loans seem generally virtuous since they are productive; consumption loans are vicious because they are, well, consumptive.

A few generations on, Victorian-era Americans had made their peace with productive credit, such as for land, "which underlay the geographical expansion and entrepreneurial business activity of the United States." According to one study, in 1895 "at least 90 percent of the country's private debt went to acquire capital goods or durable property."[28] Borrowing money was okay as long as it was "used to purchase things that increased in value or had productive uses."[29] Such debt usually took the form of an installment loan. Boiled down to essentials, this form of loan is like a rent-to-own agreement, since the buyer gets the item up front, unlike a layaway plan.

THE BLACK LINE FADES

As it happens, it was not retailers but the U.S. government that introduced installment loans. The appropriately named finance historian Lendol Calder explains that after the Land Act of 1800 the federal government "sold 19.4 million acres of northwest public lands on terms calling for a down payment of one-fourth of the purchase price and the balance due in equal payments two, three, and four years after purchase."[30] Later, installment credit allowed ordinary farmers to buy mechanical farm equipment.

The point is easy to miss. We marvel at the innovations that transformed farming starting in the nineteenth century—from the mechanical reaper credited to Cyrus McCormick to giant "combines" (combined harvester-threshers). But these inventions would have been far less revolutionary without the less tangible *credit* inventions that allowed so many farmers to own the new technologies. McCormick's grandson didn't miss the connection. He described installment lending as "the most important innovation introduced into his [Cyrus McCormick's] selling system."[31] The loans were tailored to the changing income stream of farmers, who might be in debt part of the year and then relatively flush with cash after a bountiful harvest. Not technology alone, but new technology combined with innovative credit allowed farmers to reduce "the man-hours required to harvest an acre of grain from twenty hours to one."[32]

Yet "consumptive debt" for perishable goods, such as fine wine and caviar, or even rice and beans, was still frowned upon. In fact, as late as the 1920s, the word *consumption* was still commonly used to refer to people suffering and dying from tuberculosis. Nevertheless, the thick black line between productive and consumptive loans had started to fade. The two loan types, which look quite different at first, really occupy a lot of overlapping territory.

Take the mortgage loan to buy a house. We clearly use our houses. Some folks even wear out their houses. In that way, we "consume" them. Yet even in a flat housing market—where prices don't change—buying a house with a mortgage loan can be a sort of investment. After all, if you live in a house and slowly pay off a 30-year mortgage, you end up with a house. If you had rented a house instead, at the end of that period you'd still have to pay rent and wouldn't own so much as a single two-by-four in the house you'd lived in for half your life.

As mentioned above, even in the nineteenth century, farmers bought farm equipment on credit, just as they now get loans to buy tractors, seeders, irrigators, and the like. Farm equipment doesn't retain its value like land does, but it allows farmers to produce more with their land and so to make a better living, possibly employ more people, and have more money to repay the loan. If a farmer couldn't buy a tractor until he had saved all the money to pay for it, he might be stuck in a Catch-22—unable to earn the money to buy a tractor because he didn't already own a tractor. Still, under the older reckoning, he would be taking out a consumptive loan to purchase that tractor.

Or what about a poor kid from Yazoo, Mississippi, who borrows money to help her pursue an engineering degree that lands her a job at Microsoft? She's buying short-term access to libraries, classrooms, computers, and teaching services, but for that kid a student loan is more an investment in the future than consumption in the present.

Alternately, what if that student's parents bought a piano on an installment plan when she was a child (as many people did even 100 years ago)? That's not immediate consumption. If the piano allowed her, after years of lessons, to get a scholarship to the Juilliard School, we might think of it as an investment. What if she took lessons for a few years, but eventually the piano became a nice piece of furniture in the living room? Would that mean the loan taken out years before was a consumptive rather than a productive loan? What if the piano lessons increased her IQ by six points? Or three points? Half a point, but lots of fond memories? When does it cease to be a productive loan?

If you need a car to get to work or to do your job but don't have enough savings to buy it outright, is it shameful to get a loan to buy the car and pay it off slowly? Surely not. When my wife, Ginny, and I got married, her dowry was an old Toyota Tercel that had seen too many Michigan winters. It worked for a while, but rusty parts kept falling off in the road. Eventually the monthly repairs cost more than a monthly payment on a car. I was in graduate school full-time and Ginny's job required a long commute. So we got a 5-year car loan and drove the car for 10 years. (There's a definite pleasure in driving a car that's been paid off.) Referring to the loan we got as a "consumption loan" seems to lard the act with moral opprobrium that it doesn't deserve.

These days we don't have to pinch as many pennies as we did then, but I couldn't do my job now if I didn't spend money on cell phones, Internet connections, and Advil. If we didn't have a good mattress, I would probably fall asleep in front of my computer every day. Are these expenses consumption or investment? Luxury or necessity? I happen to have enough income and savings at this point so that I don't need a loan to buy these things. Am I more virtuous than the poorer people who have to borrow money to do so? These expenses are not pure investments like an investment in a new medical device company. But neither are they mere consumption.

Now, don't get me wrong. Consumption and production are not the same thing. I'm not saying that we shouldn't exert self-control. We shouldn't pretend certain items are necessary to our daily functioning if they are really not. I have not found—nor am I looking for—a way to turn that bottle of Dom Pérignon into a necessity. We don't need to justify everything before the bar of productivity. Some luxury items are just that.

A society can't habitually and indefinitely consume more than it saves and produces (though we're giving it our best shot). Nevertheless, the economy depends not just on production and investment but on consumption as well. If no one bought cars or houses or meals, there would be no car manufacturers or builders or restaurateurs. And if having some of these things makes people more productive—as the office chair with lumbar support makes me—then it seems that credit that allows people to have access to them sooner rather than later could make society as a whole more prosperous and productive. And, if so, why would it be wrong, in principle, for finance companies to lend people money at interest to make that possible?

By the end of the nineteenth century, such considerations led Americans to put loans for items such as pianos and sewing machines on the "productive" side of the ledger.[33] This is not simply because manufacturers and consumers were overcome with avarice. With mass production, more and more consumer goods became available to the ordinary person. Goods that were a luxury and affordable only for the wealthy in an earlier age—such as pianos—were now within reach of the growing middle class. Technology and credit worked hand-in-hand. Technology lowered prices; credit lifted the reach of lower-income Americans.

The watersheds were the invention of the sewing machine and the automobile. In the nineteenth century, the sewing machine empowered millions of Americans, mostly women, to become income earners. I.M. Singer and Company is remembered because its machines found their way into so many American homes. The forgotten part of the story is that Singer and other sewing machine companies made installment credit popular nationwide.[34] Similarly, history students learn that Henry Ford used mass production to get the price of his Model T within reach of middle-class Americans. They rarely learn that installment loans, which Ford opposed at first, made up the difference. "Installment credit and the automobile were both cause and consequence of each other's success," writes Calder in his award-winning analysis, *Financing the American Dream: A Cultural History of Consumer Credit.*[35]

Despite a lingering worry, by the 1920s installment credit began to lose its stigma and slowly found its way into ordinary retail sales for everything from furniture to clothing and jewelry to appliances. Most people came to realize that the right forms of credit, with the right rules, allow us to create more wealth and improve our lives.

CREDIT EVERYWHERE

The pervasive use of credit is one of the marks of the modern world. Even paper money, when it was first introduced, was a form of debt. It represented "a promise by an issuing bank to redeem fiat money with real money," as Calder explains. "In this sense, the introduction of paper money into everyday life anticipated the arrival of a complex economy operating on the basis of sophisticated credit transactions."[36] Now practically all we use is fiat money, backed, not by gold or silver, but by the faith and credit of the U.S. government. The good news is that this is possible only because billions of people *trust* the arrangement enough that they will accept paper dollars in payment for virtually anything. The bad news is that the whole thing can collapse if a critical mass of people lose that trust.

Our age is far more complicated and diverse than the bygone era when neighbors exchanged goats for wheat. As a result, our forms of credit and debt are far more complex and diverse, and they don't fit neatly into the old contrast between capital and consumption loans. Today there are myriad ways to start, organize, and finance businesses, each with its own advantages and disadvantages. Ditto for consumer credit. Available to American consumers today are credit cards; mortgage loans, which come in different shapes and sizes; installment loans for everything from car repairs to surgery; payday loans; and even pawnshops. These meet different needs for different people at different times.

Each of these credit instruments has pluses and minuses. Each can be used or abused. When we ponder the economic and social costs of debt and credit, however, we also should remember the great *benefits* they have brought to ordinary people in the last century and a half. Especially when we're in the aftermath of a financial crisis, we shouldn't fall for bad moral arguments or throw out the good parts along with the bad. Our financial industry has helped millions of people pursue the American Dream and succeed. We should all want it to continue to do so for our children and grandchildren.

CHAPTER 3

CALIFORNIA GOLD

Herbert and Marion Sandler are a great American success story in many regards. From humble origins, they built a multibillion-dollar business together, serving for 43 years as co-CEOs of the company they built. Even as the company grew to become the second largest savings and loan (S&L) in the nation, the Sandlers preserved its mom-and-pop culture. They cared deeply about their customers—many of them poor—and retained personal connections with many long-time employees. Marion was even known to knit sweaters in business meetings, when she wasn't running them. After they sold their company in 2006, the couple didn't go on a buying spree but put most of their fortune in a charitable foundation.

Nature and nurture seemed to conspire to create what one *New York Times* story described as the ideal "philanthrocapitalist" couple.[1] Herb Sandler was born in 1931 and "grew up poor"[2] in Manhattan's Lower East Side, the "son of a compulsive gambler whose earnings were consumed by loan sharks."[3] He graduated from the City College of New York in 1951 and from Columbia Law School in 1954. Eventually he went to work as a real estate lawyer in a firm in lower Manhattan.[4] While vacationing in the Hamptons in the summer of 1960, the tall bachelor met a petite young lady on the beach, Marion Osher, from Biddeford, Maine. They were married in Boston less than a year later.

Marion's parents were Jewish immigrants from Lithuania and Russia. They settled in Biddeford, ran a hardware store and plumbing supply business, and invested in real estate. Despite their humble and challenging beginnings, they became wealthy enough to put their five kids through college and graduate school.[5] Two of their children became billionaires.

Marion graduated Phi Beta Kappa from Wellesley College, attended a one-year program in business administration at Harvard-Radcliffe, and then earned her MBA from New York University with academic honors.[6] From there, she quickly became a breaker of stereotypes and glass ceilings. She was one of only two women in professional jobs working on Wall Street and in 1955 was the first woman executive hired at Dominick & Dominick, Inc., a brokerage and investment-banking firm known as the "Tiffany of Wall Street." In 1961, she moved into the savings and loan industry when she took a position with Oppenheimer and Company.[7]

After Herb and Marion married, they found that they shared frustrations with the "quality of the management running most savings institutions."[8] So in 1963, the real estate lawyer and the savings and loan analyst moved to San Francisco to focus on what they saw as untapped potential in the industry.[9] They soon opened Golden West Financial Corporation, a holding company for Golden West Savings and Loan, which they acquired for $3.8 million using bank loans and money from Marion's brother Bernard. At the time of purchase, Golden West Savings and Loan had only a main office and one branch in Oakland, California, with 26 employees and $34 million in assets.

In 1975, they merged with another savings and loan, World Savings, and began using the World name at all their branches. At the end of the 1980s, when the savings and loan industry had been decimated, they had survived with almost $20 billion in assets.

Over the years, the Sandlers pioneered new kinds of loans attractive to thousands of poor and disadvantaged people, many of them minorities shunned by other mortgage lenders, who viewed them as high-risk borrowers. From a "chance encounter" on a beach "would spring a partnership that has become one of the more intriguing—and successful—in business," wrote the *Wall Street Journal* in 1990.[10] They were named "2004 CEOs of the Year" by Morningstar, Inc. Ten times Golden West was listed in *Fortune* magazine's annual list of the United States' most admired companies, including three of the four years prior to the sale of their company in 2006.

Because they made this sale at the peak of the market, just before the subprime crisis began, the Sandlers suffered some harsh press coverage. The *New York Times*, for instance, referred to the loan they pioneered as the "Typhoid Mary" of the housing crisis.[11] They were accused of profiting from an industry that created the crisis and harmed the poor, and of being masterminds behind "predatory" mortgage lending practices that created or at least added significantly to the mortgage bubble.

The Sandlers worked hard to correct what they believed was an inaccurate account, arguing that their lending practices were nothing like the high-risk mortgage banking that had brought the world to the brink of financial destruction. Many in the media were ready to give the couple the benefit of the doubt. Although they made a vast fortune, their public image seemed to lack the greed that marked so many players in the mortgage industry. With their 10 percent personal take from the sale of Golden West Financial, the Sandlers generously endowed their private foundation with $1.3 billion—making it one of the top 30 foundations in the country. The plan they put in place was to "give away their wealth philanthropically,"[12] spending down not only their foundation assets but the remaining money as well. As with their business, so with their philanthropy: they showed an abiding concern for the poor and less fortunate. They generously funded medical research for asthma and parasitic diseases that afflict poor countries. They tirelessly championed human rights. And they supported organizations that fight predatory lending against the poor.

"We are devoting the rest of our lives to our long-held charitable interests," Herb and Marion wrote in 2010, "to try and make the world a better place for the most vulnerable among us."[13] Marion died on June 1, 2012, at the age of 81, but Herb carries on their inspiring legacy of generosity.

A MORE COMPLICATED STORY

What on earth had happened that this seemingly wholesome couple ended up on television labeled as "Two People Who Should Be Shot"? Many analysts who have looked at the financial crisis and events leading up to it have noted that the couple made their fortune by helping to pioneer and aggressively sell an especially virulent form of the adjustable-rate mortgage loan (ARM).[14] The loans drew in the trusting soul by offering a low and quite manageable initial interest rate, with possibly higher rates to kick in far in the future. Often only dimly understood, the loans were seen almost as a gift by many borrowers who would not otherwise qualify for a mortgage. The Sandlers avoided the "greedy capitalist" label because they had the perfect cover: their work supposedly helped the poor.

While they grew their business, the Sandlers quietly funded nonprofits that looked high-minded on the surface but that secretly served their business and political interests and often harassed their competition. As "uncommonly aggressive competitors,"[15] the Sandlers managed to ride the real estate bubble to new heights.

With their intimate knowledge of their own books and the mortgage business in general, though, they knew the bubble couldn't last forever. In 2006, they made a lightning-fast sale of their company, Golden West Financial, to North Carolina–based Wachovia Bank, for $24.3 billion. The deal made the Sandlers billionaires.

For Wachovia its new assets very quickly sprouted liabilities. The day the deal was struck, Wachovia's market value dropped by a billion dollars as investors dumped the bank's stock.[16] Soon, the housing market stalled, and Wachovia—swamped with an exotic adjustable-rate mortgage called "option ARMs"—went belly-up.

Before it was over, virtually the entire market value of the Golden West purchase was gone—and Wachovia was sold to Wells Fargo at fire-sale prices, wiping out many long-term investors along with it.

One need not be a cynic to recognize that the Sandlers' brand of philanthropy, like their business, does not fit the saintly stereotype they have projected. The Herbert and Marion Sandler Foundation has supported some nonpartisan concerns, such as the American Asthma Foundation (Marion Sandler was herself an asthma sufferer). However, if one moves past the front window and to the back of their philanthropic store, one finds donations of a very different sort.

In the 2004 presidential election cycle, the Sandlers were the fourth-largest donors[17] to Section 527 organizations (tax-exempt political action committees). Their benevolence went exclusively to far left-wing outfits such as MoveOn.org. In the conservative *American Thinker*, Ed Lasky observed, "They are not merely out to elect Democrats, but to also permanently realign U.S. politics and shift our society and culture in a far-left wing direction."[18] They have lavishly funded a who's who of left-wing groups, from the Center for American Progress, created to counter conservative think tanks such as the Heritage Foundation, to the discredited and now bankrupt group ACORN.[19]

One might object that the Sandlers were just promoting a political vision that they sincerely believed would best lift up the poor and disadvantaged. This is certainly part of the truth. The whole truth, however, is more complicated. In this case, the proverbial devil is not only in the details but is also well disguised.

STRIKING GOLD

To understand the Sandlers' career, it helps to understand some quirks of the savings and loan industry. S&Ls, or thrifts, unlike investment banks and commercial banks, deal mostly with savings accounts and mortgages and are subject to different regulations than other financial institutions. The lending firm headed by James Stewart as George Bailey in *It's a Wonderful Life* was a savings and loan.

Herb Sandler traded in investment securities in the 1970s, when mortgages were less profitable. But with deregulations in the 1980s, Herb saw new opportunities in the mortgage market—and new risks. Interest rates, which were previously fixed by federal law, could now be set by S&Ls themselves. And in 1981, S&Ls were given the freedom to market ARMs—adjustable-rate mortgages.[20] The Sandlers were pioneers of what many believe was the most toxic form of these loans, called option ARMs.[21]

With a fixed-rate mortgage, the monthly payment and interest rate charged to the borrower are the same throughout the life of the loan. The loan is "amortized," so that more and more of the principal relative to interest is paid with each month's payment. In other words, the first payment on a 30-year fixed-rate loan might be almost all interest and just a little principal, whereas the last payment covers mostly principal. Therefore, the longer you make payments, the more equity on the house you build up, until finally the loan is fully amortized and you own your house free and clear.

Buyers like fixed-rate loans because they are predictable. Also, if interest rates are low when the loan is issued, eligible borrowers can lock in the rate for the life of the loan. Fixed-rate loans are worrisome to lenders for the same reason. Imagine yourself as the sole owner of a bank that markets mortgage loans, and you have a thousand 30-year mortgages on your books paying 3 percent interest. If interest rates go up, you'll be stuck, perhaps for decades, with loans yielding less than the current "price" on mortgage loans. In such an environment, you'll likely have to pay your depositors more than 3 percent just to keep saving accounts or fixed-rate CDs (certificates of deposit) in your bank. (This is one reason that banks like to get such mortgages off their books by selling them to so-called secondary lenders or investors.)

When the federal regulations changed in 1981, thrifts like the Sandlers' could avoid this problem by issuing adjustable-rate mortgages. As the name indicates, with this type of mortgage a lender can adjust the rate of the loan up or down, depending on current interest rates and the terms of the loan. ARMs are less risky for a bank to keep in its portfolio long term, since the bank is less likely to get stuck with a low fixed rate that could linger on its books for decades.

Lenders essentially borrow money from their depositors and government agencies, such as a Federal Home Loan Bank, to lend to other customers. Since they have to pay a certain rate to get money to lend, and interest rates change constantly, lenders would like to adjust the rate at which they lend accordingly. Although many lenders adjust ARMs annually, Golden West found a way to adjust them monthly (plus a little lag time). Obviously such a loan is even less risky for the lenders but more risky for the borrowers, since monthly payments could spike at any time without warning. To attract borrowers in the face of that extra risk, lenders frequently offer initial or "teaser" rates marked well below fixed rates; this shifts the borrower's focus from obvious risk to instant gratification through potential savings.

The Sandlers' offers went even farther. After 1981, Golden West Financial started offering option ARMs, which they later named "Pick-A-Pay" loans. A borrower could make regular payments, which included both principal and interest. However, if a borrower found himself in dire financial straits for a few months or even several years, he could reduce his monthly payments by paying only the interest on the loan. He wouldn't be building up any equity in the house. He wouldn't, in other words, be paying down the principal loan amount. But at least his payments would be lower and he would be less likely to default on the loan. The Pick-A-Pay loan was sold as a safety net for borrowers.

In fact, if the interest-only payment was still too much for the borrower, he could make a minimum monthly payment so low that it didn't even cover the interest. If the customer is, say, the stereotypical 21-year-old male living month to month who doesn't concern himself with the big picture, this might seem like a sweet deal. Unfortunately, however, he now has a negative amortization loan. Not only is he not paying off the loan; the principal is growing. He is getting deeper and deeper in debt.

Unlike other ARM-issuing lenders, World Savings allowed a borrower to make such debt-increasing minimum payments for up to 10 years before the loan was "recast" into a regular, fixed-rate loan. Loan officers pitched this as a perk to potential borrowers. Even though it's an adjustable-rate loan, they pointed out, borrowers could forecast the minimum they would have to pay for 10 years. Also attractive to their borrowers was Golden West's policy of not "punishing" borrowers who could not verify their reported income.

The practice was lucrative for the Sandlers. Golden West Financial became a publicly traded company in 1989 and by 2005 had issued about $275 billion in option ARM loans.[22] They went to young singles, to couples who could not afford a mortgage loan otherwise, to speculators, and to millions of buyers who lacked the good credit to get a more traditional loan.

Although Golden West/World Savings pooled and sold ("securitized") its fixed-rate loans to investors, it vigorously claimed to have held onto the Pick-A-Pay loans—94 percent of its total business in 2003—rather than sell them or turn them into mortgage-backed securities.[23]

The Sandlers clearly knew how to make this work for their company. For years, their thrift grew at an enviable rate—20 percent a year (in compounded annual earnings per share), swelling to $124.6 billion in assets by the end of 2005.[24] The only other company with such a consistently impressive performance was billionaire Warren Buffett's Berkshire Hathaway.

Some credit for this record goes to the Sandlers' famous knack for cost cutting—squeezing every nickel beyond the point of frugality. They didn't even install ATMs in their branches until the 1990s! Besides keeping costs down, Golden West focused almost entirely on mortgages for single-family residences and a few multi-family homes. They knew that, historically, even cash-strapped people were less likely to default on their homes than on loans for things like cars or boats. The company also avoided riskier loans for properties such as "shopping centers, golf courses, or million-dollar mansions."[25] Although option ARMs made it possible for borrowers to get deeper in debt, the loans' flexibility made it easier for borrowers to avoid—or at least to postpone—defaulting.

To help ensure that these loans paid off for their company, the Sandlers' option ARM loans carried stiff mandatory penalties if borrowers repaid their loans early, either by refinancing or selling the home before a given time.[26] Now think about this for a minute. Would you take out a loan with a tough prepayment penalty if you could get an equivalent loan without such a penalty? Of course not. You might be attracted to an ARM loan if you're an investor flipping houses every few months and want to keep your payments as low as possible. You might also like an ARM if you're poor now but think that your ship will come in sooner rather than later; then you'll be able to handle higher monthly payments, or perhaps pay the loan off early, and avoid much of the higher interest-rate cost looming on the distant horizon. But with the Sandlers' loans, paying it off early wasn't an option unless you ate the sizable penalty.

All of this tells us about the target market for these loans: borrowers who either didn't have a better alternative because their credit situation was bad or didn't understand what they were getting into. This becomes increasingly important as we begin to see the role these "subprime mortgages" played in the looming financial crisis and meltdown.

Despite the name, *subprime* refers less to the loan than to the borrower's credit rating. But since it sounds a little rude to talk about "subprime borrowers," we typically speak instead of "subprime mortgages." Although there is no exact definition of the word, many lenders consider a borrower with a FICO score below 660 to be subprime, and a score higher than 680 to be good.[27] (The scale runs from 300 to 850.) People with low FICO scores have some mark against their credit; perhaps they haven't paid their credit card bills on time or they defaulted on a car loan or had a run of misfortune. In any event, if you have a low credit score, you're probably in a shaky financial situation and won't appear to be a safe haven for a big loan.

Two other ingredients in the Sandlers' secret sauce were their underwriting and appraisal processes. Underwriting is the due diligence that lenders perform to make sure a borrower can handle a loan rather than default, skip the country, or otherwise leave the lender holding the bag. Appraisal is the due diligence done on the property itself, since it serves as collateral for the loan. If I'm ready to pay $300,000 for a house that I've fallen in love with because it reminds me of a beloved childhood home, but an appraiser reports that the market value of the house is only $200,000, I probably won't get the loan for anywhere near $300,000—not in normal circumstances, anyway. After all, if I default, the bank is stuck with the house. So the bank wants to make sure that it could resell the house for a price that would cover the cost of the original loan.

In 2007, a writer for *Bloomberg Businessweek* spent a day with Golden West executives in San Antonio, who regaled him with their trade secrets for underwriting loans. The lenders described their "common sense" approach, which "involved simple things like closely comparing an applicant's income to their profession—which would raise red flags if a clerk at a video rental store claimed he was making $125,000." The company also used its own appraisers rather than hiring outsiders and held them accountable for the entire life of the loan. That way, it

> ensured that IF the borrower went into default, the thrift could sell the house for as much—or even more—as it was on the hook for. That was an "asset"-based approach, rather than an "income"-based approach that put more weight on verifying a borrower's pay and assets, and then analyzing how much mortgage they could afford.[28]

So, in other words, while people at Golden West did ask borrowers to state their incomes and made sure they squared with their claimed professions, the lenders didn't do much, if anything, to verify the borrowers' personal incomes or credit histories. This may sound magnanimous, but it's not. Golden West made sure the collateral of any loan (the house) was worth enough to cover the loan should the borrower default. If the borrower did then default, who would be out? Only the borrower, presumably.

Recall that for up to 10 years a borrower could make payments so low that he would get deeper and deeper into debt, sometimes far beyond the market value of the home; and then, when the loan reset, the payments could go up, sometimes way up. When that happened, the dream of homeownership would quickly turn into the nightmare of crushing debt and almost certain default. If the home in question had appreciated in value, the borrower might escape the debt by selling the home. But if he escaped with any equity at all, the amount would be less than if his payments had at least covered the interest—and certainly far less equity than if he had made fixed-rate payments.

Again, however, Golden West was covered. If a borrower defaulted, Golden West could repossess the home, sell it, and still probably cover its costs and then some. Regardless of the outcome, Golden West would come out ahead. Many of its borrowers, though, might have been much better off renting.

I'm not saying it's wrong for a bank to develop a profitable business plan or to protect itself from loss. Far from it. My point is that the Sandlers' strategy, contrary to the way they portray and defend their work, wasn't exclusively designed to "help the poor" and certainly was no more benevolent than that of many of their competitors. It was far from friendly to the poor customers hooked by the option ARMs, though it did seem like an almost foolproof way for Golden West to make money hand over fist. I say "almost" foolproof because, as it turns out, there was a catch. As the *Bloomberg* article goes on to explain, "This 'asset'-based approach assumed that housing would never plunge in value—nor that borrowers would simply walk away from a house that plunged in value."[29] Neither of those assumptions turned out to be correct.

Did the Sandlers get burned? No. Apparently, they either knew or guessed that the prevailing assumptions about the housing market were wrong. In fact, they seemed wisely to have foreseen the possibility of a starker reality—that a distorted and overheated housing market would plunge in value, and many borrowers would

in fact walk away from their homes. Just as they had been throughout their careers, the Sandlers were ahead of the curve. They were
able to leave others holding the bag when the reality police finally
crashed the real estate party.

FROM GOLDEN EGG TO GOOSE EGG

Even as late as 2005, the Sandlers gave no evidence that they
planned to sell their company. In fact, they already had successors
in place to keep the business going. Then, in 2006 the couple suddenly decided to sell the company they had spent decades building.
The deal reportedly went through in days[30] and closed at the peak
of the housing bubble. Good news for the Sandlers; bad news for
Wachovia. And since it was part of the larger mudslide in housing
markets, it was bad for our nation's economy.

In retrospect, small details about Golden West's practices suddenly seemed significant. In particular, the thrift didn't actually
verify a borrower's employment by calling employers[31] or requiring
tax returns. Nor did the company take much stock in FICO credit
scores. This meant that Herb Sandler's insistence that Golden West
didn't make subprime loans was a meaningless ruse, since *subprime*
is often defined by credit scores.

These weren't oversights, but matters of choice, and defended
on principle. "Golden West rejected the concept of risk-based pric-
ing, believing it would invariably be discriminatory," the Sandlers
later explained. "At Golden West, any borrower who qualified for
a loan would receive a prime rate, irrespective of the borrower's
financial information or other characteristics."[32] Since Golden
West didn't bother to verify employer information and didn't look
at official credit ratings,[33] one wonders what exactly qualified a borrower for a loan, other than having a good story and some money
for a down payment. Even if you knew nothing else about its operation, these facts alone would suggest that Golden West set things
up so it could make money while leaving its customers vulnerable
to being crushed by their loans. The only hope many of its custom-

ers had was the false hope that the housing market would continue to go up.

In any case, the outcome is now well known: Wachovia bought Golden West in 2006, lost 89 percent of its value, and then was forced to sell itself for pennies on a dollar to Wells Fargo on October 3, 2008.[34]

A CRISIS OF CREDIBILITY

After the financial crisis hit in 2008, there was a media feeding frenzy. Everyone wanted somebody to blame, and the press was happy to oblige. Reporters, as prone as anyone to cultural prejudices about the banking industry, quickly concluded that the obvious culprits were greedy bankers. Even the Sandlers, who had been darlings of the media for years, suddenly found themselves cast in a somewhat dimmer light. The drubbing began with that scathing *Saturday Night Live* skit, with its ungenerous portrayal of them as "People Who Should Be Shot" (a phrase that deep-pocketed NBC no doubt realized was practically begging for a lawsuit).

A few months later, on Christmas Day, the *New York Times* continued this unprecedented trend of questioning the Sandlers and their carefully manufactured reputation. The *Times* published a major story about the Sandlers, written by Michael Moss and Geraldine Fabrickant, entitled "Once Trusted Mortgage Pioneers, Now Pariahs." ("Pariahs" was later changed to "Scrutinized.") As might be expected, the story focused on the Sandlers' option ARM. While it never directly accused the Sandlers of fraud or criminality, the story showed that the Sandlers engaged in many of the practices that had contributed to the financial crisis, and it was these same practices that the Sandlers had publicly criticized in their competitors.

Then, seven weeks after the *New York Times* story, on February 15, 2009, CBS's *60 Minutes* aired a major report featuring former World Savings mortgage salesman Paul Bishop. Bishop, who was suing World Savings, asserted that he had been fired for raising questions about the company's lending practices. He painted a picture of increasingly reckless and even fraudulent lending practices by World Savings salespeople, a picture confirmed by several coworkers who did not disclose their names.[35]

Exhibit A was one Betty Townes, an elderly black woman who was ruined by a string of refinancing deals. "World salesmen convinced Betty to refinance her mortgage four times in four years," reported *60 Minutes* correspondent Scott Pelley. "She got about $20,000 each time," thanks to rising housing prices, while World Savings raked in the new fees.

It's impossible to watch the segment and not realize that Townes had little idea what she was getting herself into. "Well," she explained, "all I know [is] that they told me this loan was best for me." Her monthly income was only $1,875, which was not enough to qualify for the loan she was seeking. The agent solved that problem by including her husband's income, which bumped the total up to $4,000 a month. The only trouble was that her husband was deceased.

"It was all about volume," said one of Bishop's coworkers. "Quantity over quality," at least in the few years before the thrift was sold to Wachovia. "By 2005, 38 percent of World's clients had subprime credit scores," said Pelley. "And customers were shown fliers that told them their income would not be checked by the bank."[36] All the while, Herb Sandler was insisting that his company did not make subprime loans.

Given the pecking order of American media, many stories appeared downstream from the *New York Times* and *60 Minutes*. *Time* magazine published a "Special" called "25 People to Blame for the Financial Crisis," which included the Sandlers. "The Sandlers' World Savings Bank became the first to sell a tricky home loan called the option ARM," *Time* explained. "And they pushed the mortgage . . . with increasing zeal and misleading advertisements over the next two decades."[37]

ON DEFENSE

Undaunted, Herb Sandler went right on pointing the finger at others. Several months after the stories by *60 Minutes* and the

New York Times, the federal government's Financial Crisis Inquiry Commission interviewed him. He blamed independent mortgage brokers, calling them "whores of the world,"[38] for transforming what should have been helpful mortgages into predatory instruments loaded with hidden fees and misleadingly low "teaser" rates. The only problem was that Herb Sandler was practically describing his own product, no matter how devious or honest the broker. "They took a loan that was borrower-friendly and made it into a toxic loan," he said, "which we warned regulators about again and again and again."[39] And yet the *New York Times* story had already revealed that by 2006 about 60 percent of the Sandlers' World Savings loans were being sold by independent brokers. Rather than take responsibility for the brokers he had hired to aggressively sell his company's loans to low-income people (and thereby make himself richer), Herb Sandler described himself as their victim.

As far as I can tell, the Sandlers never apologized. They zealously defended their record, often with help from their attorney, and sought to distinguish their practices from mortgage banking, which they maintained was the real culprit in the financial crisis.

Their defense wasn't wholly groundless. The Sandlers did do some things differently from other lenders. For instance, they reportedly qualified their option ARM borrowers for higher fixed-rate loans, so the borrowers could encounter less "shock" when the loans reset. In theory, this meant that borrowers would be able to keep up payments even when the mortgage shifted to a fixed rate. More significantly, some 70 percent of the company's loans had substantial down payments, contrary to the subprime practice of offering loans with zero down. Borrowers who hadn't put in a down payment had little skin in the game, and many defaulted on their loans at the first sign of trouble.

After the *SNL* skit aired on Saturday, it was posted to the NBC website. The Sandlers were livid. They contacted executive producer Lorne Michaels, who claimed he didn't realize they were real people, and he pulled the video.[40] Eventually NBC posted a Sandler-less version. (At some point, Guest of a Guest, a website focused on

New York City's art and entertainment scene, obtained an unedited copy and reposted it under the title "The Unedited 'Forbidden' SNL Economic Bailout Skit."[41] The website Moonbattery did the same.[42] Whether either survives long enough to be available when you read this, well, we'll see.)

NBC had gone wobbly. Happily for the cause of freedom of the press, the *New York Times* and CBS proved to have stiffer spines. In the eight months of tedious back and forth correspondence with then–executive editor Bill Keller of the *New York Times*, the Sandlers and their lawyers extracted four minor corrections, but Keller stood behind the substance of the story.[43]

After the *60 Minutes* segment aired, the Sandlers went straight to the top and contacted CBS President Leslie Moonves. CBS agreed to permanently post a 20-page response from Herb Sandler on the CBS website.[44] Paul Bishop, the whistleblower in the *60 Minutes* story, later lost his arbitration hearing. The judge ruled that his complaints failed "for lack of substantiation."[45] However, the basic accusation—that World Savings gave out billions of dollars of loans to people who couldn't afford them—is indisputable, and CBS never retracted it.

NOT SO INNOCENT

The loans made by World Savings had the same cardinal vice as the thrift's competitors: they made sense and worked well, at least for some people, only as long as the housing market continued to go up. For a lender, even zero down is not so risky if housing prices keep going up 10 percent a year, as they did in some markets in California. For a borrower, even a negative amortization loan might make sense as long as the value of the house is growing faster than the principal on the loan. But this was a risky, sophisticated loan that clearly was not appropriate for everyone.

Golden West/World Savings operated in 39 states when the Sandlers sold it in 2006, but roughly 60 percent of its mortgages were in California, where the housing bubble was as fat and fragile as an overfilled water balloon. As one analyst dryly observed, "Option ARMs were a bubble state phenomenon."[46] Option ARMs were also a Herb and Marion Sandler phenomenon.

The Sandlers admitted that they sold their company to Wachovia at the peak of the bubble, and Wachovia suffered huge losses as a result. But they defended their practices by observing that "no lender, no matter how conservatively run or whether they did ARM or fixed-rate lending, can avoid loan losses when housing prices decline at historically unprecedented levels of 50 percent or more, accompanied by surging unemployment."[47]

Fair enough, but let's remember who pushed loans to hundreds of thousands of borrowers who could least afford them. The other originators, brokers, and securitizers, whom the Sandlers denounced, can offer exactly the same defense.

In the intense after-the-fact defense of their practices, the Sandlers provided apparently self-serving and misleading accounts of their work.[48] As mentioned above, they denounced independent brokers as "whores," while employing more of these "whores" in their last several years than the richest pimp in Vegas. As a result, they cashed in big time.[49]

Despite the evidence, the Sandlers repeatedly insisted that they did not securitize their ARMs, and so they shouldn't be identified with the financial crisis. Here's how they put it in one of their responses:

1. MYTH: Golden West securitized its loans and sold them to investors.
FACTS: Golden West was a portfolio lender, meaning it kept its loans on its books and retained the risk. Unlike every other major mortgage lender in the country, Golden West maintained a conservative, risk-averse portfolio lending business model throughout its more than 40-year history.[50]

Several problems. First, their denunciations of mortgage banks for selling off loans to secondary lenders ring hollow, since the

Sandlers quite happily sold all of their loans (along with their whole company), almost all of which were option ARMs, to Wachovia for over $24 billion. If selling bundles of mortgages is bad, why was it okay for the Sandlers to sell loans totaling well over $100 billion?[51]

Second, according to Golden West's own filings with the Securities and Exchange Commission (SEC), the company actually did securitize tens of billions of dollars of its ARMs. To quote its 2005 filing directly: "We often securitize our portfolio loans into mortgage-backed securities."[52] The Sandlers claimed over and over that the company's status as a "portfolio" lender meant that it did not securitize its loans, and yet it told the SEC that it did just that.

Characteristically, Golden West seems to have securitized its loans differently than other lenders did. The company did it privately rather than publicly, and retained the servicing so that the loans continued to appear on its books.

It used funds from the Federal Home Loan Banks, a system of 12 banks organized in 1932 as part of the New Deal. (This system set the precedent for the government to enter the housing market. Its better-known sibling, the Federal National Mortgage Association, "Fannie Mae," followed in 1938. In 1970, these "government sponsored enterprises" were joined by "Freddie Mac," the Federal Home Loan Mortgage Association.)

Also damning is a so-called Pooling and Servicing Agreement between World Savings and Deutsche Bank, dated June 21, 2002;[53] apparently Golden West/World Savings used both government-sponsored and private banks to securitize its loans. This information has never been reported by the mainstream press. It was uncovered when Golden West customers who were in foreclosure, or their attorneys, did their own research to try to learn who really owned their mortgages.

More details are coming to light with mounting foreclosures on the World Savings loans that are now held by Wells Fargo. Those details include the very real subprime borrowers the Sandlers said didn't receive their loans.

Although there is still more to discover, there is strong evidence that the Sandlers played a role in the subprime housing crisis and did many of the same things they attacked their competitors for.

A COMPLEX MIX

"We are devoting the rest of our lives to our long-held charitable interests to try and make the world a better place for the most vulnerable among us," concluded the Sandlers in their response to *Time* magazine (quoted above), "including fighting predatory lending, exposing corruption and human rights abuses, and advancing scientific research to cure asthma and third-world parasitic diseases."[54] Indeed, they were among the first to join Warren Buffett and Bill and Melinda Gates in signing The Giving Pledge,[55] which committed them to giving away most of their wealth during their lifetimes. Herb Sandler continues to donate the couple's wealth freely and wants other rich people to do the same, by government force if necessary. Hence he is "devoted to the idea of preserving progressive income and inheritance taxes."[56]

The progressivism the Sandlers embody is a synthesis of particular loves and hatreds. A progressive can care about the poor and yet despise the very policies that could help the poor. That's because progressivism often mixes deeply and sometimes properly held moral convictions with what I believe are misguided political and economic beliefs, chased down with an all-too-human shot of rationalization. In Herb and Marion Sandler, we see the complete, if complex, package. In reading their responses to critics, one gets the overwhelming impression that they simply couldn't accept that their good intentions could have caused any harm.

With their complex mix of real concern and hypocritical attacks on others, at some point they were bound to cross paths with a nonprofit activist from North Carolina with the same proclivities. The Sandlers' patronage would elevate his influence and his work to unparalleled heights. He also stars in a morality tale as complex as it is cautionary. His name is Martin Eakes.

CHAPTER 4

"50 MILLION
FINANCIAL
TERRORISTS"

At a lecture hall podium of Duke University's Fuqua School of Business, wearing a T-shirt and shorts on a sultry August day in 2010, stood Matt Nash, director of the school's Center for the Advancement of Social Entrepreneurship.[1] He was introducing a man named Martin Eakes, who seemed to epitomize the social entrepreneur at his best:[2] caring, generous, shrewd as a serpent, and innocent as a dove. Martin's organization, Self-Help, was so wholesome that it had begun with $77 raised in a bake sale and was one of 12 nonprofits celebrated in the book *Forces for Good.*[3]

Self-Help, Matt explained, was "a nonprofit community development lender whose mission is to create ownership and economic opportunity for people of color, women, rural residents, and low-wealth families and communities." It had started small, but today was a sprawling operation thanks to the work of the man—the "pioneer," said Matt with a chuckle—about to come to the podium. This enterprising man had also worked with Fannie Mae, Bank of America, Citigroup, and other banks to lend more than $5.7 billion to some 65,000 low-income homeowners, small businesses, and nonprofits.

For this work on behalf of the poor, the audience heard that Martin Eakes had received death threats. Why? Perhaps because Eakes and his colleagues had more recently formed an organization, called the Center for Responsible Lending, to fight predatory lending.

The audience applauded as Eakes approached the microphone. The *Wall Street Journal* had described him five years earlier as "a 50-year-old with an impish giggle,"[4] but here, reading his speech through metal-rimmed glasses, he was professorial. Still, his face had a Peter Pan–like quality, which, coupled with his white hair, gave him a contradictory look of blended youth and experience. His clothing was nondescript—a blue jacket with white name tag still affixed, a rough-weave button-down shirt, and a modest checked tie—as modest, apparently, as the man himself.

"If I'd known that Matt was going to start off with an overly generous introduction more like a funeral eulogy," he began in a soft North Carolina accent, "I would have done the decent thing and died before I got here."

Before beginning his lecture, he "introduced" the audience to a "new way of talking"—the Southern accent—by telling a story about the shock he encountered when he first went to law school and arrived in New York City in his "old '65 Buick."[5] This was the first of several stories. There was one about a Baptist preacher, a joke about a Texas rancher and a North Carolina tenant farmer, and another tale that left more of a homespun impression than a specific memory.

Eakes then briefly described Self-Help and its offspring, the Center for Responsible Lending. Even here an engaging reminiscence was never far away. He talked about Durham, North Carolina, during the days of segregation. He mentioned how he and his wife, Bonnie Wright, founded the Center for Community Self-Help, in 1980, to give legal advice to employees who wanted to take over then-languishing furniture factories and textile mills. They started Self-Help Credit Union in 1984 to provide home and small-business loans to the working poor, as well as Self-Help Ventures Fund, in 1984, to make higher-risk loans. Ten years later, they founded Self-Help Service Corporation to do administrative and payroll work for the umbrella organization. Self-Help Community Development Corporation, founded in 1996, develops residential real estate. One of their signal accomplishments, he said, was the Walltown neighborhood rehabilitation project in Durham, which was underwritten by Duke University.

Lest he seem to be bragging, he quickly softened the description of his accomplishments with a self-deprecating reference to his inability to get to work with two matching socks. He then moved on to more recent history. In 2008, he and his colleagues established Self-Help Federal Union to "build a business base in California," on which they hoped to build a one- or two-billion-dollar institution "to serve the under-banked and unbanked in California."[6]

His summary of the Self-Help empire was routine until the end, when his tone changed slightly. "Matt mentioned the Center for Responsible Lending, which I'll talk about a little bit more later. It's an affiliated research and policy organization that started because we got really angry at the financial services sector, and in 2002 started this organization that has hired fifty lawyers, PhDs, and MBAs to basically terrorize the financial services industry for any of their abusive practices nationwide."[7]

When he said "terrorize," he thrust his left hand forward slightly, as if he were grasping at something. "At least twelve of the companies that we have engaged directly no longer even exist," he said. "And so one of the messages I will say later is that having a moral core to your business activity is important not just because it will enable you to change the world, but it's important to the very success of the very business itself. My mother used to have this saying that she would quote to her four sons: 'If you have the vision to see a problem, you have the duty to help solve it.' . . .

"We started with a $77 bake sale to raise capital to lend to minority small businesses. And now with $2 billion in assets, we've grown a lot; but we really haven't changed that much."

Eakes's telling of his story is like many third-party profiles written about him over the years. He grew up on the southwest side of Greensboro in a nice house on an old farm near a predominantly poor, predominantly black part of town. As a result, many of his childhood friends were black at a time when the South was still adjusting to desegregation. As a young adult, one of his black friends, sometimes described as his best friend, was shot and killed not far from Eakes's house. His friend's death was a watershed. "On that day, Eakes vowed to live his life for the two of them," according to a 2008 profile.[8]

He went to Davidson College, near Charlotte, double-majoring in physics and philosophy. This was a liberal arts school that encouraged such intellectual ambitions—it has graduated 23 Rhodes scholars since its founding in 1837, three-fifths the record of its nearby (and vastly larger) contemporary, Duke. Except for the matching red brick buildings, Davidson reminds me of my own undergraduate alma mater: nestled in a pastoral town on rolling hills not far from a large city; small (fewer than 2,000 students); academically rigorous; and with a religious heritage that has mostly faded into the background, leaving behind a residual progressivism.

Davidson's greatest claim to fame is that future president Woodrow Wilson spent the 1873–1874 academic year there, before transferring to Princeton University. Wilson was elected U.S. president in 1912 as an ardent "progressive," a political philosophy (shared to some degree by both major political parties) that encouraged a much more centralized government. Wilson saw much of his agenda enacted, including the first federal income tax, the Federal Reserve Act, the Federal Trade Commission Act, and the Clayton Antitrust Act—policies that all served to increase economic power in Washington. Wilson received the Nobel Peace Prize in 1919 for sponsoring the League of Nations, a first, ill-fated attempt to centralize global political power in a body of unelected technocrats. I mention all this because, while Martin Eakes likes to stress that he was shaped by the 1960s and the civil rights movement, he is also a political descendant of Wilson.

Profiles of Eakes and his wife, Bonnie, often tell how the two met one night on campus when Bonnie came upon Martin chained to a flagpole. (Some versions of this story imply this was a political stunt, others that it was a student prank.) He went on to get a law degree at Yale Law School and a public policy degree from none other than Princeton's Woodrow Wilson School of Public and International Affairs. With "Martin's vision of social justice and Bonnie's natural activism,"[9] they started the Center for Community Self-Help in Durham in 1980.

In the Self-Help origin story, the 1984 bake sale is sometimes supplemented with a reference to their first "office in the back seat of a VW Beetle."[10] Both make the same point, but the VW Beetle story has the added benefit of subtly reinforcing another Eakes theme—that despite its origin in 1980, Self-Help is really anchored to the civil rights struggles of an earlier period. "When Self-Help first started," Eakes said in an interview in 2000, "our original mission was to translate the Civil Rights and women's movements into the economic arena."[11] This is a recurring theme in Eakes's self-description.

Their initial idea was to provide legal advice to the poor in North Carolina, but they quickly discovered that their clients "didn't need advice; they needed money."[12] Specifically, they needed a reliable line of credit, usually one that would allow them to own a home. These borrowers, however, often had undesirable credit records that would bar them from getting a mortgage from a bank. Martin and Bonnie realized that if they wanted to help the poor climb a ladder of wealth out of poverty, the couple would need to be in the mortgage business.

"I did make this bet when we started Self-Help Credit Union in 1984 that has proven to make me look like a genius, even though I am not," Eakes explained at that Duke speech. "I made a bet that single mothers who didn't have many advantages in life would be great borrowers, either for small businesses or for first time home ownership. In the first ten years, we made eleven hundred home loans to families that my banker friends said had *no* chance of succeeding. I received ferocious criticism from these lenders and regulators who were convinced that we would lose incredible sums of money. But for me, these were the mothers I'd grown up with. After basketball games, I ate at their tables, and I *knew* the risk was not very great."

Eakes admitted to the *Wall Street Journal* that their first three business loans went bad, and "I realized I wasn't as smart as I thought, and my banker friends weren't nearly as stupid as I thought."[13] Not everyone is ready to own a home or start a business. But he and Bonnie taught themselves the business, and the Small Business Administration in Washington, D.C., supported some of their early projects with low-interest loans, as did the state legislature in North Carolina. They also received grants from government and private foundations.

"We wanted to be able to go to someone [at a bank] and say, this is not some academic theory that we believe in," Eakes explained in an interview for the 2000 PBS documentary *Faith, Hope and Capital.* "We're willing to put our own money on the line to prove that a single mom, who happens to be a minority, can raise her family and pay back a home loan." He then described the results, or a slightly burnished version of them: "We didn't have very much success in our early days convincing bankers that these families we were helping were good risks. But, we went for ten years, we have had our first loss of a home loan of $10,000 in a total of $120 million of lending directly and indirectly we have made, to mostly minority, single moms."[14]

The moral of the story? "If someone has a chance to get a toehold and own a home," Eakes concluded, "they will be far better borrowers than most of the rest of us. That is just a fact."

CREATING A SECONDARY MARKET

Although Self-Help had experienced some success, Eakes was convinced that without the resources and reach of commercial banks, the work of Self-Help and other, even smaller community development financial institutions would be just a drop in the bucket.

"Self-Help will never make a difference if we feel like we have to do everything," he argues in an interview for the PBS documentary.

"We're simply not big enough. We never will be big enough. . . . We will never reach 400,000 families, 200 at a time. So, we have no choice but to partner and link up with large institutions that already have developed a network that we can work with."[15]

And so Eakes began to approach larger lending institutions. Refusing to take no for an answer, he eventually persuaded some commercial banks, such as Wachovia in North Carolina, to lend to the so-called working poor and those with "less-than-perfect credit," including many minority single moms. But there was still a limit to how many nonstandard loans these banks could make. They were accustomed to selling their prime loans by the barrel to government sponsored enterprises (GSEs) such as Fannie Mae (the Federal National Mortgage Association) and Freddie Mac (the Federal Home Loan Mortgage Association) in what is called the secondary market for mortgages. (The primary market is where a lender makes a loan to a borrower to buy a house.) In the 1980s and early 1990s, Fannie and Freddie had strict rules about the kind of loans they would buy—so much so that, for decades, a "prime" loan basically meant a mortgage that met the standards of Fannie Mae. But while Fannie and Freddie were created to increase the market for home loans, their mandate did not include seemingly risky loans. This meant that banks couldn't unload their subprime loans on Fannie and Freddie, a reality that for years strictly limited banks' appetite for such mortgages.

So Eakes developed a strategy to solve the problem. Self-Help went to several large banks and said it would buy the loans from the banks in the same way that Fannie and Freddie buy up prime loans. "I could tell my banker friends," he later explained, "that what they have that I don't have is the ability to distribute and reach every little corner of the state of North Carolina because there are 2,000 branches and 20,000 loan officers for various banks throughout the state. What I have the ability to do that they don't want to do is take the risk. I don't think there's any risk in these loans. So, if they'll make them, I'll buy them and take the risk of failure."[16]

How could little Self-Help Credit Union possibly afford to buy all of those loans? When the credit union held a press conference to announce its first $100 million in home loans, an NPR reporter read the press release and wondered the same thing. She called Eakes to tell him that his press release had a typo in it. It should have said, she thought, that big banks were buying Self-Help's loans, not the other way around.[17]

It was no typo. Self-Help had been able to secure a massive $50 million grant (plus $1.8 million for overhead costs) from the Ford Foundation, which gave it a heavy ballast to make the loans. "Self-Help will concentrate on special, targeted products," said the Ford Foundation press release announcing the deal, "designed to expand homeownership opportunities for people who require lower down payments and more flexible underwriting standards, and have difficulty meeting conventional lending standards because of inadequate savings or weaker credit."[18]

But that's just part of the story. The Ford grant was part of a highly unusual partnership that Eakes managed to negotiate with Self-Help, the Ford Foundation, several private banks, and Fannie Mae. Yes, Self-Help bought the risky loans, but then the credit union got to do what banks previously could not: *securitize or sell the loans to Fannie Mae.* This subtle policy shift would eventually have profound consequences for the mortgage market. Over five years, Fannie promised to "purchase and/or securitize" $2 billion of loans that Self-Help acquired.[19]

As the middleman with $50 million in reserve, Self-Help provided a "credit enhancement" to the loans that were passed on to Fannie. As part of the deal, Eakes extracted "a promise from those banks [BankAmerica Mortgage, Chase Manhattan, and NationsBank] to lend more money to people who don't have the income, credit rating or savings to qualify for a traditional mortgage."[20] These banks had an extra motivation to give loans to low-income borrowers because of a new federal policy that strongly encouraged private banks to make loans to such borrowers. Neither the loans that Self-Help sold to Fannie Mae nor the promised loans extracted from private banks would remain on Self-Help's books.[21]

The program might seem like a drop in the multitrillion-dollar U.S. housing market bucket. However, the key players were eager to take the "North Carolina model" on the road to fill the bucket. To help that happen, the Ford Foundation also funded a multiyear study from a professor friend of Eakes at the University of North Carolina's Center for Community Capital "to measure and better understand the risk associated with non-traditional mortgages." In 2003, Ford announced, to no one's surprise, that the study showed "that minorities and low-income families have a strong track record of repaying mortgages." In response, Fannie re-upped the deal for another $2.5 billion under its new chairman and CEO, Franklin Delano Raines.[22]

By 2005, Self-Help had bought, securitized, or sold some $3.5 billion in these "subprime" loans. The loans originated in Washington, D.C., and 47 other states, most with very low or no down payments (that is, zero to 3 percent).[23]

"What we're doing today has never been done before," gushed James Johnson, then chairman and CEO of Fannie Mae, when the program was first announced in 1998. "We are combining the strengths of three very different organizations—a philanthropy, a community development organization, and a large mortgage investor—in a unique arrangement to benefit American home buyers. This initiative will have enormous implications for community lending in America." He forgot to mention two slightly less enthusiastic partners—the private banks and the taxpayers who would carry the burden if these loans failed.

"It's amazing—this little old credit union in Durham, N.C., has created a secondary market," said North Carolina Banking Commissioner Joseph Smith in 2005. "It's pioneering work, and it's the lasting legacy of Self-Help."[24]

The 1998 deal was indeed pioneering, but it was also the culmination of policies that had been stacking up for years, like wooden Jenga blocks. The purpose of these policies was to make housing more affordable for lower-income and minority borrowers.

HOMEOWNERSHIP FOR EVERYONE

Homeownership correlates with lots of good things. Most of us take better care of houses that we own rather than rent. If you own a home, you're more likely to take more interest in your community, to obey the law, and to plan for the future. You can even use your house to start a business. That's why the government has long supported policies to make it easier for people—especially lower-income people—to buy homes.

Anyone who owns a house knows about the tax deduction on interest paid on a mortgage.[25] This market intervention creates a subtle preference for one type of loan—one type of spending—over another. Yet it's far from the first or only way that government has fiddled with the housing market. As far back as 1922, Herbert Hoover led a campaign to increase homeownership. Franklin Roosevelt's New Deal brought most of the apparatus into place, starting with 1932, when Congress chartered the 12 government sponsored Federal Home Loan Banks to expand access to credit around the country. In 1934, the Federal Housing Administration (FHA) followed, to insure and thus encourage mortgages from approved lenders. And in 1938, Congress chartered Fannie Mae to create a national secondary market for mortgages. In 1970, Congress chartered Freddie Mac, to do more or less the same thing as Fannie Mae (which two years earlier had become a publicly traded company selling stocks and bonds).

Most people have heard of Fannie and Freddie, but what many don't know is that they are for-profit, publicly traded banks. They have always enjoyed favors from the federal government, which, among other things, allows them to borrow money at a lower interest rate than other banks. Their special status led investors to deem bonds from Fannie and Freddie to be as safe as U.S. government bonds. (This investor judgment was accurate—Fannie and Freddie were nationalized rather than allowed to go bankrupt in 2008.)

For years, Fannie and Freddie bought only low-risk, high-quality loans. Yet this hadn't done much to increase the percentage of Americans who owned homes. Per capita income was slowly going up in the early 1990s, but the percentage of homeowners was not. And the percentage of minorities, especially African Americans, who were approved for mortgages and who owned homes was lower than that for whites.

Much, if not all, of this could be explained by the changing nature—some might say, the breakdown—of families, especially among black Americans. In 1993, homes headed by single mothers had an average income 40 percent lower than homes with married husbands and wives. And since single motherhood was much more common among black Americans, it's no surprise that the ability to get a mortgage, and thus to own a home, would be lower among that group.

But who wants to blame family breakdown or other causes for a statistic if you can blame racist bankers instead? And as luck would have it, a 1991 study by the Federal Reserve in Boston showed that 77 percent of whites had their mortgage applications approved, but only 61 percent of blacks did. The press knew a sensational headline when they saw one. Without bothering to examine the cause and isolate the variable, the media pounced on the statistic as proof of systematic racism in the mortgage lending business. "When it comes to buying a home, not all Americans are created equal," reported the *Wall Street Journal*.[26]

THE ILLOGIC OF UNFAIR DISCRIMINATION IN LENDING

Affordable housing policies were initially justified on the assumption that lenders discriminated against minorities. There was racial discrimination in lending in the past that, while troubling, had perhaps made some economic sense to bankers. In 1950, many white populations thought that black homeowners would drive down the prices of other homes in white neighborhoods. The 1974 Equal Credit Opportunity Act and the 1977 Community Reinvestment Act, however, made banks acutely aware of the dangers of such discrimination.[27] Besides, there have always been predominantly black neighborhoods where this logic wouldn't hold.

Think about the economics of systematic discrimination by the 1990s, however. Imagine that banks all around the country were discriminating against a group of people—African Americans, in this case—who were qualified to receive loans, in defiance of laws against discrimination. That would mean these lenders were, first, willing to risk federal action against them, and second, didn't want perfectly good money because it came from black people. This would be discrimination powerful enough to overcome economic interest, more powerful even than the greed that was previously thought to dictate a banker's every choice.

However, in a free market, even fairly large pockets of overt racism wouldn't be enough to create the purported across-the-board discrepancy. That's because entrepreneurs in free markets tend to find ways to fill unmet needs. Imagine you owned a mortgage firm and knew there were millions of eligible people wanting, but not getting, home loans simply because your competitors suffered from irrational prejudice. What would you do? There's a good chance you would focus on lending to the people suffering discrimination, since you'd have few, if any, competitors. At first, anyway. Other lenders, even those purely motivated by profit, would see your success and quickly join in. You and every company whose profit motive was stronger than its racism would quickly grow as you expanded to meet the needs of this underserved segment of the mortgage market.

For the racism explanation to work, it's not enough for a third or half or even two-thirds of lending companies to be so racist they can't bring themselves to make more money by extending home loans to creditworthy minority families; instead, virtually all the lenders would have to behave this way. Or, short of this, there would have to be laws in place against lending to minorities, or the threat of vigilante "justice" would have to be so strong as to intimidate lenders from offering such loans.

There were times in America's history when this was the case, but there are no such laws on the books today and no such threat of vigilante justice. So a truly free market of mortgage lenders competing with one another, and of borrowers shopping around, would tend to expand borrowing opportunities for minorities with solid credit, even in a society that harbors some racism. You might think that this nondiscriminating type of lending is exactly what Martin Eakes's Self-Help did. But as we'll see, it became something else entirely.

MORE JENGA BLOCKS

It's impossible to understand Eakes and Self-Help without knowing a bit more of the byzantine backstory of federal policy—in other words, how that tower of regulatory Jenga blocks had been stacked beneath them.

In 1977, then-president Jimmy Carter signed the Community Reinvestment Act (CRA) to ensure that "regulated financial institutions . . . demonstrate that their deposit facilities serve the convenience and needs of the communities in which they are chartered to do business."[28] For years, this "Reinvestment Act" mostly just encouraged insured banks and savings and loans to reach out to lower-income and minority borrowers.

The next important block in our tower was put in place 15 years later, partly in response to that 1991 study comparing the success rates of white and black people's mortgage applications.[29] The Boston Fed now admits the study was deeply flawed, but in 1992, a Democratic Congress under then-president Bill Clinton used it to justify the passage of the GSE Act. Formally known as the Federal Housing Enterprises Financial Safety and Soundness Act of 1992,[30] the law was designed to increase access to mortgages for "low-and-moderate-income persons, racial minorities and inner-city residents" through the work of the government sponsored enterprises, Fannie and Freddie.

This seemingly modest addition made the tower much wobblier. Before the GSE Act, Fannie and Freddie had required conservative lending standards for the loans it purchased—that is, a good credit rating for borrowers, a 10 to 20 percent down payment, and so on. But this new act gave the Department of Housing and Urban Development (HUD) authority to mandate that a certain percentage of Fannie and Freddie's purchases had to be the mortgages of low- and moderate-income borrowers.[31]

Since Fannie and Freddie didn't originate mortgages, they had to seek them out. This created strong market demand for banks to give loans to these lower-income borrowers, which Fannie and Freddie could then buy. This also meant they were now competing for the same risky loans with the Federal Housing Administration, which had been established decades before to insure home loans to lower-income Americans.[32]

Atop this block was placed another one in 1994–1995, with Bill Clinton still president but with a newly elected Republican House of Representatives. This building block turned the government's encouragement into insistent shoving. An initiative called "The National Homeownership Strategy: Partners in the American Dream" empowered HUD to put the squeeze on still more lenders, forcing them to prove they were achieving lending goals similar to Fannie and Freddie. Banks wanting credit from Carter's Community Reinvestment Act—like the ones that partnered with Eakes and the Ford Foundation—had an increasing incentive to provide loans to more and more lower-income and minority borrowers, including those with shaky credit.

This American Dream initiative spawned many more housing programs across many departments of the federal government, adding so many blocks that our Jenga tower began to tilt like the Tower of Pisa. For instance, there was a fund in the U.S. Treasury for "Community Development Financial Institutions"—such as Self-Help Credit Union. Its purpose was (and is) "to increase economic opportunity and promote community development investments for underserved populations and in distressed communities."[33] Besides direct investment, this fund also has programs to provide "an incentive to banks to invest in their communities"—and in other community development financial institutions.[34] It is here that Eakes's ventures enter the story. Since 1996, Self-Help Ventures Fund, which deals in riskier loans, has received over $272 million through the program. Self-Help's credit unions in North Carolina and California have together received almost $6.2 million.[35]

For the budding Self-Help empire, this was just the beginning. It was growing not only in cash but also in the power to effect the change it wanted to see in society.

Credit unions originally had been built on a different tower than banks and savings and loans. Eakes figured out how to build causeways between them. Credit unions are the product of the late nineteenth- and early twentieth-century progressive era. Unlike commercial banks, credit unions are cooperatives that are democratically controlled by their members. They were first developed for people who share something in common. Employees of a large car manufacturer or teachers in a state, for instance, might get together to form a credit union.[36] Credit unions are not-for-profit, which means that they don't have to pay many of the taxes paid by banks. Since this gives them an advantage in the marketplace, most credit unions were originally limited by law in what they could do. In particular, they were directed to work with clientele that commercial banks would consider high risk. (Much of the legal line between banks and credit unions has faded over time, and many credit unions do much of what banks do.)

Thus, the plain-vanilla credit unions that Self-Help competes with can receive money from the Treasury's Community Development Financial Institutions Fund but can't receive charitable donations. Not so for Self-Help. By having nine organizations, each set up slightly differently under the *nonprofit* umbrella "Center for Community Self-Help," Self-Help entities can receive money from a number of sources: deposits, mortgage and other payments, grants and loans from government programs, and donations from private foundations and corporations.

Eakes and Self-Help have enjoyed the funding advantages and branding of a charity, even though they can receive funds from a variety of sources (rather than just charitable foundations). With the 1998 partnership of Self-Help, the Ford Foundation, commercial banks, and Fannie Mae, Self-Help's byzantine institutional structure really started to pay off.

STRICT NARRATIVE DISCIPLINE

The image of Self-Help as a benevolent charity is maintained in large part by the image of Martin Eakes. If I had heard one speech and read one article about him in 1998 and knew nothing else about him, I would have gotten the impression of a folksy, laid-back fellow from North Carolina who has spent his adult life helping poor single mothers and minorities while managing to start a platoon of influential nonprofits in the process. Self-Help sounds like an entrepreneurial hybrid of a domestic microlending operation and Habitat for Humanity.

Almost any article you pick up about Eakes and Self-Help is glowing, but the brightest glow probably comes from a 2005 profile in a North Carolina newspaper that named Eakes "Tarheel of the Year." It begins with some of Eakes's personal facts: he has a modest $60,000 salary (in 2005) and in 1996 won a MacArthur Foundation genius grant worth $260,000. A short list of his accomplishments with Self-Help follows—the thousands of home and small-business loans to low-income borrowers, the hundreds of child care centers, and 500,000 square feet of renovated property in cities from Durham to Charlotte. And then there is a detailed biographical sketch that compares Eakes to George Bailey in *It's a Wonderful Life*:

> If Stewart's character, George Bailey, were recast as a skinny, short, white-haired guy with glasses, a cheap suit and a reedy Southern accent, Martin Eakes would be a flat natural for a remake of the Frank Capra classic. To be sure, Bailey's character would need to be filled out a bit. But if Eakes stepped into the role, the good people of Bedford Falls would have to get used to an obnoxious cackle, a needling wit and a habit of wearing mismatched socks.

They would also make the slow-dawning discovery that Eakes, a Yale-educated lawyer with a public administration degree from Princeton, is a financial wizard who has pushed his belief in the working poor far beyond the confines of a storefront savings and loan.[37]

Yet even this doesn't do justice to the man who is Martin Eakes. "There's a temptation to portray a guy like Martin Eakes as a self-less saint," writer Jim Nesbitt observes, "an ego-free Mother Teresa type who drives a 13-year-old Chevrolet Corsica with a cracked rear window and who may not remember to wear a belt."[38]

Yes, Mother Teresa. Yet where the Blessed Mother from Calcutta was quietly meek, Eakes "is an evangelical firebrand with an unbendable sense of right and wrong—even allies call him Imam Martin. But he also has a steely ability to master the complex details of law, finance, and public policy. . . ."

The hagiography concludes:

> This combination places him in a league far above George Bailey or another Jimmy Stewart character in another Frank Capra movie—U.S. Sen. Jefferson Smith, the naive idealist who battles corruption in 'Mr. Smith Goes to Washington.' . . .

If Eakes was embarrassed by the short introduction before his speech at Duke University in 2010, one can only guess at the mortified blushes this 2005 profile must have inspired.

I have listened to many of Eakes's speeches and interviews. I have read profiles of him written many years apart. They differ in some particulars, but certain elements appear over and over, such as the reference to the civil rights era as well as the concern for "closing the gap between rich and poor."

Reporters always seem to know the same plot points: Eakes's mismatched socks and old cars (of varying makes and models), his self-consciously Southern accent artfully juxtaposed with his stellar academic credentials, the homespun stories, the $77 of seed money earned from a bake sale, his black childhood friends, his being "raised a Baptist" in the desegregating South, and his uniformly evil enemies. "I've had death threats from the Ku Klux Klan, death threats from drug dealers in the neighborhoods we've tried to improve," he said in 2005. "I don't scare that easily."[39]

If you read enough about him, you eventually realize that Martin Eakes, like Herb and Marion Sandler, projects a carefully constructed image with strict narrative discipline.

Take the last item. Since the KKK is pretty much a stand-in for the Devil, having the KKK as an enemy is sort of like being St. Michael the Archangel. And since no one wants to be seen in the company of the Klan or the Devil, who in their right mind would dare criticize Eakes? One brief reference to the KKK elevates and inoculates Eakes at the same time.

In 2008, Eakes was attacked and robbed by men in a parking garage elevator near his office in Durham. In a (Raleigh) *News & Observer* editorial, columnist Barry Saunders fueled speculation that it was a planned assault:

> When investigators asked Eakes whether he had any enemies, he and his staff laughed.
>
> "When we first started," Eakes said, "the KKK used to threaten us. Then it was the drug dealers" who didn't want his organization fixing up rundown neighborhoods. After that, he got on the bad side of predatory lenders with usurious rates who don't like Eakes providing lending options for poor people.
>
> "When Martin Luther King Jr. and Gandhi are your heroes," Eakes said, "chances are you have enemies."

Wow. Even when seriously injured, Eakes stays on message.[40] So far as I know, the only person ever arrested in the incident was a very unlikely Klansman—a 28-year-old black man, Harry Wayne

Massey Jr., wanted for felony possession of stolen property.[41] But the statement about the KKK is what stuck.

One final example: I mentioned that in the August 2010 speech to MBA students at Duke University, Eakes called attention to his North Carolina accent by saying that he was introducing "a new way of talking" to students in the audience who were not from North Carolina. What's weird is that the speech was at Duke. You know, in *Durham, North Carolina*. Eakes, however, is so firmly enmeshed in the narrative about the folksy fella from far-off-the-beaten-path ol' Nawth Care-a-lahna that he rolls it out even when he's in native territory. The down-home portrait is just humble enough to be endearing but not so much that it implies a lack of sophistication and intelligence.

I am not saying the biographical flourishes are made up. Rather, they are used to construct a mythic persona that camouflages the full and much more complicated reality. The enthusiastic reference in Eakes's Duke speech to hiring 50 professionals to "terrorize the financial services industry," for instance, should strike even the sympathetic ear as a tad dissonant. When later, in a moment of unguarded zeal, he refers to "50 million financial terrorists," it's a safe bet there's more going on beneath the surface.

WHAT LIES BENEATH

Many stories describe Eakes as relentless in pursuit of his goals, and Eakes himself says he thinks of himself as a younger man, with a head of hair as red as his temper. This sounds charming enough in the newspaper puff pieces about him—a kind of George-Baileyesque indignation at the mean old Mr. Potters of the world. But if you dig beneath the topsoil of Martin Eakes's humble garden of goodwill and wholesome brotherly love, you find not just compassion and indignation but what appears to be outright hatred and an unyielding desire to force others to do what he thinks they ought—and to vanquish them, if necessary, to impose his ideals.

These strong emotions are mixed with abiding economic con-
fusions to create a dangerous mixture. Specifically, Eakes combines
his passion for the poor and minorities with a perverse view of
markets. His contempt for market freedom is so profound that he
seems immune to the observations or research that might broaden
his view. Although he's financially savvy when it comes to building
nonprofits and figuring out how to get funding from a variety of
sources, Eakes has disabling blind spots when it comes to economics
(he is an attorney, not an economist), accepting as articles of faith
myths of wealth and poverty as harmful as they are misguided.[42]

"I want to say straight out," he said in his 2010 speech at Duke,
"that I believe that the prosperity theology ideology in this country,
that greed and self-interest if practiced in the market will ultimately
lead to good outcomes for all, is morally wrong and pragmatically
wrong."

Eakes conflates several things here. There is something called
the "prosperity gospel," which in rough outline teaches that if you
just have enough faith, God will bless you with great material riches.
I'm as skeptical of that idea as Eakes is, as are most serious pastors,
priests, and theologians across the political spectrum. But regardless
of one's view of the prosperity gospel, it is not the idea that "greed
and self-interest if practiced in the market will ultimately lead to
good outcomes for all."

Eakes is also confusing greed and self-interest. That's a mistake.
Every time you take a breath, take your vitamins, or show up for
work on time, you're acting in your self-interest. That's not greed;
you're simply fulfilling your basic needs. Greed is a consuming
desire for unearned gains or possessions. That's a vice.

The more serious confusion, however, is that Eakes is missing a
key insight expressed by Scottish moral philosopher Adam Smith—
that in a truly free market (which always includes the rule of law),
people can pursue their legitimate self-interests and still act for the
benefit of others. "It is not from the benevolence of the butcher, the
brewer, or the baker," Smith famously wrote, "that we expect our
dinner, but from their regard to their own interest."[43] A free market,

Smith argued, will guide the acts of individuals "to promote an end which is not part of [their] intention."[44]

Think about it. Let's say the butcher just wants to pay the rent and buy braces for his daughter. One effective way to do that is to provide meat at a price and quality better than that of his competitors. Then people will freely buy his top sirloins and pork chops. In this way the market channels his self-interest into actions that benefit others. In fact, it can even channel a butcher's greed. As we'll see later, the cost of not understanding Smith's insight can be astronomical.

Greed exists to some degree wherever two or three are gathered, but it's not necessary for a free market to work. The butcher, baker, and brewer could each be wonderfully successful business owners without having a whit of greed. They could just as well be motivated by a desire to serve their customers, or by the artist's desire to bake, brew, or cut beautifully, or by a desire to create jobs or to make their mamas proud. Successful butchers, bakers, and brewers in the real world undoubtedly are each a complex amalgam of motivations.

Untrammeled greed can bring down an economy by destroying trust and eroding the necessary links between service and reward. Extended to legislative and judicial arenas, greed for unearned gains brings rampant cronyism between political and corporate insiders. That's bad for economic growth, since less money goes to the companies that are best at serving customers, and more goes toward those best at rigging the system for special favors.[45]

A free economy isn't utopia. Contrary to Eakes's assertions, however, capitalism rightly defined does a better job of channeling self-interest and even greed into positive outcomes than do other ways of organizing an economy. That is because it provides so many constructive outlets, even for a person obsessed with getting rich. This is a crucial point, and it's very different from imagining that a market economy depends on greed.

If his words, actions, and the ultimate fruit of his activities are any indication, Martin Eakes remains deeply misguided about both of these points—that legitimate self-interest is not identical with greed, and that a free market can, to some degree, channel both self-interest and even greed for the benefit of others.

Eakes also betrays a blinkered understanding of the sources of wealth. In a 2000 interview for the PBS documentary, he was asked to explain whether providing access to credit was a way to alleviate poverty. He explained the importance of knowledge in pursuing a successful business but had this to say about markets:

> Most people believe that credit is a panacea, that it will solve all problems of poverty. And I sometimes use the metaphor of a poker game. To be a successful poker player—which is essentially what a market economy is—it takes two things. You have to have chips that you can bring to the table, but you also have to have knowledge of how to play the game. If you take either of those two away, either wealth or knowledge, the other cannot stand on its own. If you go to a poker game and you say, "Well, I've got a lot of chips," but you've never played before, it only takes a very short little time before your nest egg has been redistributed to everyone else. On the other hand, if you come to a card game and you have knowledge, but you have no chips, you can be run out of the game by someone who's willing to bet a little bit more than you have.

Spot the fallacy? If not, think about the way a poker game works: it's a zero-sum game. Somebody wins; somebody else loses. That's true of poker, but not of a normal free exchange. If there are two players who start a game of poker with $1,000 each, and one person leaves with $2,000, you know that the other player is leaving with empty pockets. That's just the nature of the game. People play because of the thrill and because they hope they might win.

Now think of the last market exchange you had. Maybe you got a sandwich at Subway or picked up some clothes from the dry cleaner. Almost any example will do. Let's go with Subway. When I enter a Subway and buy a foot-long double-meat turkey with the works, is that like a poker game? Of course not. I go in with $7 and leave with the sandwich. The store gives me the sandwich, and it gets $7. The reason this trade happens is because I wanted the sub more than the $7, and Subway wanted the $7 more than the sandwich. Since we each got what we preferred, it's a win-win exchange. This is such a simple idea that a sixth grader can get it (I've tested this), and yet it can completely escape recipients of MacArthur genius grants with advanced degrees from Princeton and Yale.

In fact, as we'll see, when Eakes compares lenders to predators, he seems to go even farther than the zero-sum-game fallacy. At least in poker, it's possible for either of the players to win and both get to leave at the end of the game. Not so with bobcats and bunnies. If the bunny eludes the bobcat, he's no better off than before the chase. If the bobcat wins, the bobcat gets dinner and the bunny gets eaten. The bunny never wins in the exchange. Does that *really* describe the normal relationships between banks and poor people who receive loans? When a poor person walks into a bank, does he get eaten, robbed blind, or barely escape with his life?

It is because of the misguided beliefs underlying these emotional and economically misleading metaphors that Eakes, like Herb and Marion Sandler, can genuinely care about the poor and yet attack the one economic system that has helped more people escape from poverty than all the poker games, bingo fund-raisers, charity giveaways, and socialist schemes in history. And these beliefs are the reason he could not be content merely to provide small home and business loans to the poor in North Carolina. More radical reform would be needed.

His old law partner, Durham lawyer Wib Gulley, unwittingly gives us a glimpse of this side of Eakes. "More than most," Gulley observes, "he's been successful at bending the world to his values and what he thinks it ought to be." Notice that Gulley didn't say *persuade* or *convince*, but *bend*. Presumably, if people pursuing their legitimate self-interest inevitably leads to disaster, and if lenders in a free economy are inherently predatory, then bending—or coercing—others is the only effective way to help the less fortunate.

I've traced only part of Eakes's story here. Eakes, as we have seen, had engineered a major deal by combining the power of the government, the banking system, his own charity, and $50 million from one of the country's largest charitable foundations. But he was just getting warmed up. To fully realize his goals on a national scale, he would need to expand the Self-Help operation, and that would take a lot of money. However, unlike most nonprofit leaders, who must pound the pavement pleading for donations, Eakes would be petitioned by a billionaire donor to go big.

CHAPTER 5

THE PHILANTHRO- CAPITALISTS

arlier, we visited the popular hagiography of Herb and Marion Sandler, and came to see why the *Saturday Night Live* satire of their business activities was closer to the truth (even if it ran off the rails with the "people who should be shot" subtitle). We only hinted at the Sandlers' philanthropy, which has gone largely unnoticed, whether on late-night comedy shows or elsewhere. It is the one area where the Sandlers might appear bulletproof. Yet, it turns out to be more like the soft underbelly of the dragon.

The Sandlers' progressive philanthropy has been as much a part of their identity as their business prowess. For years before they sold Golden West Financial in 2006, they donated to liberal causes, such as Human Rights Watch, the American Civil Liberties Union, and the now-infamous ACORN. And after they sold their company, the Sandlers allocated $1.4 billion for their foundation, putting it in the top 30 charitable foundations in the United States.

Joe Nocera wrote a glowing profile of these "Self-Made Philanthropists" in the *New York Times* in March 2008, just months before the financial meltdown that cast the work of Herb and Marion Sandler in a dimmer light. Nocera described them as doing "at least as much research into human rights organizations [potential grantees] as they did when they were thinking about making an S.&L. acquisition." He continued:

> "They are keenly interested in the management of non-profits, and they are struck by how badly managed most of them are," says Chuck Lewis, the founder of the Center for Public Integrity, an investigation-oriented nonprofit that got a few small grants from the Sandlers a few years ago. "They have almost a fetish about it. They have an absolute infatuation with focusing on management. Who are the leaders? What is their background? Is it getting bigger or smaller? They rigorously chew over what they are about to do, much more than others do.
>
> So that's one part of their philanthrocapitalist approach: they want their money to go to organizations they feel are well run and led by people they can count on to keep them that way. They want some control.[1]

Seth Lubove provided other details about their charitable work in a *Forbes* profile in 2004:

> After talking with the Sandlers, though, you come away with the impression that, for all their financial accomplishments, they're more interested in using the business as a means to the higher end of political and philanthropic pursuits. Die-hard liberal Democrats, the Sandlers support various do-gooder causes and activist outfits, as well as medical research for the asthma that afflicts Marion. The couple provided seed money alongside hedge fund scold George Soros to start up Clinton apparatchik John Podesta's Center for American Progress, a liberal version of the Heritage Foundation, and is the primary sugar daddy behind UC, Berkeley's Human Rights Center.[2]

If you don't look closely, you might merely see progressive billionaires taking time out to give back to the society that has enriched them. But dig deeper, and what you find is that their philanthropic work was not simply what they did when they weren't running the family business. It was a pivotal *part* of the family business.

MASSAGING THE MESSAGING

One of the Sandlers' first initiatives after the sale to Wachovia was in media. In October 2007, the Sandlers founded—with a $10 million seed grant to be renewed annually—a supposedly nonpartisan and independent organization called ProPublica to do "investigative journalism." Its stated purpose was "exposing abuse and neglect in powerful places." When they tapped retiring *Wall Street Journal* managing editor Paul Steiger to run it, Herb Sandler used one word to describe the stories he wanted: *outrage*.[3]

The organization has a clever strategy. Rather than just posting its well-funded investigations on its website, ProPublica offers its partially completed stories to major print publications. In this age of free digital media, from Twitter to Drudge, print publications and traditional broadcast media have not only lost their near monopoly on timely reporting but also have less money for costly investigative pieces. ProPublica gave "legacy" media a new weapon. By providing heavily funded research, ProPublica has landed major stories with partners such as the *New York Times*, the *Washington Post*, and the PBS news series *Frontline*.

The ProPublica board is chaired by Herb Sandler himself and populated by fellow liberals such as Harvard professor Henry Louis Gates Jr. Their Journalism Advisory Board enlists liberal Republican David Gergen for "balance," but he's ballast against a cadre of progressives, including University of California, Berkeley's Thomas Goldstein, and syndicated columnist Cynthia Tucker.[4]

When the initiative was first announced, some expressed worry that ProPublica would be just so much partisan PR masquerading as hardnosed reporting. "We personally are progressive," Herb

Sandler responded, "but this is going to be totally nonpartisan." Jill Abramson, another member of the Journalism Advisory Board and executive editor of the *New York Times*, typifies the pretense of neutrality that pervades the organization. When the outgoing public editor of the *Times*, Arthur Brisbane, admitted in August 2012 that a progressive worldview "virtually bleeds through the fabric of *The Times*,"[5] Abramson famously disagreed.[6] No doubt she also sees ProPublica as "playing it straight." And not surprisingly, when *Saturday Night Live* aired the skit in October 2008 criticizing the Sandlers, ProPublica president Paul Steiger called *SNL* executive producer Lorne Michaels to complain.[7]

Even more interesting, though, is the recurrence of what we might call Sandler Stories of Interest. The Sandlers' contempt for Wall Street and criticism of their own mortgage-lending competitors is well known.[8] So, not surprisingly, ProPublica has an entire investigative series called "The Wall Street Money Machine."[9] As of August 6, 2012, it included 41 stories,[10] many involving hedge fund Magnetar, which profited by shorting the housing market. In 2011, the ProPublica series reporters Jesse Eisinger and Jake Bernstein won a Pulitzer Prize for their reporting "on Wall Street's contribution to the economic meltdown."[11] Another of ProPublica's investigations focuses on the "foreclosure crisis"; as of July 3, 2012, it had 100 stories.

But perhaps the most telling investigation is of Freddie Mac. The lead story, copublished with NPR News, complained loudly that "the taxpayer-owned mortgage giant made investments that profited if borrowers stayed stuck in high-interest loans while making it harder for them to get out of those loans."[12] The only problem? The loans sound exactly like a Sandler Special: an option ARM with a prepayment penalty. The reporters' journalistic curiosity just didn't extend to the Sandlers. And although biased, ProPublica does maintain a more balanced image than, say, Media Matters—a left-wing attack dog clamped onto the ankle of conservative media and also heavily supported by the Sandlers.

Another Sandler (and MacArthur Foundation) grantee is the PBS documentary series *Frontline*. In recent years, *Frontline* has covered the financial crisis again and again. In 2009, as the crisis was playing out, *Frontline* was jam-packed with episodes such as "Inside the Meltdown," "Breaking the Bank," and "The Warning."[13] These were followed in 2012 by the four-part series, "Money, Power, and Wall Street."[14] The fifth installment came in January 2013. Called "The Untouchables," it asked why no Wall Street executives had gone to jail for fraud after the financial crisis. Were they too big to jail?[15] Although the episode revealed no clear evidence of criminality, the producers did all they could to insinuate as much. Featured expert Phil Angelides, chair of the official commission to study the financial crisis, was on hand to confirm for viewers that government oversight of Wall Street was "woefully broken."[16]

None of these called any attention to the Sandlers' role in the crisis, a role others had seen as highly significant. And worse yet, none covered the misguided political policies that planted the seeds of the crisis in the first place—except, of course, to offer the stock complaint about a lack of government regulation.

A typical treatment is "Breaking the Bank," which focused on Merrill Lynch, Bank of America, and the bailout drama of September 2008. Left-of-center commentators outnumber right-of-center commentators about three to one in the documentary. The final words, starting with the chief economist of President Obama's Economic Recovery Advisory Board and concluding with ominous words from Elizabeth Warren (whom we'll discuss later), are worth quoting in their entirety:

AUSTAN GOOLSBEE: They [Wall Street banks] created the structures themselves that got them into this position. It wasn't the government who created this problem, they created this problem. Maybe they find it inconvenient that there's a whole lot of responsibilities that come along with the government being their lender of last resort and saving them when they actually fell into the—to the pit of fire. But you know, that's where we are.

NARRATOR: As far as Washington is concerned, they're still sorting through the financial wreckage.

JOE NOCERA, *New York Times*: This is the kind of disaster, like the aftermath of the Great Depression and the crash of '29, that causes people to say, "There's something fundamentally wrong here. There's something fundamentally broken. And we can't fix it with a new agency, or you know, just a piecemeal approach. We have to kind of tear down the structure and start all over."

NARRATOR: But whatever happens, the era that propelled John Thain, Ken Lewis and Hank Paulson to the top of the financial world is over.

ELIZABETH WARREN, Chair, Congressional Oversight Panel: The party's over. The financial institutions are down for the count. This is one of those pivot points in American history. That old economy, that old way of looking at things, that old way of putting on a party—it's over. It's over.[17]

Get the message? *Wall Street—evil. Radical government expansion and control—good.* Also in 2009 *Frontline* aired an episode titled "The Card Game." The title's metaphorical reference to a zero-sum game is telling; activists like Martin Eakes persist in portraying capitalist economies as zero-sum games, like poker, in which the rich get richer by taking from the poor. But the bias doesn't stop there. The episode is billed as investigating "the massive consumer loan industry and what's ahead for customers and banks—a Frontline–*New York Times* co-production."[18] It features Democratic Senator Chris Dodd and Martin Eakes and paints a glowing picture of an anticipated Dodd-Frank Act that, in its "meticulous, provident, and kindly disposed"[19] arms, would embrace not just mortgage lending, but consumer lending as well.

The problem here is not that rich progressives support organizations that share their viewpoint. The problem is that their media beneficiaries enjoy a false presumption of neutrality. And it is that presumption that gives them real, and coercive, cultural power. Sociologist James Davison Hunter argues that cultures are influenced and changed not by majority vote but by elites and their networks, which shape the ideas of the majority. Culture is "about how societies define reality—what is good, bad, right, wrong, real, unreal, important, unimportant, and so on. This capacity is not evenly distributed in a society."[20] National media that enjoy the manufactured presumption of neutrality have an extremely disproportionate role in "defining reality" in Hunter's sense.

Think about it. To write a book like this one, I have little choice but to watch *Frontline* and read the *New York Times*. My endnotes are filled with articles from the *Times*. A major story in the *New York Times* will spawn hundreds of print and broadcast stories downstream. Similarly, the soft bias of a *Frontline* special will do far more than hundreds of opinion pieces to shape how influential Americans see an issue. These media sources need not lie. They can simply be highly selective in what they cover and how they cover it, and ignore the part of the story they think should not be told.

There's nothing inherently wrong with emphasizing one side of a story, particularly if that side has been sorely neglected. The problem comes when you can pass off your advocacy piece as a studious, neutral, and balanced assessment of a controversial issue. The presumption of neutrality attached to shows like *Frontline* constitutes significant cultural power. To be able to fund, enable, and enhance such media is an even greater form of cultural power. This is the power that Herb and Marion Sandler have wielded for years.

Fortunately there is a silver lining. This power is vulnerable. It's only when people believe that the emperor is richly garbed in the robes of neutrality that he can shape public opinion so powerfully.

If enough people see and admit that the emperor has no clothes, his authority dissipates. No one likes the rich elitist who tries to tell everyone else what they are supposed to think and do.

PROTECTIVE PUBLICITY

Unlike billionaire financier and currency speculator George Soros, who is practically a household name and stars in many a conservative conspiracy theory, the Sandlers managed to avoid the national spotlight for years. When they were in the news, the couple enjoyed fawning coverage—so fawning as to suggest that they had a knack for shaping it.

In dozens of profiles of the Sandlers over a period of more than 20 years, story after story refers to their savings and loan as a "mom-and-pop" operation. Sure, reporters pick up choice phrases from those who have gone before, but this is just too much for a company that started with $34 million in loans from a bank and a wealthy brother, had over 1,000 employees by 1990, and by 2006 boasted $125 billion in assets and 11,600 employees around the country.[21] For a while, I wondered how the Sandlers had managed to garner such uniform media coverage over many years. Then I noticed that one reporter mentioned a telling detail of his private interview with the Sandlers. Marion Sandler had brought her knitting needles and yarn. Maybe she really did knit every hour of every day, but this was also a powerful visual symbol. It communicated a warm and personal hominess, old-fashioned values, grandma, and apple pie.

The technique worked. In 1990, another reporter, Richard Stevenson, wrote a long and fulsome piece about Golden West Financial for the *New York Times*, called "Inside the Nation's Best-Run S.&L." It described the operation, under the Sandlers' leadership, as "conservative, even dull," "old-fashioned," and "stingy." Out of context, these might sound like criticisms, but Stevenson always used the terms as compliments. The stinginess, for instance, referred to the fact that the company didn't spend a lot on the superficial appearance of its branches. The Sandlers' ability to control costs was warmly depicted as an old-fashioned virtue. Reading Stevenson's profile, I could almost smell the pie.

Still, one detail stuck out. "Of the 1,050 employees who work in the branches," Stevenson mentioned in passing, "more than 500 are on permanent part-time status, keeping payroll costs low." Part-time employees often don't have retirement and medical benefits, and so they are much cheaper for employers than are full-time employees.

Now imagine if a *New York Times* reporter covering conservative Texas oilman T. Boone Pickens or libertarian businessmen Charles and David Koch discovered that almost half of their companies' employees were permanently part-time. Would that fact have counted toward their virtuous thrift or as proof positive of their hardhearted greed?

Since the Sandlers had shaped their uniformly flattering media coverage, it was a new experience when they were criticized after the subprime chickens came home to roost. What's intriguing is that they showed the same self-serving clairvoyance in this situation that they exhibited when selling their company to Wachovia. They had supported progressive media for years, but just before the financial crisis, they started positively pouring time and money into media outfits. Their first, renewable grant to ProPublica in 2007 was for $10 million—an enormous sum for a new nonprofit. Though I doubt they fully anticipated the coming firestorm that they helped create, they were well prepared.

The media criticism in late 2008 and 2009 infuriated the Sandlers, even though, for the most part, it was balanced, factual, and temporary. The *60 Minutes* segment and the *New York Times* story, which did the most to expose questionable practices at Golden West/World Savings, avoided personal attacks and even mentioned the Sandlers' philanthropic work. The *Times* story was admirably evenhanded, with the exception of the original title, which called them "pariahs," and that was quickly changed after the Sandlers complained.

When *Time* magazine wrote 90 words on the Sandlers in its piece "25 People to Blame for the Financial Crisis," the Sandlers again protested. *Time* responded by posting a link to the Sandlers' thousand-word response, which is now housed permanently on the *Time* website.[22]

It would have been shamelessly obvious for ProPublica to write a piece defending the Sandlers. But in 2010 another nonprofit media outfit, the *Columbia Journalism Review*, did so. The article is mostly balanced, but the author subtly attempts to vindicate the Sandlers against "aggressive journalism," and approvingly explains the Sandlers' responses to a misinformed press that "lumped the egregious with the unlucky."[23] Perhaps it's just a coincidence that the publication is supported by the Sandlers' donor-in-arms, George Soros.[24]

Why was it important for the Sandlers to campaign so hard to defend their reputation? Perhaps they just wanted to defend themselves and try to protect what legacy they had left. However, I suspect they understood that if a reputation as predatory lenders was allowed to stick, their righteous efforts against such lenders would lose credibility and destroy the political influence they worked so hard to achieve.

In any case, they had plenty of reason to worry. It was becoming clear how they had conducted business—and it differed from the friendly media façade they had manufactured and enjoyed.

In his March 2008 interview with the Sandlers, the *New York Times'* Joe Nocera observed that "even among the philanthrocapitalists, . . . the Sandlers stand out. Herb, in particular, can sound nearly contemptuous about how other philanthropies go about their business. Mainly, it seems, they don't do it the way he and Marion do." Nocera continued:

> But what makes them so sure their way is better?
>
> "It starts with outrage," Herb Sandler said. "You go a little crazy when power takes advantage of those without power. It could be political corruption — "
>
> "Or subprime lending," Marion interrupted.
>
> "The story of subprime is worse than anyone has written so far," Herb said, shaking his head in dismay.

"It is," Marion said, nodding in agreement.

We were sitting around a table in Herb's office talking about what motivated them to put some of their fortune into investigative journalism. But they could have been talking about much of their giving over the years. To listen to the Sandlers is to be in the presence of the kind of proud, righteous liberals who went out of fashion a long time ago. Dispassion and irony, the twin shields of the modern age, are not part of their makeup.

All this self-righteous disdain for other lenders looks bizarrely hypocritical, given the criticisms that had already been published about the Sandlers. A destroyed reputation over their longstanding business practices would blunt their longtime efforts to assert their progressive agenda on American politics. Only an ardent defense of their record could help safeguard those achievements.

The Sandlers' efforts to cast blame elsewhere also seem to have an element of denial. Had they not noticed that many of their borrowers had gone years without making even interest-only payments and were sliding ever more deeply into debt? Who knows? Call it a blind spot, but I can imagine that even behind closed doors, the Sandlers never admitted, even to each other, that they had done what their now-public accounting revealed in black and white.

A CONFLUENCE OF INTERESTS

In 2004, the Sandlers joined billionaires George Soros, Peter B. Lewis (chairman of Progressive Insurance), and others in a concerted effort to get John Kerry elected.[25] Often identified as the Democracy Alliance, the billionaires club spent tens of millions of dollars on left-wing groups, such as MoveOn.org, and created a new left-wing think tank, the Center for American Progress. An article in the *New Yorker* that same year described the Sandlers as members of a group of "hard-core partisans."[26] But there's more to the story. Their more interesting philanthropy involves nonprofits that deal with financial institutions and housing, one of which is the Association of Community Organizations for Reform Now (ACORN).

ACORN was founded in 1970 by Wade Rathke and had its origins in the radicalism of the late 1960s. A nonprofit that passed up tax-exempt status, ACORN had a sophisticated institutional structure as intricate as a spider web, with several affiliated front groups and individual state offices working in tandem with its national office. It had a dotted-line relationship with many other groups, reflecting "overlapping memberships and interlocking directorates." As best I can tell, the four main organizations of the ACORN network took in over $100 million from 1993 to 2005.[27] Officially they helped people find housing and start businesses in poor areas. They were also involved in voter drives and other "community actions."[28]

Until 2009, the average American had never heard of ACORN. Three people changed that. The first was Barack Obama. Obama's claim to fame prior to entering politics was community organizing, sometimes in concert with ACORN. He later benefitted from ACORN efforts in his 2008 election, despite various reports pointing to irregularities in ACORN's's activities.[29] But ACORN owes its infamy to two lesser-known figures, Hannah Giles and James O'Keefe.

Stories of the criminality of some ACORN employees had circulated for years, and, in 2008, media outlets such as CNN reported some cases involving ACORN in voter fraud.[30] ACORN was known for signing up individuals such as "Jive Turkey" and "Mary Poppins" in their voter drives.[31] But because the organization worked with the poor and urban minorities and received millions of dollars in government funding, it was not a convenient target for Washington politicians, especially Republicans.

In 2009, Giles, a 21-year-old college student, contacted O'Keefe, a young activist, and together they hatched a sting operation. They went to an ACORN office in Baltimore with a hidden camera and microphone. Ms. Giles posed as a prostitute, Mr. O'Keefe as her apparent boyfriend or pimp. They openly discussed their desire to get a loan to bring underage girls into the city from

Central America, implicitly to work as prostitutes.³² The ACORN officials seemed more than happy to help and provided useful information about how to avoid taxes and the law in general. Encouraged by the experience, O'Keefe and Giles did the same thing at ACORN offices in Washington, D.C., Brooklyn, and elsewhere, and often met with similar success.

They released the damning videos in a rolling barrage over a period of days, initially on Andrew Breitbart's BigGovernment.com. The story was quickly picked up on Fox News and set the blogosphere afire.

The right video is worth a million words, especially when artfully edited. ProPublica had done its best to protect and defend ACORN from attacks in 2008. But no lavishly funded ProPublica investigation has ever had more tangible effect on a target than O'Keefe's and Giles' now-famous sting of ACORN. ACORN managers found themselves firing employees while wondering what video might appear next on the Internet. Before long, Congress had cut ACORN's funding, government agencies severed their relationships with the group, and ACORN experienced a precipitous drop in donations from private sources.

There's a lot more to the drama, but even considering any questionable details, the overwhelming impression from the videos and subsequent firestorm was that ACORN employees were way too comfortable aiding and abetting criminal activity. That impression confirmed what many had long suspected—that ACORN was committed to social disruption rather than serving the poor.³³ In 2011, two Nevada ACORN leaders were convicted of voter fraud for their role in the Project Vote initiative.³⁴

Notorious for shock troop tactics,³⁵ ACORN made an art of disrupting events in order to intimidate their opponents. They stormed congressional hearings, crowded out public speeches by politicians, and occupied banks and other businesses in all manner of shakedown operations.

Despite their penchant for aggressive and intimidating tactics, they enjoyed lavish funding from respectable progressive donors—

such as Herb and Marion Sandler. From 1999 to 2008, the Sandlers doled out nearly $11 million to ACORN groups: $7.7 million to the American Institute for Social Justice and, in 2007 alone, $3.2 million to Project Vote.[36] ACORN had a huge budget and lavish funding from legions of donors, but the Sandlers' generous contributions still stood out.

In ACORN, the couple found the perfect marriage of business goals, political control, and philanthropy. According to ACORN whistleblower Marcel Reid, ACORN paid people to protest against the "predatory lending practices" of a bank with headquarters in San Francisco. Guess which bank? Yep, Wells Fargo. According to ACORN members in a TV interview, the Sandlers paid ACORN "to go out and attack their primary competition, Wells Fargo."[37]

Investigative reporter Matthew Vadum, who has studied ACORN extensively, describes the background in his book *Subversion, Inc.*: "'Wells Fargo was the Sandlers' biggest competition in California for subprime mortgages,' an ACORN insider said in an interview. 'ACORN was deployed to put so much pressure on Wells Fargo that they would not be able to do the subprime loans.'"

This well-funded harassment campaign went on for several years. In 2003, ACORN released a report denouncing Wells Fargo's practice of "predatory lending." For maximum effect, they coordinated "actions" against bank branches in 40 different cities all at once. In New Mexico, they filed 14 separate complaints on behalf of borrowers against Wells Fargo Financial, the corporate arm that sold subprime mortgages. Although state authorities could find no evidence of illegal activity and Wells Fargo had far less subprime exposure than its rivals, ACORN claimed it was able to get refunds for the borrowers it represented.[38]

In 2004, ACORN filed a class action lawsuit against Wells Fargo in Illinois and then launched a nationwide class action lawsuit, reinforced by a march in Los Angeles with 2,000 people.[39] The ACORN press release announced that victims of Wells Fargo's "predatory lending practices" would join the march. However, the number of real "victims" who joined in is doubtful. ACORN scheduled the march during its own biannual convention in Los Angeles, when it had a pool of members to call upon for the march. The press release also quoted ACORN's national president Maude Hurd. "ACORN will not allow Wells Fargo to continue to swindle and steal from our communities," she said. "We will fight until they stop their abusive loan practices, and the Wells stagecoach is no longer delivering misery to homeowners."[40]

In its nationwide suit against Wells Fargo, ACORN accused the bank of a variety of misdeeds, all under the guise of "predatory lending practices." These included "charging unfairly high rates and fees" on its loans, "misleading homeowners into refinancing out of perfectly good first mortgages and into new loans, which cost the borrowers much more," and "trapping borrowers with prepayment penalties." Sound familiar? Surely it would have been more fair to accuse World Savings Bank and the Sandlers of the same practices, since World pioneered the types of loans and practices that Wells Fargo was providing (and World, but not Wells Fargo, saw its portfolio virtually evaporate during the financial crisis). But World Savings didn't make ACORN's hit list.

This wasn't ACORN's first such campaign. By 2003, they had these operations down to a science. Just the year before, ACORN had badgered another lender, Household International, to make loans to people with sketchy credit ratings.[41] The group even held protests at the Federal Reserve and Federal Deposit Insurance Corporation (FDIC).

While ACORN's higher-ups may have thought globally, they acted locally, targeting not only abstract corporations but also individual CEOs, board members, and their families.[42] Like a pack of hyenas doing their Darwinian duty, they sought the most vulnerable members of the herd. "The idea is to go to private homes where wives and children are present and stand outside so the family members of a company official could be harassed and subject to intimidation,"[43] one vocal ACORN defector, Anita MonCrief, explained. ("The thirteenth rule: Pick the target, freeze it, personalize it, and polarize it," famously wrote Saul Alinsky, the father of community organizing, in his 1971 *Rules for Radicals*. Otherwise, he explained, "if an organization permits responsibility to be diffused and distributed in a number of areas, attack becomes impossible."[44]) Marcel Reid described the tactic in similar terms: "It's amazingly easy to find. Go to their homes and picket and do actions, use direct action to ostracize the person, which softens up the corporation for negotiations."[45]

In 2005, ACORN delivered over 100 "homeless people" to Liberty Tax Service, in Virginia Beach. After emptying four buses, "they came pouring into the building like a Mongolian horde," said Liberty's CEO John Hewitt. "There was screaming and fighting. One employee was bitten and another was scratched. They both had to go to the emergency room."[46] Hewitt had already agreed privately to improve Liberty's disclosures on loans, but that wasn't enough for ACORN. Although all the protestors were arrested, Hewitt didn't pursue legal action because of the cost. Instead, he ended up making more promises and giving the local ACORN affiliate $50,000 a year. "To me, it's just to stop them from harassing us," Hewitt explained to FOX News. "Even though I felt dirty by paying them money, I said, you know, it's a business decision."[47]

With an ongoing image problem, banks are under intense regulatory scrutiny from government. Therefore they are extremely sensitive to bad publicity, or even to the threat of bad publicity. In many cases, lenders have radically changed their lending policies not because of unsound practices, but simply to avoid the grief. In 1992, ACORN protested to prevent the Bank of New York from buying Barclay's Bank of New York. ACORN relented "after the bank agreed to lend $750 million in low- and moderate-income areas, weaken its underwriting standards for low-income homebuyers, and fund the creation of alternative schools in low-income communities."[48] This is just one of many such examples of ACORN's methods.[49]

At first, Wells Fargo resisted ACORN's more covert threats. In fact, the group began its 2003 attack on Wells Fargo only *after* they had failed to shake down the bank by less visible means. Why did the bank resist? Perhaps because it was proud of its record with poor and minority borrowers. That still didn't exempt the bank from extortion efforts by the friendly Association of Community Organizations for Reform Now.[50]

Eventually, Wells Fargo surrendered rather than engage in a nationwide knife fight with an army of shakedown masters and their lawyers. In 2007, the bank agreed to pay up to $4.4 million to certain "qualifying class members who submit claims" and to keep working to improve its "nonprime real estate–secured lending practices" and "to enact a default relief program, earmarking $2.4 million to provide relief to qualifying class members whose loans have become delinquent by more than 60 days."[51]

Once again, ACORN prevailed by intimidation, not because its target was found guilty of any crime. Wells Fargo made the same calculation that scores of other banks did. Perhaps caving seemed less costly than a tainted brand, personal attacks, and a protracted legal battle.

In hindsight, subprime lending looks unsavory, but Wells Fargo's practices were probably better than many lenders who escaped the public flogging. So why were they targeted, while other large lenders with similar or worse track records in this area were ignored? *Perhaps because Wells Fargo had competitors who knew exactly how to use their charitable giving to strategic advantage.* The Sandlers paid top dollar to ACORN, and ACORN happened to deliver a major hit to the Sandler's key competition. The effect of ACORN's actions was clear—even if most ACORN members who participated in the actions probably had no idea who was paying the bills, or why. Whether it is justice or injustice that Wells Fargo now owns its former competitor's mortgages with the long fuses is a moral riddle that may never be solved.

After ACORN's fall from grace, the Sandlers never publicly distanced themselves from the organization. At the Sandler Foundation website, however, there's no sign that it once gave the group millions of dollars.[52]

Even if it were not clear from the busloads of chaos unloaded on Liberty Tax Service in Virginia Beach, ACORN's generals and minions had shown they weren't above physical coercion and even criminality. "We do whatever it takes to get our goals met," said ACORN's Jeff Ordower.[53] That policy was both an asset and a liability. Its methods obviously worked for decades, and the ACORN grew into a mighty oak. But the lawlessness of ACORN's actions caused many of its well-meaning members to break with the organization and even denounce it. The oak rotted from within. Videographers James O'Keefe and Hannah Giles gave it a push, and it collapsed of its own weight.

Or at least that's how I'd like to think of it. More precisely, ACORN filed for Chapter 7 bankruptcy.[54] And in this case, bankruptcy does not mean extinction. If you take a tour of the Hoh Rain Forest on the Olympic Peninsula in Washington State a few hours from where I live, you will find curious mounds of earth scattered in the forest, each with scores of baby trees shooting up from them. The mounds are the decaying remains of giant fallen trees. Those remains serve as nurse logs to these many new saplings. ACORN, which sprouted decades ago, is such a fallen tree. It has been felled but not wholly finished. It is nursing saplings. Few of the masterminds behind ACORN have faded away; fewer still, the organization's corporals and sergeants, who know how to "organize communities" into mob scenes.

ACORN is not like imperial Japan, where if the head announces surrender, everyone else neatly follows. Its members are schooled in indirection and subterfuge. ACORN was not about destruction so much as infiltration and invasion. "Instead of trying to overturn 'the system,'" explains Sol Stern in his lucid *City Journal* analysis, "ACORN burrows deep within the system, taking over its power and using its institutions for its own purposes, like a political *Invasion of the Body Snatchers*."[55]

Many ACORN seedlings have sprouted and are spreading their branches, infiltrating new forests. In particular, and oddly enough, they have infiltrated several religious groups and created religious fronts.[56]

THE OTHER TRACK

Now, as any good strategist knows, you don't bet everything on one track. A robust campaign needs at least two—one highbrow and the other lowbrow. If you've watched James O'Keefe's hidden-camera videos, you know which track ACORN took. The Sandlers were good strategists. In 2002, around the time ACORN started its intimidation campaign against Wells Fargo behind the scenes, the Sandlers laid the other track—the Center for Responsible Lending, perhaps the most successful cause to benefit from the Sandler money. It was a strategic investment.

CHAPTER 6

"WE'RE GONNA DRIVE YOUR DAMN COMPANY INTO THE ATLANTIC OCEAN"

In late 1998, a Durham school bus driver named Freddie Rogers came to a Self-Help credit union to inquire about its new "fix-it" loan. The loan's stated purpose was to help homeowners repair or improve their homes. Rogers's home had drainage problems, which had led to a flooded basement and mold so bad that he and his daughter couldn't live there.

Lanier Blum, the Self-Help employee who met with Rogers, learned that Rogers had a mortgage with Associates First Capital, a Texas-based lender that at the time was a subsidiary of Ford Motor Company. Blum called Associates to find out how much Rogers owed. The lender's phone operators were evasive, and so she called over and over—"We absolutely harassed those people."[1] Eventually she learned that Rogers had incurred a lot of late fees on a mortgage with a 13.7 percent interest rate. But that only explained two-thirds of what he owed. Upfront fees made up the other third—fees, which, among other things, financed mortgage insurance to protect Associates if Rogers defaulted. All told, after 10 years of making payments on a $29,000 loan, he now owed $47,500.

Soon the folks at Self-Help realized Associates was writing many such loans. Martin Eakes decided to call Associates himself. The woman in customer service who had the misfortune of answering the phone was less than forthcoming about the details of Roger's loan—Self-Help was a competitor, after all—and, as Eakes remembered, "I just snapped."

"You've picked the wrong fight with the wrong person at the wrong time," he told her. "If it takes me the rest of my life, we're gonna drive your damn company into the Atlantic Ocean and you'll never make a loan in the state of North Carolina ever again."[2]

The incident doesn't paint a flattering picture of Eakes; it has entered the Self-Help hagiography nonetheless as the moment when Self-Help expanded its portfolio to include lobbying and activism.

Associates was much larger than Self-Help. In North Carolina alone, the lender had some 80 branches, to Self-Help's half-dozen. One would think Associates would therefore enjoy economies of scale and so have a competitive advantage. But Eakes claimed that if Rogers had gotten a loan from Self-Help, the bus driver would already have paid it off and even saved $10,000.[3] This is just one of the recurring economic perplexities one encounters in studying Self-Help. If the credit union really could offer better, cheaper loans than Associates—and Self-Help had the advantage of heavy support from the Ford Foundation and the government—why wasn't it already beating Associates in the market? Why would borrowers choose a loan with huge upfront fees, a prepayment penalty, mandatory mortgage insurance, and a high interest rate, if the Self-Help alternative was so much better? Curiously, this question never seems to occur to journalists who write friendly stories about this episode in Self-Help's history.

Apparently neither did the question occur to Eakes. Instead, Self-Help's lawyer, Mike Calhoun, drafted an "anti-predatory lending" law, and Eakes began his lobbying career—to make North

Carolina the first state in the country to pass such a law. Perhaps he thought, why compete in the marketplace when you can outlaw the competition's business plan? Or, less cynically, maybe he just thought he was on the side of the angels. Either way, if you can paint your opponents as minions of Satan, all the better.

FROM HELP TO ACTIVISM

Eakes began gathering allies under the banner of the Coalition for Responsible Lending. An early member of the coalition was housing activist Peter Skillern, who ran an operation called the Community Reinvestment Association of North Carolina. Skillern's group had been staging protests against Charlotte-based Nations Bank, citing, as proof of unfair discrimination, studies showing that black North Carolinians were more likely to end up with a subprime loan from Nations Bank than whites were. (They failed to mention far more relevant differences, such as credit history.)

Atlanta housing activist Bill Brennan contributed to the cause with emotional video interviews of poor borrowers trapped in "abusive" loans. Brennan had been doing this for years in Atlanta (even appearing in an episode of ABC's *Primetime Live* on the subject). A bank may have a thousand satisfied customers to one unsatisfied customer, but happy customers don't make for politically potent videos. Brennan knew how to find the really sad case. He would contact a friendly TV reporter, and "in short order, a story would air about an elderly black woman living on meager means who had been ruined by Associates," writes Gary Rivlin in a book highly sympathetic to Eakes and his allies, "or the short-order cook with diabetes who struggled to stand on his feet all day, or the hardworking couple with two children, and there would be Brennan, eyes moist, bathing the viewer in sincerity, decrying the injustice that had been done. With the heat turned up high, negotiations [between the bank and the activists] would commence and an accord would be reached contingent upon everyone's future silence. Brennan's friends dubbed it the 'media-induced settlement.'"[4]

Armed with a sampler video compiled by Brennan, Eakes spent months dragging a TV-VCR combo around the halls of the state Capitol, showing sad stories to as many state legislators in Raleigh as he could persuade to meet with him. He distributed more than 7,000 of the tapes around North Carolina, and testified at least eight times in favor of the proposed "anti-predatory lending" law, eventually getting the AARP and NAACP to join the fight.[5] He even managed to persuade many other banks that they ought to support the legislation. (Businesses are more than happy to support regulations that limit their competition, especially if their support also ingratiates them with the local bully or shakedown artist.)

The final bill limited fees to 5 percent, while making illegal both prepayment penalties (for mortgages under $150,000) and mortgage insurance (when rolled into the loan). The bill became North Carolina law in July 1999. A couple of years later, California had followed North Carolina's lead, as had Philadelphia and a few other cities. But Eakes and his friends were just getting started.

After the 1999 law passed, Self-Help legal counsel Mike Calhoun helped Freddie Rogers, the Durham bus driver with the flooded basement, "get an out-of-court settlement with Associates that allowed Rogers to refinance with Self-Help under terms he could afford. A few years later, a developer seeking to gentrify Roger's neighborhood paid him a substantial bounty for his home."[6]

It's a heartwarming story, as long as you ignore the long-term consequences of the tactics and shakedowns that were first perfected in North Carolina.

GOING NATIONAL

By the next year, Eakes's reputation had reached Washington. Then-Congressman John LaFalce of Buffalo and Senator Paul Sarbanes of Maryland summoned Eakes to the capital. The two were the ranking Democrats on the banking committees of the House and Senate, respectively; together they represented over 45 years of experience in Congress. (Two years later, just before his retirement, Sarbanes would sponsor the accounting reform act bearing his name—Sarbanes-Oxley—which, under a flood of paperwork costing an average of $2 million to implement, would help bring American small-company initial public offerings to a screeching halt in the twenty-first century.)

The two senior politicians wanted to talk to Eakes, the up-and-coming activist. Citigroup, the banking behemoth then headed by Sandy Weill, was planning to acquire Eakes's Texas target, Associates First Capital. Over his 45 years on Wall Street, Weill had built a fortune in consumer credit, and he saw potential in the beleaguered Texas-based lender. Sarbanes and LaFalce, like Eakes, saw a predator who would get a lot more prey as part of Citi. They "basically deputized me," Eakes said, to make a stink about the acquisition.

Citigroup was as big and visible a target as Eakes could ever have hoped for. He showed up with his guns drawn. "You will change these practices," he warned the first time he met with Citigroup. "Or we will bring you to your knees."[7]

When representatives from Citigroup went to Durham to meet with Eakes, they found him surrounded by several dozen North Carolinian rabble-rousing protesters who were still in the glow of their statewide legislative victory from the year before. The activists made a long list of demands, including that Citi should dispense with any prepayment penalties, cap its fees at 3 percent, and stop making mortgage insurance part of the loan. The bank agreed to shorten the prepayment penalty period on the loans in question from five to three years, but it was not enough for Eakes. And he had another trick up his sleeve.

On Sunday, November 12, 2000, "Five Questions for Martin Eakes; An Advocate for the Poor and a Thorn for Citigroup," appeared in the *New York Times*. Eakes told his interviewer, Julie Flaherty, that "nothing can be worth the loss of reputation that Citibank will suffer."

"What is your next step?" asked Flaherty.

Eakes answered with his staple rhetorical device. "I have been in meetings where black ministers made the statement that this will become the civil rights movement of this decade, the confronting of the systematic destruction of wealth by abusive lenders. Will it take street demonstrations? Boycotts of specific Citibank products? I hope not. But many of us are prepared if necessary to spend the next 15 years battling Citibank."[8]

Back in Washington, Eakes petitioned federal regulators to hold hearings on the Citigroup acquisition of Associates, while he launched a harassment campaign to send thousands of e-mails every week to Citigroup CEO Sandy Weill. "Look, if Citigroup thinks we're going to go away, they're in for a big surprise," he told the *News & Observer* in Raleigh, North Carolina. "We're just getting warmed up."[9]

Indeed. In March 2001, the Federal Trade Commission (FTC) sued Citigroup in U.S. District Court over Associates' high interest rates, high fees, and "high-cost credit insurance." The next month, Citigroup held its shareholders meeting at New York City's Carnegie Hall, a long-time recipient of Weill's philanthropy. Astonishingly, a group of prominent Citi shareholders, including Bill Gates Sr. and Warren Buffett, invited Eakes to read a resolution asking for Weill's compensation to depend on his adopting "standards of responsible lending." (Enough shareholders recognized the imprecise words as a carte blanche to activist litigators, and the resolution was defeated.[10]) Eakes' efforts paid off nonetheless, reinforced—intentionally or unintentionally—by the federal government. In September 2002, Citigroup settled the FTC suit, without an admission of guilt, for $215 million. The federal agency announced it as "the largest consumer protection settlement in FTC history."[11]

From the outside, this episode does indeed look like a tale of a righteous David fighting a fat and corrupt Goliath, especially since some practices by Associates loan officers, even if they were legal, were unsavory. Campaigns like this one against Citigroup, however, were simply the visible, public relations part of a much larger campaign, one that would have destructive, even if unintended, consequences.

PAY DAY

While fighting mortgage lenders, Eakes and Self-Help had also gotten interested in small-dollar lending, such as payday loans, tax-refund anticipation loans, and installment loans. Each of these small-dollar nonbank loans is based on a different business plan. Payday lenders ask borrowers for a postdated check, and they charge a fixed fee. H&R Block and other tax preparers were offering loans using expected tax credits as collateral. Installment loans, unlike the better-known mortgage installment loan, typically are given without collateral for relatively small amounts of money with terms of six months or more. Because collateral isn't required, installment loan officers must spend relatively large amounts of time on underwriting. This includes a personal interview and budget planning with the borrower, as well as verification of the borrower's income, to gauge his or her ability to repay the loan in installments over a fixed amount of time.

Each of these loan products is different from the others and is subject to different regulations. Traditional installment loans, for instance, are heavily regulated, much like banks, whereas pawnshops are often loosely regulated. What is more, practices differ from one loan company to another. Nevertheless, Eakes and other "consumer advocates" consistently lump these loans and lender types all together as "fringe" or "payday" loans, which they have deliberately worked to make synonymous with "predatory."

The state legislature in North Carolina had approved payday lending in 1997 for a three-year trial run. If lawmakers did not reauthorize it in July 2001, payday lending would disappear from the state. A coalition of consumer activists saw that as an opportunity, and in January 2001 they published a booklet, *Too Much Month at the End of the Paycheck*. The coalition included Peter Skillern and his Community Reinvestment Association, along with the University of North Carolina, Chapel Hill's Center for Community Capital (the same group mentioned in Chapter 3, which the Ford Foundation had funded to do a study on loans to low-income mortgage borrowers).

Funded with private foundation grants and funds from HUD, the booklet appeared fairly balanced, featuring short interviews with both payday lenders and borrowers. Among these were the stories of six North Carolinians—five African American women and one white man—who had availed themselves of payday loans but had not repaid them and had ended up in bad situations. (A seventh borrower, an African American woman, told a different story, of using a payday loan in an emergency and paying it off. Her reaction: "It's good to know they're there.")

Skillern noted in the introduction that these borrowers were "not a scientifically representative sample of payday patrons."[12] But no matter. Sharpened by the accompanying campaign, the booklet, with its two scholarly articles and poignant vignettes, did what it was meant to do: payday lending ceased to exist in North Carolina on July 31, 2001. For most people, who don't frequent such lenders, payday's move from the state probably seemed irrelevant or even welcome.

EXPANDING ON TWO FRONTS

Meanwhile, Eakes's victorious two-front war against Citigroup and the payday lenders in North Carolina got the attention of Herb and Marion Sandler in faraway California. In 2002 Herb started urging Martin Eakes to expand the scope of his work beyond the Tar Heel state. Sandler even offered to fund a national operation if the folks at Self-Help would come up with a proposal. Eakes supposedly resisted the idea at first, but once he put his mind to it, he decided the operation would need an annual budget of $8 million or $9 million. Furthermore, he did not want to use up time and resources on fund-raising, which meant that the organization would require an endowment of something like $100 million to get off the ground. Herb Sandler balked at the sum—the sale of his savings and loan to Wachovia was still four years away. Nonetheless, he kicked in perhaps $10 million, and Herb and Marion Sandler became the generous founding donors of a new nonprofit. It would expand the war of the Self-Help empire and Martin Eakes far beyond the borders of North Carolina. It was named the Center for Responsible Lending (CRL).[13]

With Eakes as its CEO, the center essentially acts as Self-Help's lobbying, public relations, and research arm. Mark Pearce served as its first president—until, in quick succession, he became North Carolina Commissioner of Banks, and then went to Washington to lead a newly created consumer protection unit at the Federal Deposit Insurance Corporation in 2010. Since Pearce made his move into government, long-time Self-Help counsel Michael Calhoun took his place as president.

Backed by the wealth of Herb and Marion Sandler, in 2003 the Center for Responsible Lending moved its headquarters to Washington, D.C. For $23 million, it bought the Barr Building on 17th Street NW, on Farragut Square, just a few blocks north of the White House—prime lobbying real estate.

Among the scads of "consumer rights" organizations in Washington, none has commanded the kind of access that the Center for Responsible Lending has enjoyed, to politicians, regulators, and private foundations.

Getting exact funding information on the Center is tough, but the Sandlers, by their own admission, have given it "well over" $20 million since 2002.[14] It has received additional funding from a who's who of progressive philanthropists, including George Soros, the John D. and Catherine T. MacArthur Foundation, the Ford Foundation, and the Annie E. Casey Foundation, which together have helped push the organization's annual budget to over $8 million. Since 2011, Eakes has served on the board of the Ford Foundation; and in 2012, the MacArthur Foundation awarded the Center a $2 million grant, which it is using to begin building an endowment.[15] The donor profile alone reveals that, whatever else it may be, the Center for Responsible Lending is definitely not a humble mom-and-pop consumer advocacy outfit.

The only donation that deviates from the profile of progressive activist support is a massive $15 million grant from John Paulson—

the largest single grant in the Center's short history. Paulson is a hedge fund manager who was one of a handful of people who had bet heavily against the subprime housing market. Beginning in 2006, he "shorted" various pools of mortgages, mortgage companies, and banks that were invested in these assets—that is, he bet they would crash because defaults on the underlying loans would start to spike. The gain from all of Paulson's bets, often called the "greatest trade ever," netted $14 billion for his hedge fund, and almost $4 billion for himself.[16]

In 2007, Eakes managed to get Paulson to give that giant grant, with no strings attached, increasing the Center's budget by almost 250 percent. The same year, Republican Congressman Darrell Issa began an investigation of possible collusion between the Center for Responsible Lending—lobbying for laws that would further devalue subprime mortgages—and Paulson with his "big short" against subprimes. Although the Center denied that any of the money would go to lobbying, its lobbying budget rose 220 percent the next year.

The timing was wrong, though, to incriminate Paulson, who had already made most of his money by then. Most likely the suddenly rich investor, who also supports the pro-market American Enterprise Institute, was trying to fend off a potential threat to his winnings from Eakes's litigious and well-connected Center, with its talk of "cramdowns" and "clawbacks."[17]

Fortuitously prominent in any federal inquiry (at least during 2009 and 2010) would have been Eric Stein, the Treasury's Deputy Assistant Secretary for Consumer Inspection. Stein's previous position? Senior Vice President of the Center for Responsible Lending and chief operating officer of the umbrella organization, Center for Community Self-Help. In that capacity, in 2007 Stein had testified before the U.S. House Judiciary Committee's Subcommittee on Commercial and Administrative Law in favor of a mortgage bankruptcy law, also favored by Paulson, which would have forced lenders to accept changes in their contracts by judges.[18] Two years later, President Obama appointed Stein specifically to oversee the creation of a new consumer financial protection bureaucracy.[19] Once those plans were solidly in place, Stein resigned from Treasury and returned to the Center for Responsible Lending and Self-Help as Senior Vice President of both organizations.[20] Infiltration is much easier when you have an unlocked revolving door.

IT'S ALL BEEN PROVEN

So how has the Center for Responsible Lending used its clout and its hefty financial windfall? Well, for years it has lobbied for more state and federal control over financial industries. It has also commissioned many less-than-credible "studies" designed to justify its presumptions about predatory lending. I surmise that Eakes and other activists in North Carolina understood that sketchy agitators such as ACORN had a valuable role to play in imposing their agenda on banks, but that legislators and the media needed more credible and apparently objective sources in order to pursue lenders. For that purpose, there's nothing like having a study to cite in editorials and news stories.

Since many reporters already share the viewpoint of the Center for Responsible Lending, the studies don't need to be rigorous enough to withstand much scrutiny. They just need to seem credible to the casual observer. For instance, in the 2001 booklet, *Too Much Month at the End of the Paycheck*, that helped kill payday lending in North Carolina, University of North Carolina, Chapel Hill professor Peter Coclanis admitted that Americans have used consumer credit in some form for centuries. Yet rather than treat this diverse and complex subject in a nuanced or evenhanded way, he labeled all consumer credit as "predatory lending." When it involves African American borrowers, he dubbed it a legacy of slavery. Other essays in the booklet explained that payday lenders put their storefronts in middle-income rather than destitute neighborhoods because their patrons would by definition be people with checking accounts. Somehow this was assumed to be scandalous.

Even more essential to the rhetoric than statistics and allegations, however, are the sad stories accompanying or worked into the Center's studies.

I could fill many pages with stories of people who took out World Saving Loans and subsequently lost their homes and destroyed their credit. Ditto with Martin Eakes's Self-Help loans. I could, for instance, fixate on the dire details in the story of Norman and Orianne Rousseau, of Ventura, California. A World Savings broker had persuaded the couple to refinance and take out an option ARM. They spent years trying to resolve their financial nightmare after they were accused (apparently by mistake) of missing a payment. At every step, their situation grew worse until, finally, foreclosure became unavoidable. Two days before he lost his house, Norman Rousseau walked into his garage with a gun and shot himself.[21]

This is a very real, and very sad, story—and there are many others like it. Treating such stories as representative samples, however, would be manipulative and dishonest. We should not, I believe, evaluate entire companies or industries based on a few sad outcomes.

Imagine you own a bank that makes hundreds of thousands of home loans, and only one-tenth of 1 percent of your loans has ever gone into default. That's well below the historical norm, but even that rate would mean dozens of sad stories. The studies that the Center for Responsible Lending issued played exactly this game—cherry-picking the inevitable worst-case outcomes and holding them up as representative.

Often just as misleading is the Center's use of statistics. One of its notorious "issues papers," released in 2005, goes after one of its favorite targets—payday lenders. "Race Matters" offered statistical evidence that payday loan stores were three times more common in black than in white neighborhoods.[22] "This study shows in the starkest terms that African American neighborhoods bear the brunt of predatory payday loans—loans that are no longer even legal in North Carolina," said Mark Pearce, then president of the Center for Responsible Lending. Although payday lending was banned from North Carolina in 2001, some payday lenders continued to operate there by affiliating with out-of-state lenders.

Let's assume for now that the study was accurate. At best, it simply confirmed that lenders understand marketing. One usually finds payday stores in neighborhoods near their customers—people with jobs and checking accounts but not a lot of extra money. That describes many urban African American neighborhoods. You rarely find payday stores in tony, boutique malls nestled between Restoration Hardware and Williams-Sonoma. Why? Common sense dictates that a business put its stores near its most likely customers.

To find payday stores near their customers is shocking only if you *assume*, ahead of time, that payday and small-dollar lending are predatory by definition. But if these loans are predatory *by definition*, why waste time and money with utterly unremarkable statistical studies?

The Center for Responsible Lending is not making a rigorous argument at all. It is performing a rhetorical sleight of hand. Throw in a sad story or two, quickly pivot to a "study," toss in some statistics about the stressed economic status of many African Americans, imply a distasteful racial bias, and pivot back to another sad story—all before skeptics have a chance to ask why lenders shouldn't set up shop where their services are wanted.

The Center is quick to denounce payday lenders for seeking repeat customers. They could very well criticize barbers for the same reason. In one 2005 paper, the Center for Responsible Lending defined "abusive" and "predatory" lending in terms of a "debt trap," which in turn they defined as having five or more loans in a single year.[23] The paper confuses the scenario in which a borrower takes out five separate loans at different times with "flipping" the same loan multiple times. A 2006 paper, "Financial Quicksand,"[24] made the same mistake. Again, most businesses want repeat customers, and customers generally don't return to businesses that abuse them.

However emotionally satisfying it may be to see other people's villainy as the cause of someone's misfortune, it doesn't follow that, because someone ends up in a bad situation after taking out a loan, the lender caused the bad situation or intended it. The Center for Responsible Lending has a tendency to treat stories of people who find themselves bogged down in a cycle of debt as proof that the loans were designed to do that in the first place.

Double standards are another common feature in the Center's reports. For instance, as we've seen, the Center for Responsible Lending and other activist organizations attack small-dollar lenders for giving too many loans to African Americans and other minorities but criticize mortgage lenders for giving minorities too few. In any case, if marketing to likely customers is evidence of predatory "targeting," then one could just as well attack Self-Help for "targeting" minorities, single mothers, and borrowers with bad credit.

Most important, it simply doesn't follow that if payday and other types of loans are prohibited, borrowers will be better off as a result. We already read in Chapter 1 of payday loans mitigating the effects of natural disasters in California. A 2011 review by Kelly Edmiston, senior economist at the Federal Reserve Bank of Kansas City, found—in studies ranging from Oregon to South Africa—that restrictions and bans on emergency finance have had unintended negative consequences for lower-income people. For example, Donald Morgan and Michael Strain of the Federal Reserve Bank of New York found that after payday loans were banned in Georgia and North Carolina, "households . . . bounced more checks, complained more to the Federal Trade Commission about lenders and debt collectors, and filed for Chapter 7 bankruptcy protection at a higher rate."[25]

Edmiston reported his own analysis of access to payday loans as it relates to people's credit scores, looking at county-by-county data across all 50 states. He found that in counties where payday lending is unavailable, poor people tend to have worse credit scores than they do in counties where they can access payday loans. He found a similar correlation between payday lending and on-time bill payment: "Consumers living in counties where payday lending is legally accessible were less likely to have late bill payments than consumers in counties under restrictive state payday lending laws and regulations."

Despite the hopes of the Center for Responsible Lending, Edmiston found, in a further analysis, that outlawing payday loans does not encourage people to seek out "more traditional forms of lending" (such as a Self-Help credit union loan); instead, "the results suggest that those living where payday lending is inaccessible . . . typically tap other nontraditional forms of credit in lieu of payday lenders, or do not have credit at all."[26] The Center's studies seem blind to the unintended consequences of their policy proposals.

They seem almost equally blind to small loans other than payday, such as installment loans. These loans are much harder to knock, since they've been around for decades, helped eradicate loan sharks, and have a strong track record with a diverse cross section of customers, including military service members. Rather than making careful, analytical distinctions between different loan products, the Center's public campaigns seem designed to confuse payday loans, which they have spent years vilifying, with installment loans.

PREDATORY FOR THEE, BUT NOT FOR ME

The prevailing theme of the research papers done under the auspices of the Center for Responsible Lending is that entire classes of lenders are "predators," "exploiting the poor" and "draining" money from the community.

This language reflects the favored terminology of Martin Eakes and his lead donors, Herb and Marion Sandler, but, as it happens, Eakes and Herb Sandler don't agree on what the terminology means. Eakes deems "predatory" all adjustable-rate mortgages (ARMs) and prepayment penalties.[27] The Sandlers' savings and loan, however, sold hundreds of thousands of such loans, and Herb Sandler has hotly defended the practice. At the same time, the Sandlers frequently attacked their competitors for "predatory lending."

So what exactly *is* a predatory loan? Does *predatory* refer to the structure of a loan? To the motives of the lender? To the lender's profit margin? To the opacity of the loan's terms to the borrower? Are some forms of credit, such as payday and other small-dollar loans, predatory no matter who does the lending or how the loan is structured? Or does the financial status of the borrower or lender make a loan predatory? Is an option ARM predatory if it comes from Angelo Mozilo, the disgraced former CEO of Countrywide Financial? But if the same loan is issued by a self-proclaimed soft-hearted progressive, is it just a cuddly bear hug?

Excepting cases of criminality, it's actually not easy to define predatory lending. "There is no definition of predatory lending," former Senator Phil Gramm once wrote. "I don't know how we can hope to address the problem before we have decided what it is."[28]

If we are going to define small-dollar loans as predatory, then Self-Help is equally guilty, since it also makes such loans. If our definition includes, say, complex adjustable-rate mortgages with prepayment penalties sold to people of modest means in the run-up to the financial crisis, then we have no good reason to exempt the Sandlers either. Their loans involved the largest purchase most people will ever make. The loans were structured to protect Golden West's but not the borrower's interests, even going so far as to penalize borrowers who prepay. They encouraged low-income borrowers to go deeper and deeper into debt, and their terms were bewildering for all but the savviest borrowers. The Sandlers also pushed their loans aggressively to a segment of the population who could least afford the risk those products entailed. Add to this the facts that the Sandlers often securitized Golden West's loans and used independent brokers while denouncing their competitors for doing the same. Finally, they festooned their entire enterprise with high-minded rhetoric about helping the poor and minorities and fighting predatory lending. It makes your mind spin.

If, on the other hand, we define predatory in a way that excludes the Sandlers' lending practices and loans (rather than merely exempting them arbitrarily), then virtually none of the legal lending in the years before the crisis could be called predatory. None. This is simple logic, not high finance.

Another problem with the phrase "predatory lending" is that it treats borrowers as innocent bunnies who get eaten by raven-ous wolves. However, no one is chased down, dragged into a bank by the scruff of the neck, and forced to take out a mortgage or a small-dollar loan. Since regulations can't cover every scenario, borrowers—the same people we allow to marry and bear and raise children—must assume some responsibility for the exchanges they freely make.

Don't get me wrong. We all know there are con artists who trick people into buying things they don't want or need. Heck, every time I go to the grocery store with my kids, we have to run the gauntlet of candy and gum come-ons in the checkout line, and that's after we've resisted (or not) the towers of sugary cereals in splashy, colorful boxes in aisle 7. It's a small miracle our pantry isn't filled with boxes of Count Chocula and Froot Loops. If you're a parent, or even just a person with a sweet tooth, you know what I'm talking about. And yet no one talks about predatory grocers.

Of course, mortgages are far more complicated than sugary snacks, so there's a great deal more at stake and more room for mischief when buying them. Still, we should not assume that if a borrower ends up in dire straits it's because she's been cheated by the lender. If a lender really misrepresents the nature of a loan, that's wrong *and* illegal. Call it predatory if you want to, but we already have a perfectly good word for that: *fraud*. It's punishable by large fines and, in some cases, extended prison sentences. Ask Bernie Madoff.

So why don't Martin Eakes and Herb Sandler spend their time seeking out real cases of fraud? And why do they often prefer the nebulously defined term "predatory lending," whose meaning and application can shift ground like, well, a good con artist?[29] Given the combination of hypocrisy and fuzzy terminology, we can be forgiven for questioning the Norman Rockwell image that Martin Eakes and Herb and Marion Sandler so fastidiously created of themselves.

CONSUMING CRITICS

Self-Help and the Center for Responsible Lending have enjoyed almost universally positive coverage by the media, but a few perceptive souls have criticized their work. In response, the Center has used its war chest and connections to indulge in a bit of its own predation.

For instance, in 2010 a libertarian organization called the Consumer Rights League asked the Clerk of the House and the Secretary of the Senate to investigate whether the Center for Responsible Lending was failing to disclose much of its lobbying activity and, at the same time, lobbying for policies beneficial to its donors. (As we've seen, this is a plausible and real complaint.) Rather than responding objectively, the Center went after its fellow "CRL" for . . . being lobbyists. "This is an industry-funded front group, also known as Astroturf, that can't win on the merits of their arguments so they have to attack people personally," sniffed Kathleen Day, spokeswoman for the Center for Responsible Lending. "They lack transparency. That should make everyone wonder why. Whose water are they carrying?"[30]

Her objection is obviously a two-edged sword. After all, the Center for Responsible Lending has donors of interest as well and attacks individuals personally as part of a standard policy. By itself, this is little more than a hypocritical diversion that uses the same methods of attack that it condemns in its target. It doesn't even touch the substance of the Consumer Rights League's arguments.

The Center's response to economist Thomas Lehman of Indiana Wesleyan University had the same flavor. Lehman explained and defended payday lending in several scholarly articles and editorials. In one, he cited a technical article by two other economists, which indicated "that payday borrowers are more likely to have poor credit histories and to have worked with credit counselors in the past, and are more likely to have had one or more bounced checks in the previous five years." So any payday lender that wanted to avoid bankruptcy would need to charge commensurate fees or interest rates to cover the risk of lending to such borrowers. "This is a simple enough business model," he observed, "and would seem to be a legitimate means of extending credit to poor and low-income households who may not otherwise be able to obtain loans due to poor credit histories."[31]

The Center for Responsible Lending did not respond to these arguments. It homed in on one extremely arcane statistical objection that few reporters or policymakers would understand and that had no particular relevance to Lehman's central points. Even this was wrapped in a snarky attack on Lehman himself for receiving financial support from the payday lending industry. Again, since the Center for Responsible Lending also receives a great deal of funding from interested parties, it can hardly be a serious argument. And again, this seems to be little more than a personal attack designed to divert attention from the issues Lehman raised.

The intellectually honest approach in responding to arguments and research is with good counterarguments and good research, not mudslinging. The fact that the Center for Responsible Lending consistently opts for mud over logic implies a lack of truth and evidence on its side.

NEVER LET A SERIOUS CRISIS GO TO WASTE

Eakes's center had the good fortune of establishing itself in Washington, D.C., well before the financial meltdown in 2008. Eakes and other partisans from the Center for Responsible Lending claim they were early warners of the subprime mortgage crisis, though their warnings tended to be contemporaneous with the events they warned about. Their warnings also had more than a whiff of red herring. "The economic problems we've seen in subprime lending came about through a narrow focus on self-enrichment among brokers, lenders and investors on Wall Street," Eakes claimed after the crisis began.[32]

The truth is, for years Eakes and Self-Help were in the very thick of the subprime market and bragged about the fact that they were leading subprime lenders. They used their influence and cajoled private banks to get into the market. They orchestrated partnerships between banks, risky borrowers, and Fannie Mae, and made money as the middlemen. And they helped degrade the underwriting standards on home loans that figured prominently in the financial crisis. With their clout and connections, however, they were able to help provide the disingenuous official spin on that crisis—while editing out their own aggressive role in causing it.

In fact, for all the talk about predators, it was Eakes, the Sandlers, and the Center for Responsible Lending who zealously solicited the power of state and federal governments to eliminate their competition. The 2008 financial crisis provided the perfect opportunity for them to do just that.

CHAPTER 7

MELTDOWN

On Friday, September 12, 2008, Timothy Geithner, president of the New York Federal Reserve, called the CEOs of the major Wall Street banks in to the Federal Reserve for a last-minute meeting. Joining Geithner was Treasury Secretary Henry "Hank" Paulson and Christopher Cox of the Securities and Exchange Commission (SEC).[1] The meeting's purpose was to persuade the executives in attendance to work together to save one of their ailing competitors, Lehman Brothers. Lehman, a Wall Street fixture since 1848 and the fourth-largest investment bank in the United States, was on the verge of collapse. Paulson and Geithner told the CEOs that if the investment bank failed without remedy, the ensuing financial death spiral would suck in not just the U.S. economy but the world economy as well.

The CEOs who had gathered at the New York Fed knew that Lehman's ills were epidemic—or, as bank regulators put it, systemic. The other banks also knew that while Lehman may have caught the bug early and gotten an especially virulent strain, the same virus coursed through their companies' veins as well.

Six months earlier Paulson and Geithner had arranged a forced wedding, with a $29 million dowry, between Bear Stearns and JPMorgan Chase. Bear Stearns's stock price plunged, and JPMorgan Chase eventually bought the company for a punishing $2 a share. After wails of protest from Bear Stearns's shareholders,

JPMorgan Chase upped its buyout price to $10 a share. JPMorgan Chase appears to be losing money as a result.[2]

Paulson decided he wasn't going to let the same thing happen with Lehman Brothers. Lehman had decent options. Even as the company's stock price plummeted, CEO Dick Fuld had rebuffed several reasonable offers to buy the firm, on the hope that the housing market would recover or that the government would save Lehman as it had Bear Stearns.

Now Paulson and Geithner were urging the CEOs gathered at the New York Fed to pool their resources to save Lehman Brothers without any government buffer. Among other aims, Paulson seemed intent on teaching everyone a lesson on the dangers of moral hazard, in which bailouts induce more risky behavior—the very moral hazard that the Fed and the U.S. Treasury had encouraged with the Bear Stearns deal.

Confusing the Treasury's stance of instructive stinginess was Secretary Paulson's announcement just four days earlier of a federal takeover of the mortgage giants Fannie Mae and Freddie Mac (after insisting previously that the two government sponsored enterprises were fine and dandy). Fannie and Freddie owned or guaranteed more than half of all U.S. mortgages, so they were close to ground zero when the housing bomb exploded in 2006 and 2007. Even though Fannie and Freddie could already borrow money at a lower interest rate than their private competitors, the two mortgage behemoths had lost some 60 percent of their market value in a two-week selloff of their shares (80 percent for the year). They didn't go bankrupt, of course. They had always enjoyed government privileges, and this time the government went all in, nationalizing them in the blink of an eye.

Up to the last minute, Lehman Brothers seemed to have prospective buyers. One was Bank of America under CEO Ken Lewis, but John Thain of Merrill Lynch cut Lehman off at the pass by persuading Lewis to buy Merrill Lynch instead. Finally out of options, Lehman filed for bankruptcy early on Monday, September 15. The Dow Jones dropped almost 500 points within a few hours.[3]

The fun was just getting started. The very next day, the government lent AIG $85 billion and took an 80 percent stake in the insurance giant. AIG had sold financial products called "credit default swaps" to other banks around the world to insure against default of hundreds of billions of dollars in subprime assets. In response to the government action, investors pulled assets out of AIG and other investment banks and fled to the safety of government bonds. Suddenly, banks would not lend to other banks, even overnight. Worldwide capital markets were starting to freeze out even the non-financial sectors of the economy. The moon had not turned red and the stars had not fallen from the sky, but it was clear that Paulson and Federal Reserve chairman Ben Bernanke thought economic Armageddon was imminent.

Paulson and Bernanke met with key members of Congress, including Senator Chris Dodd and Representative Barney Frank, to ask them to authorize a bailout of some $700 billion for the nation's leading financial institutions. They called this omnibus bailout TARP, the Troubled Asset Relief Program. Those "troubled assets" were mortgages and various compound financial instruments composed of mortgages or insurance against their default.

Paulson and Bernanke conjectured that enough government money for the banks would allow them to buy up the toxic mortgage-based assets and restore confidence. But for House members two months away from an election, supporting a plan to bail out a bunch of fat cats was like swallowing a snake. How were they going to sell it to voters, most of whom were far less financially flush than the major bank CEOs they were seeing on the evening news? The first time TARP came up for a vote in the House, it failed.

When markets opened on Monday, September 29, the Dow dropped 778 points, the biggest one-day drop in history. Fear of an economic apocalypse now filled the halls of the U.S. Capitol. Congress quickly passed a modified version of TARP, and President George W. Bush signed it into law on October 3, 2008. This gave Paulson permission to act. His initial idea was to endow the banks to absorb their toxic assets in the same way that the government had awarded the dowry to Bear Stearns. But he discovered that it could take months to isolate and extricate those assets from the rest. The week of October 6 through 10, 2008, became the worst week in the history of the Dow Jones Industrial Average. It lost 18 percent of its value, with no bottom in sight. So Paulson opted for a direct cash injection into the banks, which the final version of TARP permitted.

On October 13, Paulson, along with FDIC Chair Sheila Bair and Timothy Geithner, abruptly summoned the heads of nine major banks to the Department of the Treasury in Washington, D.C. Many of the participants of the September 12 meeting in New York were present, but this time Richard Kovacevich, chairman and CEO of Wells Fargo, also flew in from California.[4]

Paulson announced that the U.S. Treasury was going to "invest" in those nine banks through the purchase of a portion of their preferred stock (stocks that offer a dividend); thus, it would become a nonvoting member of each of their boards. Paulson's gamble was that if the banks had this money to lend, they would do so, and this would cause the credit markets to thaw.

All the CEOs knew this was the proverbial offer they couldn't refuse. With their agreement, the U.S. government bought a $125 billion stake in nine of the largest U.S. banks. Although the country quickly entered a deep recession, the worldwide economy did not collapse. For his efforts, *Time* magazine named Paulson a runner-up for 2008 Person of the Year,[5] which ultimately went to Barack Obama. Even if Paulson's final action prevented a greater panic in the short term, it set a dangerous precedent for political intervention in the economy.

SUBPRIME

If you were like most people, you probably watched this spectacle with some mix of consternation, confusion, and frustration. From a distance, the whole thing wreaked of cronyism. A former CEO of Goldman Sachs persuades Congress to authorize him to give hundreds of billions of dollars to well-connected banks, starting with the most well connected, and does so in a matter of nanoseconds on a legislative time scale. Why the giveaway?

Worse, while everyone knew that the crisis had been triggered by the so-called subprime mortgage crisis, there had been no "bailout" for the Americans who had been directly affected by it. In 2006 there were 1.2 million foreclosure filings, 42 percent higher than the year before.[6] In 2007 foreclosures swelled to 2.2 million.[7] In formerly hot markets such as Las Vegas, Florida, and coastal California, many people found themselves "underwater": they owed more on their mortgage than the current market value of their house.

Many of these same people had received "subprime mortgages." While "subprime" refers mainly to the shaky credit history of the borrower, it can also apply to the structure of the loan itself, which we might call a "nontraditional" mortgage. A prime loan is a traditional 15- or 30-year fixed-rate loan, with a down payment of around 20 percent, lent to a borrower with good credit. By contrast, a nontraditional loan might allow a nominal down payment and lack documentation on employment or salary (due to self-employment, for example), as in many so-called Alt-A loans. A nontraditional loan might also be an adjustable-rate mortgage (ARM). "5/1" ARMs start with a low fixed rate for five years but adjust annually after that. The option ARMs sold by the Sandlers through World Savings were a sort of "all of the above" subprime loan. Although many World Savings loans had down payments, these loans often lacked documentation and allowed interest-only payments or even negative amortization (where the outstanding balance increases over time) for up to 10 years before resetting to a fixed rate.

In the period leading up to the subprime mortgage crisis, these nontraditional loans began to dominate the market; huge numbers of them were being made to people with shaky credit records. One result was that the most complex loans were often going to people least able to understand their terms.

Still, these loans weren't all that risky as long as housing prices went up year after year. Even if the borrower wasn't making progress paying down the principal, the increase in his or her home's value would ensure that the homeowner wasn't going underwater. But when home prices began to drop, the loans, and many of the securities based on the loans, turned toxic. Foreclosures, and projected foreclosures, devastated not only borrowers but mortgage lenders as well. The best known was Countrywide Financial, based in California, which in 2006 financed 20 percent of all U.S. mortgages. Founded in 1968 by Angelo Mozilo and David Loeb, Countrywide reached $200 billion in assets at its zenith.

Though the lender is now a pariah, at the time, its former executive Adam Michaelson preened sanctimoniously over Countrywide's vow to "lower . . . the barriers to homeownership for African Americans, Latinos, and other minority groups who could face potential challenges within the existing lending system."[8] Near the end, Countrywide was able to secure funds from the Atlanta Federal Home Loan Bank (one of 12 such banks, which together comprise the lesser-known sibling of the government sponsored enterprises Fannie Mae and Freddie Mac). It lent Countrywide over $50 billion when no one else would; but the bailout didn't help.[9] When, at the urging of Washington, Bank of America acquired the mortgage lender on the verge of bankruptcy in 2008, the purchase price was a paltry $4.1 billion. Its value had dropped almost 50-fold.[10]

In the midst of the crisis, on September 25, 2008, the Office of Thrift Supervision seized another lender, Washington Mutual (WaMu), after a frenzied run on the bank. The FDIC split WaMu's assets (nominally worth $307 billion) from the bank holding company and sold them to JPMorgan Chase for a mere $1.9 billion. The bank holding company was stuck with the liabilities, and it promptly declared Chapter 11 bankruptcy. It was the largest bank failure in American history, two-thirds as costly as all the bailouts and buyouts put together during the long S&L crisis of the 1980s.

Amid all the conflagration of bank values, however, a savings and loan based in California, headed by Herb and Marion Sandler, was a shining exception. Their World Savings was purchased by Wachovia in 2006 for $25.3 billion, at the peak of the housing bubble. In less than two years, Wachovia—now with a Trojan horse of subprimes from World Savings—imploded like Countrywide, thus making World Savings one of the linchpins in the entire collapse. In the middle of the tense TARP debates in Washington in September and October 2008, Wells Fargo bought ailing Wachovia for $15.1 billion in stock.[11] The Sandlers, meanwhile, walked away from the carnage with their massive fortune intact—and ready to do a different kind of damage.

IT'S COMPLICATED

These and other lenders had originated hundreds of billions of dollars in nontraditional mortgages. Many of those mortgages were then sold for a profit to secondary buyers, such as the government sponsored enterprises Fannie Mae and Freddie Mac, and investment banks such as Goldman Sachs and Morgan Stanley. Most adults understand perfectly well what mortgages are, but anyone who followed the news at the height of the crisis also heard about all kinds of exotic financial instruments somehow connected with mortgages, many of which had turned toxic. If they weren't mortgages, what were they?

In the fictional 2011 film *Margin Call*, an investment bank has to decide what to do during one tense, 24-hour crisis. The character Peter Sullivan, a risk assessor working for the bank and played by Zachary Quinto, figures out that the bank's assets are worthless, thanks to a flawed mathematical model used to calculate its risks. The executives call an emergency meeting at 3:00 a.m. with the CEO, played by Jeremy Irons. Sullivan, whom we learn has a PhD in engineering (a "rocket scientist" as they say in the film), is brought to the meeting to explain what he has discovered. When he starts to provide a few of the technical details that had escaped almost everyone's attention, the CEO interrupts him. "Speak to me as if I were a young child or a golden retriever," he says calmly. "It weren't brains that got me here."

The scene is pure Hollywood cliché, but it does capture a truth about the credit instruments at the heart of the financial crisis: to most people they seem like a black box. They know there's something inside the box. They're told that the something has caused a lot of mayhem. The rest is darkness. If you don't know, or don't remember, what a collateralized debt obligation or mortgage-backed security or credit default swap is, you're part of a very large club that includes some extremely bright people. Unlike previous financial crises, this one involved markets that most people had never heard of and that only a few people, including many bank executives, understood. The good news is that while these credit instruments are complicated, they are not impenetrable. With an analogy or two and without any complicated math, we can break open the black box and shine a light into the darkest corners. Learning even a little bit about these financial instruments is essential for getting past the distorted conventional wisdom on the financial crisis; it will also dispel much of the mystery that surrounded the crisis.

INSIDE THE BLACK BOX

Let's imagine you have a 30-year fixed-rate loan from a bank. The bank might simply keep the mortgage and receive your monthly payments. But if it has many of these, it might like to sell them and have cash rather than a bunch of IOUs promising monthly payments for 30 years from homebuyers in Cincinnati and Schenectady.

The institutions that buy mortgages from other banks are called *secondary buyers*. These could be private investment banks, such as Goldman Sachs or Morgan Stanley, or government sponsored enterprises, such as Fannie Mae and Freddie Mac. They don't want to hold an asset that takes 30 years to pay off either. So they *securitize* the mortgages, bundling them and selling pieces of the bundle as bonds[12] called *mortgage-backed securities*. The monthly mortgage payments then pass from the home buyers through the security to the owners of the securities.

In a properly functioning market, these securities serve the important function of diversifying risk and opportunity. As with any real-world investment, however, these financial instruments still come with real-world risks, resulting from people paying their mortgages off early or the Fed changing the interest rate. So, in 1983, investment banks Salomon Brothers and First Boston invented a new type of mortgage-backed security for the new government sponsored enterprise, Freddie Mac. These *collateralized mortgage obligations*[13] were designed to distribute the risks.

Let's say you're an investment bank, and you've just bought 1,000 fixed-rate 30-year mortgages from 10 different banks—that is, you now have the contractual right to receive monthly payments from 1,000 homebuyers. Imagine each mortgage as a 30-story-high skyscraper, with the first floor of each skyscraper as the part of the mortgage promising the payments for the first year, the second floor promising payments for the second year, and so on up the building. All 1,000 "skyscrapers" would be side by side in a big city.

Now imagine that you could connect the 1,000 individual skyscrapers together with a series of skywalks. All the thirtieth floors are now connected to make one giant thirtieth floor, and so forth, all the way down.

Like giant penthouse condos, you can sell each floor—or *tranche* (French for "slice"[14])—separately. You might sell the first tranche to a mutual fund tailored for retirees that requires a supersafe AAA rating. They now own the first year of payments coming from those 1,000 mortgages. Since this is paid off first, it carries both the lowest risk and the lowest return. People willing to risk a bit more for the chance of a greater reward might buy a tranche in the middle, called the "mezzanine" level. And the high roller who bought the top floor is promised a much higher return on his investment in exchange for a much higher risk; he might get stuck with a security that pays him less than he was promised because the mortgage collateral backing his tranche is in partial or full default.

In this transformation of mortgages, the investor, the originating lender, and potential homebuyers all benefit. Since a lot more money is now available for mortgages than if banks just sat on their mortgage contracts, more people can get loans. Banks also will tend to charge lower interest rates on their home loans, thanks to the law of supply and demand.

Derived from mortgages, these collateralized mortgage obligations are called *derivatives*. Other derivatives can include other things as collateral; for example, collateralized *debt* obligations (CDOs) can include all sorts of assets, bonds, and loans.[15] Rather than being structured according to the payment schedule of mortgages, the tranches in a collateralized debt obligation are structured according to the quality of the credit used as collateral, with really risky subprime and Alt-A loans, for example, at the dizzy top.

Okay. We're almost done with this tour of Securitization City. Let's say you're an investment bank, and you have leveraged your money (that is, borrowed) to buy some mezzanine-level collateralized debt obligations that yield 10 percent annual interest. Now, these bonds have a BBB rating, which means that they're just risky enough to keep you awake at night. (In fact, they're making me nervous just writing about them.) Here's where *credit default swaps* come in: they provide a way to hedge against that risk. As with any insurance policy, you pay the issuer of the swap a little bit at a time, on a schedule, and the issuer promises to cover your losses if your bonds go belly-up.

Unlike most insurance policies, you could buy a credit default swap on a security even if you do not own that security—like buying collision insurance on your neighbor's car rather than on your own. Perhaps you know that your neighbor (despite his perfect driving record and low car insurance rates) has been driving erratically. There's a company willing to sell you coverage, no questions asked, which will pay off if your neighbor has a wreck. Macabre, yes. But not a bad investment, if you can get it. Such are credit default swaps.

But how to hedge against a whole portfolio of securities, not just one? In 1997, the *synthetic collateralized debt obligation* was invented, where the tranches are slices of bundled credit default swaps. After the financial crisis, Goldman Sachs was criticized for buying such synthetic CDOs to hedge against the very mortgage-backed securities they sold. Essentially, the investment bank was denounced for being smart enough to take precautions against losses—losses that turned out to be real.[16]

When people at the Fed opened up the books of Bear Stearns—the first Wall Street investment bank in danger of collapse in March 2008—they discovered that Bear Stearns had sold credit default swaps to cover billions of dollars of assets for other banks. This was far more than they could cover if the entire housing market went south. Bear Stearns assumed, along with almost everyone else, that housing prices would keep going up, at least for the time being.

SO, WHAT HAPPENED?

Those who wrote the 2010 Dodd-Frank Wall Street Reform and Consumer Protection Act insisted that the crisis happened because securitization is complicated, bankers are greedy, many lenders are predatory, and the Congress (mostly Republicans) deregulated Wall Street by repealing so-called Glass-Steagall, two acts regulating banking that became law in the early 1930s.

This is the official story, and much of the media has done an excellent job of peddling it. The story requires that federal regulators play the heroes who came to the rescue; private lenders, and especially Wall Street, play the villains who caused the problem.

But there is one hiccup in this narrative: in 2008 and 2009, Wall Street and Washington seemed to be in cahoots. The Treasury, the Fed, and Congress were busy bailing out the largest banks. This apparent complicity created a sticky situation for the politicians now in power: how could Washington save Main Street from Wall Street, if Washington was colluding with Wall Street? The 2012 *Frontline* series "Money, Power and Wall Street" shows how this awkwardness was overcome: by identifying the politicians who bailed out Wall Street with that *other* administration. In this narrative, President Obama simply inherited the crisis, but, by working with the forces for good in Congress, he was able to pass reform in the face of relentless resistance from the Wall Street lobby.

Never mind the inconvenient truths: Obama had already reappointed the previous Federal Reserve chief, Ben Bernanke, and selected the head of the New York Fed, Timothy Geithner, as his Treasury secretary. (Geithner's father, as it happens, spent 28 years at the Ford Foundation and once worked with Ann Dunham, Obama's mother, on microfinance programs in Indonesia.)[17]

And never mind that Chris Dodd and Barney Frank played key roles in the policies that precipitated the financial crisis in the first place and opposed reforming these policies until the bitter end. These inconvenient truths had to be brushed under the rug, because it was now time to defend Dodd-Frank and the Democrats against the swelling ranks of their detractors. Representative Frank claimed in 2011 that the financial overhaul with his name on it was "clearly the best we've ever done in the history of the country to protect consumers and investors from abuses."[18]

Those ranks of detractors were swelling because the official story rested on a rickety foundation of half-truths and falsehoods. But the truth has a way of getting out, even if only a discerning few notice it at first.

CHAPTER 8

THE
OFFICIAL
STORY

I n 1996, President Bill Clinton appointed Brooksley Born as chair of the little-known Commodity Futures Trading Commission—to oversee, among other things, the special markets for trading derivatives. Some derivatives are purchased directly from the supplier, with no inter-mediary. Known as "over-the-counter" derivatives,[1] these were outside her purview. Born lobbied the president and Congress unsuccessfully to give her agency oversight of these private, "off-market" transactions.

For this, Born is lionized in a 2012 PBS *Frontline* special, "Money, Power and Wall Street," as the "lone regulator who warned about the risks of derivatives—and was ignored."[2] Three years earlier, in October 2009, *Frontline* dedicated an entire one-hour episode to her story. "The Warning" presents Born as a lone voice crying in the wilderness and fighting for the truth, as she urged regulation of over-the-counter derivatives against a trium-virate of free marketers—Robert Rubin (former head of Goldman Sachs and Clinton's Treasury secretary), Rubin's "top deputy" Larry Summers, and Federal Reserve Chairman Alan Greenspan—all straight from central casting to play the older white male villains.

The promotional graphic for "The Warning" shows the visages of the three men glaring coldly at the viewer. The episode presented Alan Greenspan as the most dangerous of the three:

NARRATOR: [. . .] Alan Greenspan was not your stereotypical economist.

ROGER LOWENSTEIN: He was also very charming and a man about Washington.

NARRATOR: He played jazz clarinet, had made himself rich on Wall Street. And he had embraced an unusual political guru . . .

We then see Ayn Rand from an old *60 Minutes* interview:

AYN RAND: I'm challenging the moral code of altruism.

NARRATOR: . . . the Libertarian philosopher Ayn Rand.

AYN RAND: Everybody is enslaved to everybody.

JOE NOCERA, *The New York Times*: Greenspan is a disciple. She [Rand] is the great champion of government as a destructive force that just gets in the way.

MIKE WALLACE, *60 Minutes*: Can I ask you to capsulize your philosophy?

AYN RAND: I am opposed to all forms of control. I am for an absolute laissez-faire, free, unregulated economy. Let me put it briefly. I am for the separation of state and economics.[3]

Well, you get the point. According to the producers of "The Warning," the financial crisis happened because of rich white guys who hated regulation—one was even a *disciple* of Ayn Rand. They, in turn, let Wall Street cowboys wreak havoc. But it could have been averted if they'd just listened to Brooksley Born.

New York Times columnist Joe Nocera appears throughout "The Warning" as a Born booster, and at one point describes a private lunch meeting the CFTC chair supposedly had with Greenspan. Greenspan, we're informed, had told Born that he didn't believe there should be rules against fraud: "I think the market will figure it out and take care of the fraudsters."[4]

When she is asked if the lunch actually happened, however, she demurs, "I'm not going to talk about it. I'm not going to talk about it on camera." In other words, even though *Frontline failed to confirm that such a conversation ever took place*, and even though it contradicts Greenspan's public statements about the way fraud disables markets,[5] the program included Nocera's charge.

This 2009 *Frontline* episode is as pure a distillation of the conventional wisdom about the financial crisis as we're likely to get: causing the crisis was widespread fraud, enabled by deregulation and lack of regulation in financial markets, especially in complicated derivatives. By the time a congressional inquiry was launched in the spring of 2009, the narrative had been carved in granite.

WHITEWASH

Aiming to "improve enforcement of mortgage fraud, securities fraud and commodities fraud, financial institution fraud, and other frauds," President Obama on May 20, 2009, signed into law the Fraud Enforcement and Recovery Act.[6] Along with its fraud enforcement redundancies, this law authorized formation of a 10-member Financial Crisis Inquiry Commission, composed of 6 Democrats and 4 Republicans.

Commission Chairman Phil Angelides, a liberal politician from California, selected almost all of the research staff as well as the panelists who would testify during the 19 days of public hearings spread out over eight months. The Center for Responsible Lending had its say on the very first day of hearings; its senior policy counsel Julia Gordon appeared on a panel on January 13, 2010.[7] Of the 700 named panelists, only about 150 appeared in the public hearings. The rest were interviewed in private by staffers. Gearing the evidence and the results toward a predetermined conclusion, these sources never faced questioning by other commissioners; in most cases other commissioners didn't even know who was being interviewed.

Angelides so dominated the proceedings that the body was often referred to as the "Angelides Commission." As California state treasurer, he had channeled billions of dollars from state employee and teachers' unions into green energy initiatives,[8] "private equity businesses in underserved areas," and "affordable housing."[9] (Both unions' pensions are now in serious trouble.[10]) As chair, Angelides could shape the commission's view of national affordable housing goals and suppress any inkling of their role in the crisis. He was a beneficiary of the Sandlers' largesse in California politics, and his commission issued a report that carefully respected Herb Sandler's self-defense and rationalizations.

On January 27, 2011, a year after the commission began its proceedings—and months after the president had signed the Dodd-Frank "Wall Street Reform" act—the six Democratic-appointed commissioners issued a 400-plus-page majority report. The four other commissioners had received it in its final form 10 days before it was to go to press.

The majority report had a few critical remarks for public institutions. For instance, it chastised the Federal Reserve and government regulators for failing "to stem the flow of toxic mortgages, which it could have done by setting prudent mortgage-lending standards."[11] And it concluded that "the government was ill prepared for the crisis," that financial industries took dangerous risks, and that "excessive borrowing" took place. Furthermore, the report stated that mortgage-lending standards collapsed, credit rating agencies failed to do their jobs, and "there was a systematic breakdown in accountability and ethics."[12]

Of its several conclusions, however, the central one is this:

We conclude widespread failures in financial regulation and supervision proved devastating to the stability of the nation's financial markets. The sentries were not at their posts, in no small part due to the widely accepted faith in the self-correcting nature of the markets and the ability of financial institutions to effectively police themselves. More than 30 years of deregulation and reliance on self-regulation by financial institutions, championed by former Federal Reserve chairman Alan Greenspan and others, supported by successive administrations and Congresses, and actively pushed by the powerful financial industry at every turn, had stripped away key safeguards, which could have helped avoid catastrophe.[13]

In particular, the majority fingered the market for over-the-counter derivatives, which it called "shadow banking." At the same time, the majority dismissed the role of government-imposed housing goals, conceding only that they "contributed marginally" to Fannie Mae's and Freddie Mac's risky business practices.[14]

The *New York Review of Books* gushed that the report was "the most comprehensive indictment of the American financial failure that has yet been made" and "the definitive history of this period."[15] Since I had studied the crisis in detail before I read the report, I had a different response. In reading the report—or rather, the summary of comments from the people Phil Angelides had allowed to speak—I imagined a scenario in which a group of statisticians from the United Nations (UN) are sent to Haiti to investigate a reported rise in the country's death rate. The group arrives in Port-au-Prince, Haiti, on February 10, 2010, to study the situation carefully. They conclude that hundreds of thousands of people are dying because of an unprecedented lack of clean water, exposure to the elements, and an unusual number of collapsed buildings. Also to blame are devastated water-purification plants, dilapidated housing, and too many old buildings. Since the group has been commissioned to provide a single underlying explanation, they identify shoddy Haitian building codes as the culprit. Despite their thorough research, in their 400-page report, it never occurs to them that the 7.0-magnitude earthquake 16 miles west of Port-au-Prince on January 12 might have been worth mentioning.

ON THE CONTRARY

The two official dissents are far more illuminating. The Democratic majority limited dissenters to nine pages each in the commercially published book, which became a *New York Times* bestseller. But there was no page restriction on the official version submitted to the president and Congress. Commission members Keith Hennessey, Douglas Holtz-Eakin, and Bill Thomas wrote a 26-page dissent, and Peter Wallison wrote a devastating 99-page dissent. Here and elsewhere, I refer to the official version of the minority report, since it contains the real meat of the case against the whitewashed report of the majority.

The 26-page dissent charged that while the majority report avoided giving "simplistic," "single-cause explanations," it did make the mistake of being overly broad. "The majority's almost 550-page report," they wrote, "is more an account of bad events than a focused explanation of what happened and why. When everything is important, nothing is."[16]

There is certainly one clear example of this problem in the majority report. The majority pushed the "deregulation" argument as a major cause of the crisis as far as they could. And yet, in the very section where they emphasize this most strongly, they say: "Yet we do not accept the view that regulators lacked the power to protect the financial system. They had ample power in many arenas and they chose not to use it."[17] In other words, regulators need not have been hampered by deregulation. But if, as the majority report argues, deregulatory zealots took this protective power away from the regulators, how was it that the regulators still had the power to prevent the crisis? The trouble here is not so much a lack of focus as a lack of coherence.

The three dissenters also faulted the majority for "focusing too narrowly on U.S. regulatory policy and supervision, ignoring international parallels" and using vague or prejudicial terms such as "shadow banking" and "derivatives" to refer to all sorts of different practices.

When the 26-page dissent fingered causes, it pointed to "appallingly bad risk management" and a widespread assumption that housing prices would always go up, or at least not drop everywhere at once.[18] This point was stated more concisely than in the majority report. Unfortunately, it was not the prelude to deeper insights. As with the majority report, the three dissenters said little about federal housing policy.

Perhaps the subject was too close for comfort. Bill Thomas, the dissenting vice-chair of the commission, had served in Congress from 1978 to 2007, and for years was chairman of the powerful House Ways and Means Committee. Douglas Holtz-Eakin had served on President George H. W. Bush's Council of Economic Advisors and was director of the Congressional Budget Office under President George W. Bush. Keith Hennessey was also an economic advisor in the White House from 2002 until the end of President George W. Bush's second term. Although affordable housing goals were laid and incubated by the left, they continued to be hatched during President George W. Bush's two terms.[19] For the three Republicans to indict affordable-housing policies, they would have had to indict, at least in part, the Bush administration's decision to go along with those policies. As a result, they also followed the pattern of the UN statisticians analyzing the death rate in Haiti and failing to mention the earthquake. The Republicans blamed bad risk management and a plunging housing market.

Policy wonk Peter Wallison, in contrast, had no such need to avoid the obvious. He was free to dismantle the majority's arguments and then point to the unusually high winds that wreaked the wreckage: a relentless siege of government-imposed policies, including "affordable housing goals" supported by an activist national campaign that degraded lending standards.

Wallison is a scholar at the American Enterprise Institute who attended Harvard College and Harvard Law School. Among his previous posts, he served as general counsel to the Treasury

Department and later counsel to President Reagan. He had warned of a coming crisis from the government housing policy for years, and his dissent is a tightly argued brief, jam-packed with documentation and evidence. Before getting to his explanation, however, let's do what Wallison also does first: unmask the official narrative of the financial crisis.

WALL STREET GREED

By late 2008, the optics of the financial crisis couldn't have been starker: millions of poor, lower-income, and middle-class Americans losing their homes while a few fabulously wealthy, greedy, well-connected bankers got billions of dollars in bailout money from the government. And all because the bankers had created mysterious financial products that almost no one had heard of or understood. Those avaricious bankers simply had to be the main culprits behind the crisis. It was the perfect source material for an Oliver Stone movie.

Too perfect. If Wall Street greed caused what became a worldwide economic crisis, why were the problems in the markets related to home mortgages and nothing else? Why would greedy bankers zero in on mortgages and mortgage-backed securities when there are so many other sectors of the economy to be irrationally greedy about? And why the sudden spike in high-roller greediness? Did they suddenly get greedier in the new millennium, just as they developed a weird obsession with home loans? Why not drug manufacturing or silver mining or foreign currencies or soybean futures?

As Steve Forbes has observed, saying that greed caused the financial crisis is like saying that gravity caused a plane crash. Greed is a constant in all cultures at all times in history. To find the ultimate cause, we must, as statisticians say, *isolate* the variables and look at them one by one.[20]

DEREGULATION

The majority report spoke of "more than 30 years of deregulation,"[21] even though the financial industry is one of the most regulated industries on the planet and had been layered with new regulations year after year for much of those 30 years. For instance, in 1991, the tough Federal Deposit Insurance Corporation Improvement Act was approved in the wake of the savings and loan crisis.[22] When the deregulation claim is accompanied by actual specifics, its vacuity is even easier to grasp, so let's consider the two examples mostly commonly offered.

Glass-Steagall

The 2012 *Frontline* special "Money, Power and Wall Street" invoked deregulation as a cause of the crisis—specifically the "repeal" of the Depression-era Glass-Steagall Act, which had drawn a black line between commercial and investment banks.[23] As one might expect, the Financial Crisis Inquiry Commission majority report did so as well.

In 1999, Congress did pass, and President Clinton did sign, the Gramm-Leach-Bliley Act with overwhelming bipartisan support. That act repealed *parts* of Glass-Steagall. For instance, it allowed financial firms to diversify, and commercial and investment banks to affiliate.[24] That is a rare, though modest, example of deregulation, but just on the face of it, what does it have to do with the financial crisis? Not much. And where it does, the evidence suggests a positive rather than a negative impact. Everyone from President Bill Clinton to libertarian economist Tyler Cowen to Peter Wallison pointed out that the partial repeal of Glass-Steagall almost surely made the crisis *less severe.*[25] If all of Glass-Steagall had been in place in September 2008, JPMorgan Chase (a commercial bank) could not have bought Bear Stearns (an investment bank), and Bank of America could not have bought Merrill Lynch—purchases that helped to slow the snowball of panic. Similarly, although they weren't bought out, investment banks Goldman Sachs and Morgan Stanley raised private funding and converted to bank holding companies at the peak of the crisis. That made these companies subject to *more* regulations, not fewer; those purchases would have been impossible if Glass-Steagall had not been modified.[26]

Credit Default Swaps

Okay, but what about all those unregulated derivatives, and especially credit default swaps (CDSs)? Those CDSs made millions for some people, but did they cause the crisis?

As mentioned earlier, the official story of Bear Stearns is that the Fed and Treasury saw tens of billions of dollars of credit default swaps on Bear Stearns's books and feared that the industry was so interconnected through these swaps that if Bear Stearns failed, it would take down others as well. The insurance giant AIG was even worse—initial reports suggested the company held $440 billion worth of credit default swaps. (Others put the total in the trillions.[27]) In any case, if either of these firms got downgraded and were no longer allowed to issue the swaps, and the counterparties who traded with them couldn't get comparable insurance elsewhere, then Bear Stearns and AIG could be forced to hunt for more reserves—an impossible task when capital markets are frozen.[28] And so, the official story goes, then–Treasury secretary Hank Paulson and then–New York Fed president Timothy Geithner had little choice but to step in and bail out Bear Stearns.

But if that was the rationale for the Bear Stearns bailout, why on earth would Paulson and Geithner let Lehman Brothers fail? Lehman was both a major dealer of credit default swaps and "a borrower on which many CDSs had been written." If Lehman failed, these swaps would have to be paid to their owners. Yet, as Peter Wallison observed in December 2008 after Lehman failed, "There is no indication that the Lehman failure caused any systemic risk arising out of its CDS obligations—either as one of the major CDS dealers or as a failed company on which $72 billion in notional CDSs had been written."[29] And despite all the buzz about credit default swaps, only AIG collapsed because of them.[30] For every loser in a swap there is a winner; it's a zero-sum game. The problem wasn't credit default swaps but something much more mundane: lots of investment bets on AIG and Lehman's books that went very, very bad.

RISKY BUSINESS

The majority report, submissively following the official story of the crisis, also criticized the "originate-to-distribute" model—securitization itself—which supposedly destroys the natural incentives of lenders not to take on too much risk.[31] "If I can make a whole bunch of loans and sell the entire right to collect those to somebody else," said Congressman Barney Frank on NPR after the meltdown, "at that point I don't care. . . whether or not they pay off. We have to prohibit that."[32]

The market of mortgages, securities, and derivatives does depend on communicating accurate information about risk. For this superstructure to work over the long haul, loan originators must accurately evaluate borrowers as well as the value of the homes on which they issue mortgages. In other words, the quality of the mortgages that make up the securities and derivatives must be clearly and accurately described. One way to ensure this happens is for the loan originators to keep on their own books a part of or all of every mortgage they sell. That way, their self-interest will encourage them to get details right so they don't get stuck with bad loans.

The argument against securitization is that lenders were far less diligent because they knew they could sell the mortgages to a secondary buyer. In this scenario, a loan officer thinks to himself, "Who cares how good this mortgage is? We're going to unload it on some poor sucker in a few weeks anyhow." This explanation for the flood of bad loans collapses under even a cursory cross-examination.

If it were a valid argument, then practically any market exchange would fail. Imagine a grocery store chain that buys produce from farmers and then sells that produce to customers. Sure, if a grocer buys heads of romaine lettuce for herself, she's going to have a personal incentive to make sure they are not rotten. If she plans to sell them to customers, though, she still won't be indifferent to their freshness. After all, she has to compete with other grocers. The last thing a grocery store wants is a reputation for rotten produce.

The same incentive would even apply if the person were a middleman distributor between farmers and grocery store owners. The distributor is two removes from the end user, and yet his entire business still hinges on giving his buyers and, by extension, the end users, a product they'll want to keep coming back for in the future.

Ditto with mortgages. In a normal market, secondary buyers will also do their due diligence. They won't want rotten assets any more than folks want rotten lettuce, so they will check out the methods of the originators who sell the mortgages and avoid ones who cut corners. That, in turn, will inspire the originators to make sure their mortgages are solid, because they want to sell them to secondary buyers again and again.

In a normal market, the investors who buy mortgage-backed securities and collateralized debt obligations are subject to the same incentives. They wouldn't want bonds that are riskier than advertised, since they would be incurring risk but not benefitting from a correspondingly higher yield. Normally investors won't look at every little detail of a mortgage-backed security, just as computer customers don't inspect the insides of every computer before they buy it. They'll rely on reputations and ratings agencies. And as elsewhere, if the incentives are arranged properly, the rating agencies and those who trust them will *suffer* when they make bad judgments and *profit* when they make good judgments. The ratings agencies will have a strong incentive to get things right.

The Financial Crisis Inquiry Commission majority report correctly described the rating agencies as "essential cogs in the wheel of financial destruction" and "key enablers of the financial meltdown."[33] Their role in the mess worked like this: banks found it hard to sell lower-rated tranches of mortgage-backed securities; to fix this problem, they bundled tranches of many different low-rated securities (BBB and lower) based on houses in many different places. In this way they were able to get some 75 percent of the resulting collateralized debt obligations rated as AAA. This made all the difference in the securities' attractiveness to large investors, since many pension funds and institutional investors are required to invest only in the highest-rated bonds, which rarely default. By elevating bonds based on the riskier mezzanine tranches to an AAA rating, banks could offer higher-yielding assets to major investors. And since the agencies rated them as safe, those investors around the world bought them—big time.[34]

If you suspect that this implies a certain coziness between the banks and ratings agencies, you're right. The three big ratings agencies are paid by the banks selling the bonds. That's more than a little screwy. Guess how that happened? Government regulation. In an earlier time, a ratings agency such as Moody's charged the buyers—that is, the bond investors—for its research and ratings. In the 1970s, however, the SEC changed that arrangement, under pressure from unions and public pension plans that didn't like paying the ratings agencies. That set up a potential conflict of interest: agencies should be rewarded for being accurate, not for giving good grades to those being rated.[35]

Was fraud involved? The Justice Department says so. It filed a civil suit against Standard & Poor's, charging the ratings agency with fraud in its earlier assessments of mortgage-backed securities. At the time of this writing, however, I am unaware of widespread corruption in the rating process. It seems just as likely that the Justice Department, under the Obama administration, is simply punishing Standard & Poor's for downgrading the credit of the federal government and, at the same time, issuing a warning to Moody's and Fitch, who have threatened to do the same. What took the Justice Department four years to bring these charges? What did Standard & Poor's do that the other agencies did not? We should follow this suit with an open but critical mind.

In general, ignorance is more likely than malfeasance. The actions of the ratings agencies can be fully explained by ignorance and bad incentives without recourse to fraud. They did not systematically fail in other sectors, and they did adjust their ratings of the mortgage-backed bonds in question in 2007, once they realized they had made a big mistake. Like most everyone else, the ratings agencies thought, and acted on the thought, that housing prices would keep going up, and even if prices dropped in one place, the agencies assumed the drop would be offset by increases elsewhere. Each individual mortgage-backed security might contain 1,000 mortgages from one state, but the collateralized debt obligation would be made up of tranches from 100 different mortgage-backed securities from all over the place. What are the chances that large numbers of the underlying loans from hither and yon would default all at once?

As it turned out, of course, the chances were quite good. Despite the geographical diversity of the mortgages underlying the bonds, the bonds were all built on the same flood plain.[36] When the dam burst, defaults and delinquencies suddenly surged everywhere.

REDUCIBLE COMPLEXITY

Where else did the Inquiry Commission majority report point its finger? Another charge related to the one above, from the majority report and elsewhere, is that overly complex and opaque assets caused the financial crisis.

But the market for securitized mortgages is far *less* complicated than many other markets that work just fine. If you're reasonably smart, have an aptitude for math, and study it fairly closely, you can learn just about every aspect of the mortgage and mortgage-backed securities market.

In contrast, consider any piece of modern technology, such as a smartphone. Before you can buy an iPhone at the Apple store, the work of *millions* of people, from miners to truck drivers to software programmers and silicon wafer fabricators, has to be coordinated. Everyone involved in this process is ignorant of the vast majority of these steps. In fact, most people involved in bringing an iPhone to fruition know only about their own step, and many may not even know that their work contributes to iPhones. The guy at the bauxite mine in Australia doesn't know anything about how the aluminum he extracts from the earth will be molded to become part of an iPhone body. The assembler doesn't know how to fabricate wafers for computer chips. The woman putting computers in boxes in

China doesn't know how to organize the transport of the boxes on a ship to the United States.

No one person on the planet could build an iPhone or even one of its components from scratch. And yet corporations such as Apple sell high-quality smartphones to hundreds of millions of customers. Somehow a complex network of information connects mines to manufacturers to retailers to customers, even though no one person knows more than a fraction of the details. A manual that fully described every step required to create an iPhone from scratch would fill many rows of shelves in a library. But no such manual exists, or needs to. For markets to work, participants simply need to have access to certain facts relevant to their part of the transaction, including especially price.[37]

The process that gives rise to an iPhone involves an information chain. And as with all information chains, every link doesn't need to connect to every other link. It just needs to connect to the links on either side of it. If all the links are strong, the chain is strong.

The complexity of mortgage securities pales in comparison to high-tech markets for smartphones, so complexity per se wasn't the problem.

SINE QUA NON

When there are many contributing factors and necessary conditions for an event to take place, the trick is to find out which proximate factor or condition, if it had been absent, would have significantly altered the event or kept it from happening at all. "Using this standard," Peter Wallison contends in his dissent, "I believe that the *sine qua non* of the financial crisis was U.S. government housing policy, which led to the creation of 27 million subprime and other risky loans—half of all mortgages in the United States, which were ready to default as soon as the massive 1997–2007 housing bubble began to deflate. If the U.S. government had not chosen this policy path . . . the great financial crisis of 2008 would never have occurred."[38]

By now, at least this should be clear: something happened in the market so that most actors—home buyers, mortgage brokers, appraisers, lenders, secondary buyers, ratings agencies, and investment bankers—incorrectly assessed the risk involved. So the real causes of the crisis are whatever jammed the signals concerning risk in the mortgage-related market. As we'll see, if you're open to the evidence and ask the right questions, the answer becomes clear.

CHAPTER 9

AMERICAN
DISSENT

From Herbert Hoover and Franklin Delano Roosevelt to Bill Clinton and George W. Bush, presidents have upheld homeownership as the defining feature of the American Dream. "A nation of homeowners is unconquerable," declared Roosevelt as the United States entered World War II; almost sixty years later, Bush was affirming his belief that homeownership has the power to transform people.[1]

For half of a century the federal government piled one policy on top of another to increase homeownership. The 1930s saw the establishment of Federal Home Loan Banks (to expand access to credit), the creation of the Federal Housing Administration (to insure mortgages that might otherwise be too risky for banks to sell), and the formation of Fannie Mae (to buy mortgages from banks in order to increase the money that lenders have to lend). In the 1970s came Freddie Mac and the Community Reinvestment Act (to exert pressure on federally insured lenders to keep up with Fannie and Freddie). The total effect was to exhort—some might say, to extort—and entice lenders to weaken the standards they used to evaluate loan applications.

In 1992, House Banking Committee Chairman Henry Gonzalez, a Texas Democrat, "informally deputized" ACORN and other activist groups to write affordable housing guidelines for a new law. ACORN members also demonstrated and even stormed hearings to intimidate opponents.[2] The resulting Federal Housing Enterprises Financial Safety and Soundness Act had been originally intended to create commonsense regulation of Fannie Mae and Freddie Mac. Instead, as Peter Wallison points out, this "GSE Act" gave the Department of Housing and Urban Development authority to establish "what was in effect a mortgage quota system in which a certain percentage of all Fannie and Freddie mortgage purchases had to be loans to low- and moderate-income (LMI) borrowers."[3] As a result, a law originally intended to create commonsense regulation of Fannie Mae and Freddie Mac instead established "affordable housing goals"—functionally, quotas for these two government sponsored enterprises.

Over the next 15 years, Congress proceeded to greatly enhance and increase those quotas. Initially 30 percent of the mortgages that Fannie and Freddie purchased needed to meet these goals. In 1995 the quota rose to 42 percent, then to 50 percent in September 1999, and to 56 percent in 2008. Former BB&T Corporation CEO John Allison thinks the 1999 goal was the straw that broke the camel's back. Even the *New York Times* thought it was a bad idea.[4]

Fannie Mae and Freddie Mac did what the law required them to do, and met the new goals every year from 1996 to 2008.[5] At times, to do so, they had to "window-dress" their records, as Allison puts it, by acquiring loans temporarily.[6] In its own 2006 SEC filing, Fannie Mae admitted that it had had to "relax some of their underwriting criteria" to meet the goals.[7] In other words, in order to comply, it had to buy risky loans. Since the government sponsored enterprises had originally helped define safe loans for the industry, these policies meant that the traditional features of home loans—a sizeable down payment, verification of employment, and ability to repay—had withered away.[8]

As with the 1992 GSE Act, these government efforts worked fist-in-glove with the intimidation tactics of ACORN, Self-Help, the Center for Responsible Lending, and other activists to coerce banks into loosening their lending standards. More than one bank CEO has told me in interviews that Martin Eakes "blackmailed" his bank into making risky loans that it would not have made otherwise. In 2007, an umbrella organization for community activist groups, called the National Community Reinvestment Coalition (NCRC), "reported that between 1997 and 2007, banks that were seeking regulatory approval for mergers committed in agreements with community groups to make over $4.5 trillion in CRA [Community Reinvestment Act] loans."[9] Translation: "That's a nice merger plan you've got there, buddy. You wouldn't want anything *bad* to happen to it."

There's more. In 1994, HUD developed a best practices initiative, which Wallison shows "was explicitly intended to encourage a reduction in underwriting standards so as to increase access by low-income borrowers to mortgage credit." These "best practices" included much lower and looser standards for down payments, approval of borrowers with a history of delinquency, and so forth. The now-notorious Countrywide was only the largest of 117 mortgage banks to comply with this initiative.[10]

Perhaps the people at HUD, ACORN, and Self-Help thought that loosening lending standards wouldn't be a problem because they believed that people were getting turned down for loans, not because they didn't qualify, but because the lenders were racist. The activist horde apparently thought that for the average banker, racism trumped even avarice.

The effects of all this pressure should be obvious. In a normal market, loan originators will do everything they can to issue mortgages that are likely to be repaid, and secondary buyers will do everything they can to ensure that they buy just these types of mortgages. But what if secondary buyers are under more and more government pressure to buy mortgages issued not merely to poor people but to poor people with bad credit histories? And what if these secondary buyers succumb to this government pressure? The answer, of course, is that these buyers will create a demand for risky loans in the secondary market.

How did the typical lender respond? Lenders were already being badgered by government regulators and noisy activists to lower their underwriting standards. Now they had a good economic reason to do so, since they knew that investors in the secondary market would snatch up the lenders' mortgages in bundles, despite the rotten quality of the credit underlying them. Suddenly, many home loan companies wanted to originate as many of these risky loans as possible, since they represented a new and untapped lending market. A market once walled off from them by a commonsense concern about unreliable borrowers defaulting on their loans had now been opened wide by government interventions in the market. In short, these interventions *encouraged* lenders to quickly unload the mortgages onto the secondary market and encouraged secondary buyers to snatch them up.

Keep in mind, there wasn't just a single foolish buyer in the secondary market. Government policies put Fannie Mae, Freddie Mac, the Federal Housing Administration (FHA), and banks under the Community Reinvestment Act all in competition for the same risky mortgages. And since government and government sponsored entities had economic advantages, they could out-compete the private buyers, pushing private banks toward the even riskier loans that remained. One result: in 1990, only 1 in 200 mortgages had a down payment of 3 percent or less. By 2007, it was 1 in 3![11]

HOMEOWNERSHIP AND THE VIRTUOUS CIRCLE

There's a difference between earning a million dollars from hard work and winning a million dollars in the lottery. There's also a difference between merely having property and disciplining yourself so that you can acquire and keep property. In housing policy, politicians left, right, and center made the classic mistake of confusing correlation with causation. Homeownership, all things being equal, is correlated with good behavior. Policymakers decided that they could boost good behavior by boosting homeownership.

But ownership doesn't automatically make people financially wise, capable, or virtuous. Instead, in a country with property and other basic rights, wise and virtuous behavior tends to lead people to accumulate enough capital and credibility to be able to buy a home. This incentive has spurred a virtuous circle among countless American immigrants. The dream of buying a house encouraged good financial practices, hard work, and thrift. Once people owned their homes, they valued them all the more because of what they'd had to do to get them in the first place. The equity they put into the loan spurred them to stay on the straight and narrow.

In a healthy mortgage market, people get a mortgage loan because of what they have already done—they've worked hard, kept their jobs, paid their debts, delayed gratification, and saved for a down payment.[12] In this virtuous circle, wise behavior makes it possible to acquire a home, and acquisition of a home reinforces wise behavior.

When government short-circuited that loop of incentives, a vicious circle of bad financial decisions was the result.

OF BUBBLES AND BLACK HOLES

In the years before the subprime crisis, borrowers were putting less and less into down payments, so much so that the amount of residential real estate actually owned by households—as opposed to being financed with debt—went *down* from 2001 to 2009. The housing boom, in other words, didn't provide households with more assets. Instead, it created staggering debt.

Temporarily, the government's strange policy brew stimulated demand, leading to a surge in new construction and home prices.[13] After the dot-com crash of 2000, returns on real estate seemed much better than returns on many stocks and bonds. Those returns drew more money into real estate, mortgage-backed securities, and other housing-related derivatives. The housing bubble suppressed default rates for years—since there's no reason to default if you can sell your house in two weeks for a profit. This made higher-yielding subprime loans look like a good investment, and such loans started getting bundled, sliced, and diced into various bonds (i.e., securitized). The extra capital this activity provided, in turn, drove interest rates for mortgages even lower and provided more money for more bad loans to people with bad credit—loans that would have never been made if the mortgage market had been kept free of government tampering.[14]

The bubble also drew in speculators—people who bought houses simply to "flip" them a few months later. The high return on investment made this inevitable. House flippers were willing to take on more risky loans because they were planning to hold them only for a few months or years. Although these folks did not have "subprime" credit ratings, many still defaulted in bubble states such as Florida and California when the market collapsed, since they weren't fighting to keep the roof over their heads; they were just trying to limit their investment losses.

The bubble was a bit like a black hole: the bigger it got, the better it got at sucking things in. Unlike a black hole, however, an economic bubble doesn't remain stable as it grows. And, also unlike a black hole, the housing bubble wasn't a natural phenomenon.

GOVERNMENT-SPONSORED MORTGAGES

As a result of the arduous efforts to expand homeownership, by 2008 *about 27 million loans "were subprime or otherwise risky loans"*[15]— that is, nontraditional loans. That was half the mortgages in the United States! (It would take a couple of years after the meltdown to discover the full magnitude of the problem.) Fannie Mae and Freddie Mac held 12 million of those loans. FHA and other federal agencies (such as the Veterans Administration and Federal Home Loan Banks) held 5 million, and Community Reinvestment Act and HUD programs had another 2.2 million. That's a total of 19.2 million risky loans held by entities controlled by or within the federal government, leaving 7.8 million for Countrywide, Wall Street, and so forth. Let that fact sink in, because this is the one that shatters all the mythology surrounding the financial crisis. *Two-thirds of all risky loans in the system "were held by the government or entities acting under government control,"[16] and they existed because of aggressive government housing policy.*

Edward Pinto—a former chief finance officer for Fannie Mae who had become Peter Wallison's colleague at the American Enterprise Institute—first approximated these staggering numbers when the Financial Crisis Inquiry Commission was still holding hearings. In two carefully sourced documents produced in March and August of 2010 and given to the commission, Pinto showed that Fannie Mae and Freddie Mac had grossly underestimated the number of risky loans in the system, which he estimated at 25 million at the time of the crisis.[17] Pinto's documents were never made available to the commissioners. The majority report focused its attention on the 7.8 million mortgages in private hands, and more or less ignored the 19.2 million "government-sponsored mortgages."[18]

The commission's clueless investigation and report did not happen by accident, and it did not happen for lack of pleading from Peter Wallison. Drawing on Pinto's research, Wallison frequently asked people speaking before the commission if they knew there were 25 million bad loans in the system. No one ever said yes, apparently because to the panelists it was new information. And no journalist ever reported the number or asked Wallison where he got it.

The commission was like a jury in a trial with a corrupt judge, in which only the prosecution could call witnesses, enter evidence, and make its case. It is not a stretch to say that the majority report was based on a politically motivated cover-up of the facts and arguments that countered its foregone conclusion. It's no wonder Wallison described the report as a "disgraceful" and "thorough whitewash."[19]

THE FED AND MORAL HAZARD

Although it's a bit harder to prove, two other government actions surely helped set the stage for all these bad loans. One was the Federal Reserve's policy of increasing the money supply and keeping interest rates artificially low after the recession brought on by the September 11, 2001, attacks.[20] If housing prices in a growing city are going up at, say, 10 percent a year, and the Fed has artificially pushed borrowing rates down to 4 percent, then buying a second house or a much more expensive primary house suddenly looks like a sure bet. If the Fed hadn't suppressed interest rates, the bubble might have been much smaller. Still, this doesn't explain why the federal government pursued "affordable lending goals" or why underwriting standards were degraded. Federal Reserve policy wasn't a sufficient condition for the financial crisis, but it surely played a role.

Second was the government's known tendency to bail out financial institutions deemed "too big to fail"[21] (really, too big to *be allowed to* fail). Perceptions of what government will do in a crisis affect the decisions of those in markets. And what government has done in the past shapes current perceptions. If teenagers know from experience that parents in their town clean up their kids' legal and financial costs in the case of a car wreck, those teenagers will tend to drive much more recklessly than if they regularly hear stories of friends or siblings working long hours at Burger King to pay for the repair and insurance costs or if they hear stories about the kid who lost his license and must take the bus to school because of a drunk driving charge that Daddy didn't make go away.

Bankers and teenagers have something in common—they're human beings. They tend to respond to incentives and disincentives in much the same way. What this means is that if bankers believe the government will bail out their bank if trouble strikes, they will be inclined to pursue riskier investments in pursuit of bigger returns, since they know the government will rescue them from financial ruin should the risky investments crash. This happened with Lehman Brothers. Although Bear Stearns was the smallest of the Wall Street investment banks, the Fed was quick to orchestrate a rescue. Thus, Lehman CEO Dick Fuld spent months *not* preparing for bankruptcy, and even at the end he rejected several viable purchase offers because he was holding out for the deal that Bear Stearns had gotten.[22] Once the Fed and U.S. Treasury helped Bear

Stearns, everyone expected the same for Lehman Brothers. When that didn't happen, the uncertainty sent panic through the markets. It's possible that the panic wouldn't have happened if the Fed and Treasury had held tough initially and let Bear Stearns file for bankruptcy.

Really, *the whole system* suffered from moral hazard because of the way the mortgage market, and securities based on them, separated the consequences of risk from the risk takers. Some big financial firms, especially Fannie Mae and Freddie Mac, expected that if they got into trouble, the federal government would provide a soft landing. It had certainly done that in the past. And for the most part, that's exactly what happened during the crisis, with the government lifting losses off the shoulders of too-big-to-fail firms and passing them on to healthier banks and on to current and future American taxpayers.[23]

SCRAMBLING THE SIGNALS

Government distortions in the housing market scrambled the normal market signals until the market was little better than a stadium-sized game of "telephone" played by people with severe speech impediments. At some point, the whole operation was bound to grind to a mumbling and incoherent halt.

Our cast of players from Martin Eakes to Barney Frank didn't merely encourage lenders and secondary buyers, such as Fannie Mae and Freddie Mac, to find reliable borrowers who had had some bad luck and low-income earners with good credit. As we've seen, they threatened, enticed, and, in some cases, coerced lenders to effectively degrade their lending standards for lower-income and minority applicants, to the point that these institutions were making loans to more and more people with a track record of irresponsible financial dealings.

If we understand that a market is an information network, it's easy to see why this situation couldn't end well. Picking up on *Saturday Night Live's* tongue-in-cheek portrayal of one subprime borrower ("no credit history, no job, minor criminal record, dishonorable discharge from the Army, drug problems, alcohol problems, gambling addition, pregnant girlfriend"), imagine if the Seattle city council did a study and discovered that most drug addicts were not well dressed and had a hard time getting credit in department stores, which made it hard for them to interview successfully for jobs and thus improve their lives.[24] Now imagine that newspapers ran the story, and, in response, sociology majors from the University of Washington protested outside of Nordstrom and Macy's stores, demanding that these stores extend credit to the poor drug users who are trying to turn their lives around. Just because of their past actions, the writers cry, these addicts are being penalized and not allowed to improve their lot! Wouldn't we all be better off, they reason, if we helped the addicts participate in the American dream? Yet, here they are, frozen out of the system by the greedy capitalists running those big chain stores. In response, the city council members, fondly recalling their heady protest days at the University of California at Berkeley, decide to pass an ordinance requiring stores to give out 10 percent of their credit cards to drug addicts, with credit limits of at least $10,000.

Now imagine that, each year, the required percentage of drug-using credit card holders is ratcheted up by 5 percent. So the second year, these department stores would need to give 15 percent of their credit cards to druggies. Then 20 percent. Then 30 percent, and so on, all the way to 50 percent. At some point, Nordstrom and Macy's would lose so much money that they would need to stop giving out credit cards altogether or go bankrupt and cease to offer credit cards or anything else.

What if Nordstrom and Macy's could somehow sell those drug addicts' credit accounts to another company for a profit? The stores could then continue their credit card program long after it should have died a natural death, delaying and expanding their inevitable crash. If this were happening in Nordstrom and Macy's stores all over the country, the crash and burn would not only knock out two giant retailers but also ripple out into industries that depend on them.

This is just an analogy, of course. Obviously, subprime borrowers are not typically drug addicts. Many are just people with poor or no credit histories who are not likely to be better off if they get stuck with a mortgage. And, no doubt, many work hard to make their mortgages work and keep their homes. But in both the fanciful fictional scenario and the real financial crisis, a government entity has pressed businesses to extend credit to people whose past behavior indicates they are not exactly financial safe havens.

The "self-correcting nature of the markets," which the majority report of the Financial Crisis Inquiry Commission dismissed again and again, couldn't prevent the crisis for the obvious reason that the proper market signals had been scrambled from top to bottom.[25] The false signals guided investment banks on Wall Street, bankers on Main Street, and all manner of actors in between—Realtors, mortgage brokers, home builders, home buyers, appraisers, the manufacturers of products used in home building and home remodeling, and so on.

While the commission's majority report whitewashed all of this, Wallison's minority report laid out the reality in stark detail. The activists, lobbyists, and policymakers ultimately responsible for the bubble and the ensuing crash were, to put it mildly, not amused.

THE EMPIRE STRIKES BACK

When the Financial Crisis Inquiry Commission report came out on January 28, 2011, its majority report began getting powerful PR help not only from the *New York Review of Books* and the *New York Times*, but all over the media, from documentaries to op-eds. Fannie Mae and Freddie Mac—the elephants in the room, holding half the high-risk mortgages in the country and nationalized in the middle of the crisis—received scant attention in the press either before or after the report. A few months after the government took over the mortgage behemoths, *Frontline* ran a special in February 2009, "Inside the Meltdown," covering the key events of the 2008 crisis. It gave two of its 60 minutes to Fannie Mae and

Freddie Mac.[26] This is a bit like giving two minutes to the bubonic plague in an hour-long documentary about the deadliest medieval epidemics. In the gripping 2011 HBO movie *Too Big to Fail*, based on the equally gripping book by Andrew Ross Sorkin,[27] the incident is similarly just a small aside in the larger drama between private bank CEOs and government officials.

Wallison's dissent, in pointing to the elephants, jarred harshly on the ears of the government apologists. Too substantial to ignore, it needed to be marginalized. That January, on the release date for the report, Joe Nocera of the *New York Times* was first out of the starting gate, calling the dissent "a lonely, loony cri de coeur." Wallison's case was "so contrary to the facts," he wrote, "that even his fellow Republican commissioners did not agree with him." But Nocera had the commercially published version of the report, which contained not the full dissent but only a nine-page summary.[28] It was he who was unacquainted with the facts, an especially curious failure since a book he coauthored in 2010 with Bethany McLean, *All the Devils Are Here: The Hidden History of the Financial Crisis*,[29] noted that Fannie Mae and Freddie Mac were buying loans as early as 2000 to conform to HUD's affordable-housing goals. Perhaps he didn't read that part of his book.

In February came a report from a law professor, David Min, at the Center for American Progress, the Sandler-funded think tank a few blocks away from Wallison and Pinto's American Enterprise Institute in Washington. Its cover—a photograph of a "wrong way" sign—displayed the considered title, "Faulty Conclusions Based on Shoddy Foundations." Min explained, "Pinto's controversial conclusion that federal housing policies were responsible for 19 million high-risk mortgages is based on radically revised definitions for the two main categories of high-risk mortgages, subprime loans and so-called Alt-A mortgages." He concluded that "it would be unfortunate if policymakers relied on Peter Wallison's claim that federal affordable housing policies caused the financial crisis."[30]

As Wallison's media critics multiplied—many referencing Min's "Faulty Conclusions" paper—*The American Spectator* invited

Wallison to reply. "What Pinto did, that no one had done before, is show that loans made to people with FICO credit scores lower than 660 (which he called 'subprime') had substantially higher rates of delinquency and default than loans to people with credit scores above 660," Wallison explained in late May. Pinto included "Alt-A" loans, those loans with no documentation, low down payments, or other deficiencies, and unsurprisingly found that these, too, had much higher rates of default. Wallison continued:

> Min is arguing that it's unfair to use the terms "subprime" or "Alt-A" in a way different from how others had used those terms in the past. Even if we grant him that and call subprime and Alt-A something else (perhaps "bananas" and "peaches") the important point is that bananas and peaches—which had far higher delinquency and default rates than prime mortgages—were *half* of all mortgages in the financial system as we approached the financial crisis of 2008. . . . By 2008, 19.2 million bananas and peaches were on the balance sheets of government entities or entities that the government could control. That is one reason that the government was responsible for the financial crisis.[31]

In December, the SEC filed charges against executives of Fannie Mae and Freddie Mac for making "materially false" claims about how many risky loans (subprime and Alt-A) were on their books by 2008. Even allowing for the fuzziness of the word *subprime*, some executives clearly had made false statements. For instance, Richard Syron, former head of Freddie Mac, "told an investor conference in May 2007 that the company had 'basically no subprime business.'"[32] For Joe Nocera, this was the SEC "taking its cues" from the "Wallison/Pinto school of inflated data."[33] But it was hard to deny what was obvious to any fair observer: the SEC had just independently verified and vindicated Wallison's *cri de coeur*. (Perhaps Nocera was rattled by the fact that his *New York Times* colleague, Pulitzer Prize–winning business reporter Gretchen Morgenson, had that May coauthored a book laying much of the blame for the crisis at the feet of Fannie Mae.[34])

Nocera seemed to have limited his research to a *New York Times* story about the SEC complaints. As a result, he made several false claims, which Wallison kindly pointed out the next day in *The American*.[35]

The gall! On Christmas Eve, Nocera fired back, accusing Wallison and Pinto of telling, as he put it, "the Big Lie," which succeeds not by virtue of its truth but by the frequency with which it is asserted. The Big Lie, according to Nocera, was their "primary data point"—that *27 million* risky home loans were issued before June 2008. He asserted that Wallison and Pinto had repeated it so many times that the Republicans in Congress, the editorial page of the *Wall Street Journal*, and even the apparent simpletons at the SEC had bought it. Nocera accused Wallison and Pinto—and now the SEC—of using a definition of "risky" that included plenty of great loans. Apparently he had forgotten that these supposedly winning loans would have wiped out Fannie Mae and Freddie Mac if the government hadn't rushed in and made the companies wards of the state.

Wallison and Pinto responded promptly.[36] They noted that the SEC's finding actually *raised* the total of risky loans over what Wallison and Pinto had previously reported. In his dissent, Wallison, drawing on Pinto's work, had estimated that Fannie Mae and Freddie Mac had made 12 million risky home loans. The SEC put the total at 13.37 million. This wasn't just the SEC's number. Fannie Mae and Freddie Mac signed nonprosecution agreements with the SEC in which the two government-owned enterprises confirmed the facts cited by the SEC. Suddenly Joe Nocera had put himself in the absurd position of insisting he knew more about Fannie Mae and Freddie Mac's books than those organizations themselves did.

Unfortunately, winning an argument is not the same as making policy. Many of the misguided policies that gave rise to the financial meltdown are still in play today. Even now, as Wallison points out, the Community Reinvestment Act "requires all insured banks and [savings and loans] to make loans to borrowers at or below 80 percent of the median income in the areas the banks service."[37] And only the 2010 election, which put Republicans in the majority in the House, prevented a bill to extend the Community Reinvestment Act's authority to all "U.S. nonbank financial companies"—something Barney Frank claimed as his "top priority."[38] Meanwhile, the cost to U.S. taxpayers from the Federal Housing Administration's 5 million subprime loans has still not come due in full.[39]

As Thomas Sowell has said, demagoguery beats data. The commission that studied the financial crisis took no account of the facts that Wallison and Pinto had uncovered. Even if the majority had done so, however, Congress and the president announced their sentence before the rigged trial (authorized by them) had rendered a verdict. By the time the SEC vindicated Wallison and Pinto's claims in 2011, Dodd-Frank was already the law of the land.

CHAPTER 10

AN ARBITRARY
AND SOVEREIGN
POWER

The natural progress of things is for liberty to yield,
and government to gain ground.

—Thomas Jefferson

More than 800 pages long, the Dodd-Frank "Wall Street Reform and Consumer Protection Act" makes some 398 rulemaking requirements. These will translate into thousands of pages of regulations spread over a dozen government agencies—two brand-new, and one endowed with unprecedented power.[1] Since this is a book rather than a multi-volume encyclopedia, we can't unpack the details of it here. What we can do is shine a spotlight on a few frightening and dangerous characteristics of the act and the actors behind it.

WHO REFORMS THE REFORMERS?

In a sense, the fact that the act is named after then-Senator Chris Dodd and then-Representative Barney Frank tells us much of what we need to know. More than any other members of the U.S.

Congress, these two men bore the most responsibility for championing the housing policies that, as we have seen, spawned the crisis. Were they really the best choice to assign blame and reform the system that caused the crisis?

Now retired, Barney Frank was a longtime, scandal-prone fixture of the House of Representatives from 1981 to 2011. For years, he shaped financial regulations from his perch on the House Financial Services Committee, which he chaired from 2007 to 2011. Hypocrisy didn't seem to perturb him. For all Frank's talk of regulation *after* the crisis, for years before the crisis struck, he was an ardent defender of loosening the rules that governed Fannie Mae and Freddie Mac's lending standards.

In September 2003, the George W. Bush administration proposed a new agency to oversee the two government sponsored enterprises because of worries that their lending had started to bear too much risk. Frank, the lead Democrat on the House Financial Services Committee, blocked it. "These two entities—Fannie Mae and Freddie Mac—are not facing any kind of financial crisis," he claimed. "The more people exaggerate these problems, the more pressure there is on these companies, the less we will see in terms of affordable housing."[2] He continued to oppose the Bush administration's efforts until the subprime writing on the wall became clear to everyone in 2007,[3] at which point he started blaming Republicans for the crisis.

Perhaps Frank's finger-pointing was a diversionary tactic to make sure his pet project was not implicated. In any case, the press mostly followed his lead. But the facts about the cause of the crisis point back to him and his close political and personal associates.

Frank's longtime partner, Herb Moses, was an executive at Fannie Mae from 1991 to 1998. While there, Moses "helped develop many of Fannie Mae's affordable housing and home improvement lending programs," explained the *National Mortgage News*. During the financial crisis, one GOP House aide asked on a national news program, "C'mon, he writes housing and banking laws and his boyfriend is a top exec at a firm that stands to gain from those laws?"[4] Unfortunately, the answer to the question is yes.

Frank, for his part, received $40,000 in campaign contributions from executives at Fannie Mae and Freddie Mac.[5]

Barney Frank won 17 consecutive elections in his Massachusetts district, but he faced probably his toughest race before his 2010 win. That victory was vital; it gave him time to push for the act that bears his name. His work done, in November 2011 he announced that he would not stand for reelection in 2012. The ranking Democrat on the House Financial Services Committee is now Maxine Waters of California, an even more avid fan of affordable housing policies than her predecessor.[6]

Over in the Senate, Chris Dodd, chairman of the Senate Banking Committee, also had a long career as a "consumer advocate." His advocacy was put at risk when it came to light that he had gotten discount mortgages through a VIP program at Countrywide Financial Group, the giant subprime mortgage lender acquired by Bank of America in January 2008. At the time of its collapse, Countrywide was servicing 9 million home loans in the United States worth $1.5 trillion. The sweetheart deal looked suspiciously like payment to Dodd for political favors, but the Connecticut senator was never convicted of a crime. Still, the House Committee on Oversight and Government Reform, chaired by Representative Darrell Issa, issued a report in 2012 concluding that former Countrywide CEO Angelo Mozilo had used the VIP program to buy influence in Washington.[7]

One thing that helped Dodd escape relatively unscathed is that he announced his own retirement at the beginning of 2010. The decision may have helped get the Dodd-Frank bill to the president's desk, because it allowed Dodd to take his gloves off in the remaining rounds of the fight over Dodd-Frank. "Now he can be bolder," said Graham Steele of the progressive group Public Citizen, "because he won't have to worry about continuing a working relationship with other members of the banking committee after the legislation is approved, particularly if negotiations go sour."[8]

The bill was rushed through the conference committee on regulatory reform—the group appointed by Congress to resolve disagreements on the bill—in two weeks. Despite stiff opposition from the financial industry and Republicans in Congress, the final 848-page bill passed both the House and Senate. On July 21, 2010, President Obama signed the Dodd-Frank Act into law.

TOO BIG TO (BE ALLOWED TO) FAIL

Among the bureaucratic consequences of Dodd-Frank was the creation of the Financial Stability Oversight Council. This financial supergroup is made up of the heads of the financial regulating agencies as well as the Treasury secretary, the chairman of the Federal Reserve, and an independent insurance expert appointed by the president for a six-year term.[9]

One of the new council's first jobs was to come up with the name "systemically important financial institutions" (SIFI), which is bureaucratese for "too big to (be allowed to) fail."[10] These are companies judged to be so integral to the national economy that if one of them failed, it could spell disaster for the entire economy.[11] To qualify initially, a bank or bank holding company simply needs to have at least $50 billion in assets. That's a wide enough net to capture all the American banks involved in the harrowing meetings in New York in the fall of 2008.[12]

As we've already seen, knowing that the government will bail out a failing firm creates all kinds of dangerous incentives, but at least there's a specific threshold for banks to be dubbed "systemically important." This hard-and-fast line could at least limit cronyism by curtailing the power of politicians to curry donations and other favors in return for promising SIFI status to individual banks. Unfortunately, the council is now applying the label to *nonbank* institutions that are "predominantly involved" in finance. The guidelines for assigning systemically important status are vague, leaving plenty of room for sweetheart deals among political-corporate cronies and no way to know where it will all lead. What does seem clear is that not just major banks but a slew of other firms—large holding companies, insurance companies, securities firms, finance companies, hedge funds, and even money-market mutual funds—will surely begin receiving their SIFI seal of protection. That's provided, of course, they learn how to play well with their political friends in Washington.[13]

Once the council dubs a company a systemically important financial institution, that firm will be subject to more stringent regulation, such as being required to hold more capital on its books compared to smaller companies.[14] This might be reasonable, if it were handled differently. But the practice of designating *specific* firms as "systemically important" goes far beyond commonsense regulation. It will have at least five effects as predictable as they are perverse. These effects could be the cause of a meltdown far worse than anything we have seen in our recent crisis.

SHIELDED FROM THE CONSEQUENCES OF BAD DECISIONS

One perverse effect is that investors, capital markets, and the world will see the SIFI label as a form of special protection by the U.S. government. Sound familiar? Recall that, leading up to the financial crisis, investors rightly expected that the government wouldn't let Fannie Mae and Freddie Mac, as well as some of the larger private banks, collapse. Investors are likely to treat systemically important financial institutions in the same way, and this will give those firms an artificial advantage that some researchers suspect will be worth billions of dollars.[15]

Bankruptcy scholar David Skeel argues this point in one of the first thorough books about Dodd-Frank, *The New Financial Deal*.[16] Dodd-Frank, he says, creates provisions for an "orderly liquidation authority" (a fancy name for a bailout) and for "resolution planning" (code for "government takeover"). More specifically, if a systemically important financial institution gets into trouble, the government will put the firm under the control of the FDIC and preserve it from having to file for Chapter 11 bankruptcy. It's no wonder that in a 2012 presidential election debate, Mitt Romney described Dodd-Frank as the "biggest kiss that's been given to the

New York banks I've ever seen." To judge from past liquidations by the FDIC,[17] however, it may be the kiss of death for employees who find themselves replaced by federal agents.

Dodd-Frank mandates that the more solvent competitors pay for the liquidation of a troubled firm—yet another source of perverse incentives. But this unfair provision is unlikely to prevail in the long term—meaning that the bill will actually get passed onto taxpayers.

FAVORING THE BIG OVER THE SMALL

Second, we'll see even more consolidation of banks and financial industries. That's because smaller firms will likely suffer from being outside the SIFI zone of protection and so will feel strong pressure to merge or sell themselves to firms within the zone. This will not only reduce competition; it will make the new larger firms even *more* systemically important. Already the six biggest banks in the United States have assets totaling 62 percent of our country's gross domestic product, up from 18 percent in 1995.[18] That's twice as big as the next 50 largest banks combined.[19] Do we really want even more of this concentration of power, money, and government protection?

The same thing will happen to nonbank institutions such as insurance companies. At the moment, insurance is a very competitive industry. But imagine, says Peter Wallison, "what the industry will look like if the [Financial Stability Oversight Council] declares three or four insurers or their holding companies to be too big to fail and subjects them to special regulation by the Fed. Creditors and customers will come to feel more secure working with them than with others, seriously distorting competition in the insurance market."[20] Although we may rightly assume that it is government's job to break up monopolies in the private sector, in reality, monopolies are usually formed and maintained by collusion between big business and government. Large companies are often only too happy to have regulations that weed out competitors. That will certainly be the case here. Real competition among insurance companies lowers costs and increases quality for consumers. A lack of competition will do the opposite.

If you thought the megabanks were too big to fail before, just wait to see what happens now that they've been officially dubbed "systemically important." The ultimate effect could very well be bailouts that make the 2008 bailout look like lunch money.

CENTRALIZING POWER

A third perverse effect of the act stems from Dodd-Frank requiring deep and abiding relationships among the Financial Stability Oversight Council, private firms, and their taskmasters in the Federal Reserve—relationships that won't exist for community banks and other smaller firms. The natural outcome is that the systemically important financial institutions will have both greater incentive and a greater capacity to curry favor with their regulators, and less incentive and capacity to serve their customers. Rather than being a counterbalance to the centralization of power in Washington, these firms will further entrench and expand that centralization. "In the future," Wallison argues, "SIFIs will be added to the timid group that will fear to challenge the Fed or the administration in power, and will be susceptible to demands for backing administration policies."[21] We will end up with an economy that is not merely regulated by the government but dominated by it—an economy of command-and-control cronyism among well-connected insiders rather than one of competition and free enterprise.

PLEASING REGULATORS RATHER THAN CONSUMERS

A fourth perverse effect of the Dodd-Frank Act is that it will transform the mission of big financial firms from pleasing consumers on Main Street to appeasing politicians and bureaucrats in Washington. Think of the Volt electric car released by General Motors. In 2009, the federal government took over General Motors; as a result, GM's incentives changed. The Volt was largely the product not of strong consumer demand but of political pressure to produce greener cars (both before and after the takeover). Not surprisingly, GM sold about half as many Volts as they had projected, and this despite taxpayer-funded rebates for buyers ranging from $2,500 to $7,500.

STAGNATION

Fifth, and perhaps ironically, the burdens of being designated "too big to (be allowed to) fail" could lead to moribund growth for the systemically important financial institutions. The new rules will lead to more than 10,000 pages of regulations. Just complying with the first 224 of the almost 400 rules will add more than 24 million work hours in the private sector every year. Republican Representative Randy Neugebauer has noted that it took less time to build the Panama Canal, the great sea bridge connecting two oceans.[22]

You might think that, well, at least the many millions of hours that must now be poured into paperwork creates jobs, but this misses the bigger picture. This is human time and effort that might have been spent creating, building, improving, and delivering goods and services that people want and need. Instead it will be spent sifting, interpreting, and tracking miles of red tape that stretches to the horizon in every direction. Paying people to dig holes and then refill them also creates jobs in the short term. What it doesn't do is create new wealth, which can, in turn, be used to generate fresh demand and capacity for new market exchanges, new forms of labor, and hence a more competitive, thriving economy.

At the moment, it's hard to predict whether the benefits of being designated too big to fail will outweigh the regulatory costs for systemically important financial institutions, but one thing is clear: if their regulatory burden hinders them from competing with smaller, less regulated competitors, the SIFIs will seek still more "protection" by the U.S. government. And they will likely get it. "Either we will have large, successful, government-backed firms that swallow up smaller competitors," argues Peter Wallison, "or we will have large, unprofitable, heavily regulated giants that are gradually driven to failure by their more nimble and less regulated competitors. In the former case, small firms and consumers are the victims. In the latter case, taxpayers will pay for the bailouts. Pick your dystopia."[23] Either way, we'll end up footing the bill.

It may seem paradoxical that being dubbed a systemically important financial institution could be both helpful and hurtful, but it's not. For a business, special treatment by the U.S. government can look a lot like special treatment from the Mafia. Sure, Cosa Nostra offers you protection for a price and keeps your competitors at bay. But if you're good at delivering value to customers, you don't do nearly as well as you would without the mob in your neighborhood. Besides, with such protection, you can't shake the feeling that you have traded freedom for bondage.

In short, rather than fixing the problems that caused the financial crisis, Dodd-Frank has transformed some of the most harmful of those problems into permanent features of the financial landscape.

MORAL HAZARD 2.0

This mistake is especially obvious when it comes to Fannie Mae and Freddie Mac. Prior to 2008, Fannie and Freddie were publicly traded private companies that also enjoyed perks that private companies did not. They are now owned and controlled by the federal government—officially under the new Federal Housing Finance Agency—and no longer traded on the New York Stock Exchange.[24] The loss to the U.S. Treasury for this venture so far is $141 billion—a staggering sum even for our government. Yet, the federal government still has no plan to sell them. "Four years after the takeover of Fannie and Freddie," wrote Jim Millstein and Phillip Swagel in a *Washington Post* essay in October 2012, "the government now backstops 90 percent of all new mortgages and has no plan to reduce its market share, no plan to protect taxpayers against future losses on the trillions of dollars of mortgage credit underwritten since the firms were placed under government control and no plan to recover the taxpayer money invested in Fannie and Freddie."[25]

Now that Fannie Mae and Freddie Mac have graduated from being government sponsored enterprises to being fully nationalized entities, the growing class of companies dubbed SIFIs will in effect become the *new* GSEs. Even the Federal Reserve Bank of Dallas observed in a recent annual report that "for all its bluster, Dodd-Frank leaves TBTF [too-big-to-fail] untouched."[26] In fact, the act *encourages* "too big to fail." The moral hazard that distorted incentives and scrambled signals in the mortgage market before the crisis has not been expunged by Dodd-Frank. Instead, it has been compounded and institutionalized.

And that's just the beginning.

COUP DE GRÂCE

If all you knew about Elizabeth Warren was what appeared on the front pages during the 2012 elections, you'd probably be surprised to learn the important role she played—and continues to play—in the infiltration of the American financial system by the ideological left.

Most Americans outside the financial industry and state of Massachusetts didn't know much about Elizabeth Warren until a controversy erupted over her ethnicity, real and alleged. In the spring of 2012, Warren was a sixty-something professor at Harvard Law School and the newly minted Democratic Party candidate for the U.S. Senate against Republican incumbent Scott Brown. She was about to learn that the limelight can also be the spotlight.

In April 2012, the *Boston Herald* revealed that Harvard Law had for years listed her as contributing to the ethnic diversity of their faculty, apparently because she listed herself as Native American in law school directories. When questioned, Warren said that, according to "family lore," she had a great-great-great grandmother who was Cherokee. Perhaps she really was one thirty-second Native American and so had added mightily to the Harvard Law faculty's ethnic smorgasbord. Unfortunately, as several later news stories reported, there was no evidence that the blonde, blue-eyed native of Oklahoma had Cherokee lineage.

When I heard the story, I understood it at once. I grew up in the Texas Panhandle. From my hometown of Amarillo, if you get up in the morning, hop on I-40 and drive east, you can be in Warren's hometown of Oklahoma City by lunch. Nonnatives would have a hard time telling these places apart. Besides the hot summers, wide-open spaces, and latitude, they have something else in common: practically everyone with deep roots in the area has heard family lore about Cherokee ancestry. The Cherokees had been moved to the region from Georgia in the early 1800s, and claiming Cherokee lineage added a noble and exotic flare to otherwise nondescript personal bios. But these stories were largely the province of teenage bragging sessions—and best left there. Elizabeth Warren is that rare instance of a public figure who has tried to parlay such unsubstantiated lore to career advantage.[27]

Had she been running in a less progressive state, her career might have been over the day the *Boston Herald* broke the story. As it was, there were some amusing follow-up pieces about "Fauxcahantas" and "Sacajahwarren," but the media soon stamped the subject "old news." It had mostly dissipated when she took the stage in September 2012 at the Democratic National Convention in Charlotte, where she delivered a populist barnstorming speech perfected on the campaign trail.

Drawing heavily from the humble origins playbook, the speech had many of the same features found in the rhetoric of Martin Eakes and Herb and Marion Sandler. Warren told of her modest beginnings in a working-class family in Oklahoma—her dad a janitor, her mother working the phone for Sears, her three brothers serving in the armed services. Well, okay, it's true she was a bankruptcy law professor at one of the most elite and well-heeled universities on the planet, and she was headlining the Democratic Party's national convention; but deep down she was just a humble servant defending a hardworking and hard-bitten middle class.

Warming up, she described the noble progressive vision, starting with Teddy Roosevelt's campaign to save children from labor and protect everyone from dangerous food and drugs. For decades, government was all about helping the common man. But that had changed recently. "For many years, our middle class has been chipped, squeezed, and hammered," she charged. The blame rested squarely on greedy Wall Street bankers and Republicans. "The Republicans have made their vision clear," she announced. "They have said, 'I got mine. The rest of you are on your own.'" Perfecting the caricature, she continued, "Republicans say they don't believe in government. Sure they do. They believe in government to help themselves and their powerful friends."

There are merits to having at least two political major parties, since each serves to check the power of the other. But when one side uses demagoguery, it spells danger.

It's hard to imagine any major Republican figure saying or thinking any of the things that Warren ascribed to the entire party. Warren was a Republican herself until 1996, a year after she accepted a full-time position at Harvard. Most Republican politicians emphasize economic freedom as the best way to empower the poor and middle class to improve their lot. Conservative Republicans in particular argue that a limited government—one that refuses to endlessly regulate and redistribute an economy—best encourages human creativity and opportunity, whereas a bloated government does just the opposite. It's one thing to disagree with these views, but quite another to mangle them beyond recognition. All the same, Warren's speech fired up the convention.

The following week, Jeffrey Toobin in *The New Yorker* quoted someone who described Warren as "a throwback to a more combative progressive tradition."[28]

The significance of Elizabeth Warren for our story, however, starts earlier. In 2007, she wrote an article for the progressive journal *Democracy* where she laid out a proposal for what she called a Financial Product Safety Commission.[29] She derived the name from another federal agency, the Consumer Product Safety Commission, started in 1972 by the Nixon administration. She argued that the commission, rather than damaging the market for Christmas lights, toasters, and so forth, protected consumers from things they would not otherwise know about. Because of that agency, she explained, consumers today can continue to exercise their freedom to choose between vertical and horizontal, white and stainless steel toasters, and they can do so with the confidence that all their options are safe.

Her point, of course, is that while toasters are properly regulated, financial products are not. According to Warren, many unsafe financial products have flooded the market since the 1970s—from confusing and term-changing credit cards to subprime mortgages to payday loans—and consumers desperately need protection from them. To back up many of her claims, she cited the misleading "studies" discussed earlier, the ones from the Center for Responsible Lending that described "predatory practices" without ever providing a definition.

She conceded that regulators could not be expected "to provide the self-discipline that customers lack." Still, "lenders have deliberately built tricks and traps into some credit products so they can ensnare families in a cycle of high-cost debt." Credit card disclosures had grown from one page in the 1980s to "thirty pages of incomprehensible text"—not because lenders feared lawsuits, but because "they were designed in large part to add unexpected—and unreadable—terms that favor the card companies." She also complained of mortgage brokers that charged home buyers a rate of interest higher than they qualified for and pocketed the difference.

Yet she saved her sharpest barbs for the payday lenders. They "have a bad reputation for taking advantage of people," she argued. "No one should expect to be treated well by them." Conclusion: like unregulated toasters, "financial products are dangerous, and any consumer who is not careful is inviting trouble."

There's something almost surreal about Warren's *Democracy* article: she passionately asserted that the financial services industry needed a new arm of the government to start regulating it. But that's like contending that pro basketball needs to introduce a Basketball Player Safety Commission with the power to go onto the court and enforce the rules—making sure, for instance, that the burly centers don't use their superior size to beat the shooting guards into a bloody pulp. Never mind that the National Basketball Association already has referees.

And no, that's not a far-fetched analogy. It's putting it mildly. Think about it: the financial services industry already is encrusted with layers and layers of government regulation and regulators—state audits, the FDIC, federal regulations (such as Truth-in-Lending), Fair Credit Reporting, rules against discrimination, the Federal Reserve, the Office of the Comptroller of the Currency, the Federal Trade Commission, and the Office of Thrift Supervision (which was replaced by the new regulatory bureau that Warren was advocating). She gave the impression that new financial products were springing up like saloons and brothels in the Wild West, but it would be hard to characterize the facts less accurately. Perhaps sensing that her straw man needed a fig leaf, she did admit in the essay that some regulation already existed, but then she quickly insisted that these were weak reeds against the tsunami of industry lobbyists. Hence the need for a new, powerful, "independent" agency to police the financial industry.[30]

Throughout the article, she claimed that her proposal would not harm the "free market"; instead, it would regulate the market. The aim was to "produce value for both buyers and sellers, both borrowers and lenders," she explained. "But the basic premise of any free market is full information." This sounds almost sensible, but it's impossible to have full information in almost any transaction, and yet we freely exchange goods and services all the time—from bananas and disposable razors to undershirts and laptop computers—using only a few key pieces of information. I'm using a MacBook Pro, and when I bought it, I shopped first for brand, which in the case of computers is a hugely important data point. After that, screen size, processor speed, and price. I didn't know a thing about 99.999 percent of the construction and supply chain of the machine. Neither did anyone in the Apple Store where I bought it. If a free market required the parties in the sale of a personal computer to know *everything* about the transaction before the sale, no one would ever get around to buying a computer. In place of Warren's utterly unworkable call for "full information," what's needed is a far more modest standard: for a market trade to be free, consumers should not be coerced and should have access to relevant information.

Warren's claim about "full information" seems plausible, however, because on almost every page she mentioned a case where a credit card company changed the terms and rates of its cards without notifying customers, or buried the notice so deeply in the fine print that no one but a contract lawyer could be expected to comprehend it. That is a bad practice, since the terms and rate of a loan are *exactly* what borrowers need to know to make a free exchange. Economists call this "information asymmetry." At a certain point, such deception amounts to fraud, but we need to be discriminating here. Just because customers don't do their homework, their confusion is not evidence of fraud. Certainly, credit card fraud is sometimes a problem, but there are over 7,000 banks in the United States, along with countless other large- and small-dollar lenders. Warren made it sound like fraud was the norm for all of them.

Besides, the Harvard professor didn't merely propose for the government to protect us from fraud in the financial sector. Though in her rhetoric she called for Americans to be protected from another financial crisis, her proposal was not about eliminating the causes of the meltdown. Instead, she called for a new and unprecedented federal agency that would move into the regulatory space occupied by dozens of local, state, and federal oversight and enforcement entities. This new agency was to take on the role of regulating every jot and tittle of the financial industry in all its variety, and businesses as diverse as college loan providers, credit card companies, collection agencies, mortgage lenders, traditional installment lenders, payday lenders, and pawnshops.

In 2007, Warren might never have imagined that in just three years, her proposal would become a reality. In 2010 the Dodd-Frank Wall Street Reform and Financial Protection Act established the Consumer Financial Protection Bureau. Warren worked with others behind the scene—including Eric Stein of the Center for Responsible Lending, then ensconced at the Treasury—to establish the agency. Clearly the financial crisis didn't *necessitate* a new agency to police pawnshops in Tuscaloosa, Alabama; rather, the crisis was an *opportunity* to create an agency. What we got was one with unprecedented power and little oversight.

HOW WE GOT SADDLED WITH
AN UNNECESSARY AGENCY

Elizabeth Warren's role in this work is well known. Equally certain, if far less well known, is the connection between Dodd-Frank, the Consumer Financial Protection Bureau, and the Center for Responsible Lending—*The Little Engine That Could*, built by Martin Eakes and the Sandlers. The mainstream media scarcely noticed the link, but it didn't go wholly without public acknowledgment.

In 2012, the MacArthur Foundation credited the Center for Responsible Lending for Dodd-Frank,[31] and in his August 2010 lecture to Duke MBA students, Eakes did the same, quite openly and more colorfully. For a moment, he set aside his carefully crafted public image and showed his true colors. "Just this year the financial reform bill that just passed, and the chief operating officer from Self-Help was hired to be the director of consumer protection in the U.S. Treasury," he said proudly. "And the Center for Responsible Lending—that by now we had put eight million dollars a year into funding these 50 million [sic] financial terrorists, if you want to call them that—we got to the point where we were basically shaping the very principles that we sat down in a little conference room on the sixth floor of our building in Durham in 1998 and designed. Every one of those ten principles were designed into law with this financial reform bill twelve years later."

If Elizabeth Warren was the mother of the Consumer Financial Protection Bureau, then the Center for Responsible Lending was its father. To help fulfill the Center's vision to "basically terrorize the financial services industry," its acolytes are now beginning to populate the Consumer Bureau and other agencies. Leslie Parrish, formerly a research assistant at the Center for Responsible Lending with no experience in private industry, has become a program manager at the Consumer Bureau overseeing payday and small-dollar loans. The Center's first president, Mark Pearce, became director of the newly created Division of Depositor and Consumer Protection at the FDIC, and Center for Responsible Lending policy analyst Keith Ernst became its associate director.

Given Warren's DNA and Harvard credentials, however, why was she not appointed as director of the bureau? The short answer is that she had too many well-placed critics. Before coming to Harvard Law in 1995, she had coauthored several books on bankruptcy law. Other experts in the field subjected this work to withering criticism in respected academic journals. One law professor from the State University of New York at Buffalo criticized her methods and conclusions, which made it impossible for her to confirm her claims. A professor of economics at the University of Michigan challenged Warren's treatment of his field: "[The] authors [of this book] are quite hostile to economics, and they attempt to discredit economic models and their predictions.'"[32] And a Rutgers Law School professor even charged Warren and her coauthors with "scientific misconduct" for the way they handled data.[33]

Most of the media treat these scandals as old news—how could she be a bad scholar if she went on to teach at Harvard Law School?—but these are serious charges that have never been cleared up.[34]

Despite devastating criticism of her poor scholarship and concern about her grasp of economics, she somehow earned a spot on a federal commission to study bankruptcy in 1997. This was followed by her really big break in 2008, when Senator Harry Reid appointed her to a panel charged with monitoring the recent bank bailouts: the Troubled Asset Relief Program.

The position gave her a bully pulpit to rail against lenders and to blame Wall Street greed and deregulation for the crisis. The problem for her career wasn't that she wasn't progressive enough. It was that her progressivism was flamboyantly principled rather than merely partisan. She loved being the watchdog and quickly became a pit bull in her position. She went for the jugular in her questioning of President Obama's Treasury secretary Timothy Geithner, who had helped orchestrate both the bailout of Bear Stearns and the larger TARP bailout in September 2008. She pressed him, even though Geithner would play a major role in choosing the first director of the Consumer Bureau, a post she surely coveted. It's hard to imagine that her grilling had no effect on Geithner's choice.

By 2010, Warren was also considered a pariah by the U.S. Chamber of Commerce and many on Wall Street. So it's no surprise that she (along with another likely choice, Eric Stein of the Center for Responsible Lending and the Treasury) was passed over for the job. Instead, the Consumer Bureau directorship was given to Richard Cordray, a credentialed but unassuming Ohio politician without a sharp ideological edge. Politically, that made sense. Not only was Warren an excitable ideologue who could not be trusted to keep her whistle-blowing focused on the issues at hand, she also came with baggage. Besides having exploited a tenuous and possibly faux Native American ancestry, she had made big money apparently practicing law in Massachusetts without a license.[35] In the most publicized case, Travelers Insurance paid her $212,000 for successfully representing that company in a case with asbestos victims.[36] The news broke shortly after President Obama nominated Cordray. Perhaps the White House knew about Warren's actions before the story broke. In any case, if she had been perched at the top of a controversial agency, this baggage would have invited unwanted attention.

But when one door closes, another often opens. In February 2011, Representative Barney Frank told President Obama that if Warren was passed over for director of the Consumer Financial Protection Bureau, she would run for the Senate.[37] She did just that, and she didn't shy away from touting her role in birthing the new regulatory bureau. On the campaign trail, she referred to it maternally as a "baby agency."[38] Her baggage may have kept her from becoming its first director, but she connected—baggage and all—with Massachusetts voters, beating incumbent Republican Scott Brown by more than seven points. Firmly in office, she has already generated buzz about running for president in 2016. Yet the influence she now wields may be enough to keep her satisfied for the foreseeable future: she sits on the powerful Senate Banking Committee, the perfect perch from which to nurture her Consumer Financial Protection Bureau offspring and contemplate a larger brood of bureaucracies.[39]

CLOSING THE DEAL

Herb and Marion Sandler, Elizabeth Warren, and Martin Eakes have all worked toward a common goal: to empower the federal government and its well-connected friends to infiltrate every nook and cranny of our financial system. They have parlayed the financial crisis into a golden opportunity to take power into their own hands while continuing to promote the same policies that brought on the crisis.

As should be clear by now, the Sandlers, Warren, and Eakes are far from alone. Despite the implausibility of the claim, many in the media—especially in Washington, D.C., and Durham, North Carolina—have worked hard to connect unrelated credit card and small-dollar lenders to the financial meltdown—and then to use that connection as a bridge to greater government control of all financial institutions, large and small.

In November 2009, the PBS *Frontline* series, funded by the MacArthur Foundation and the Sandlers, aired an episode coproduced with the *New York Times* called "The Card Game." It featured the *New York Time's* Joe Nocera, along with Timothy Geithner, Senator Chris Dodd, Elizabeth Warren, and Martin Eakes. In the opening, the narrator informs viewers that "the credit card industry even played a hand in the economic meltdown." Most of the episode is concerned with giving examples of confusing credit card policies and telling stories of people who didn't understand those policies, spent too much, and got into trouble.

Clearly the credit card industry needed to do more to smoke out bad actors, and the Credit Card Accountability Responsibility and Disclosure Act of 2009 (Credit CARD Act) addressed some problems with transparency. But as with Warren's 2007 article, the *Frontline* documentary portrayed deception and criminality as the norm in consumer lending. At one point, expert Robert McKinley offers a line about deregulation that could have served as a blurb promoting the film: "The credit card industry has always been the Wild West. . . . Competition ramped up to such a level that it created an industry that was out of control."[40] From here the report drifted seamlessly into an attack on payday lending.

Watching "The Card Game" in hindsight, it looks like a middlebrow infomercial for the Consumer Financial Protection Bureau and Dodd-Frank, even though its apparent goal was to defend the rationale for the 2009 Credit CARD Act. For instance, lest someone conclude that the Credit CARD Act would render the upcoming Consumer Financial Protection Bureau legislation redundant, the documentary made clear that more was needed. "We need to fix the rules and make them tougher with a simple, clear, single mission to protect consumers," said Timothy Geithner. The problem, he went on to explain, is that existing regulations were spread around in an army of agencies, which created "a complicated mess." Dodd-Frank, in contrast, stipulated that the Consumer Bureau have a *single* director appointed for a five-year term. (Most other independent federal agencies are governed by bipartisan commissions.) And it gave the agency authority to write rules over almost every consumer finance transaction in the United States.

When Richard Cordray was nominated to head the new agency in 2011, nearly all Republican members of the House objected. Their problem wasn't with Cordray, but with the appointment itself. The Consumer Financial Protection Bureau, unlike most regulatory agencies, had been placed under the quasi-private Federal Reserve System, which meant that Congress would not hold its purse strings. "I'm sure that you have a good background . . . but you're caught between a big substantive debate," said Senator Richard Shelby (R-Alabama) to Cordray during the committee hearing on Cordray's confirmation. "And that's going to have to be resolved, I think, before we move this nomination farther."[41]

To break the stalemate, the White House released a paper in December 2011 defending the importance of the new agency and its need for a single director.[42] The document liberally cited studies from the Center for Responsible Lending—that factory of "research" that artfully combines sad stories and misleading statistics. The White House paper framed the debate as a struggle between ordinary Americans and powerful, predatory bankers and other lenders.

The move failed to allay the Republican House members' concerns about a powerful appointment that circumvented the Senate's constitutionally ordained role to advise and offer or withhold consent on political appointments. No matter. On January 4, 2012, President Obama simply appointed Cordray to the post, during what the president claimed was a Senate recess.

AN ARBITRARY POWER

Keep in mind a few important points we mentioned at the beginning of this book. Although the Congress and president created the Consumer Financial Protection Bureau, it's not funded or overseen by Congress. The bureau gets its considerable funding from the Federal Reserve and from the fines it imposes. The president can only remove the director for "good cause," for something like gross negligence or criminality. Neither the Fed chairman nor board can remove the director for any reason. In fact, the Fed has no control over any employee of the CFPB or over any rule that the CFPB implements. The agency is basically a sovereign entity.

As a sovereign standing astride the financial world, the CFPB has a wide range of enforcement tools and sanctions at its disposal. For instance, against businesses it can issue cease-and-desist orders that go into effect immediately. Such actions are already happening, though you'll have a hard time finding news stories about them. I have spoken to employees of firms who describe the experience of being ordered by the CFPB to cease and desist as a sort of SWAT raid—except that the officers wear suits and carry briefcases and don't bring search warrants. The descriptions add bones and muscles to Martin Eakes's abstract homage to "financial terrorists." Almost any pretense will do for such raids, since Dodd-Frank gives the agency the power as it sees fit to "declare" that a company has engaged in "unfair, deceptive, or abusive acts or practices."[43] Companies targeted by the sovereign Consumer Bureau are guilty—and effectively shackled—until proven innocent. At the moment, the agency is examining financial institutions to make sure they practice "fair lending."[44] Sound familiar?

Legal scholar Michael Greve notes that at least the words *unfair* and *deceptive* have clear meanings, which have been developed over "decades of regulation and litigation." But what does *abusive* mean? The power given to the CFPB implies that some financial transactions could be fair and truthful but still "abusive." That doesn't even make sense. In practice, *abusive* is likely to do the same work as *predatory*. It's a catchall word, used to designate whatever firm or practice Consumer Bureau officials want to punish, control, or destroy.

The bureau's arbitrary power includes the ability not only to condemn but also to exempt. When it issued its lengthy standards for a "qualified mortgage" in January 2013, it captured large banks, savings and loans, credit unions, and community banks in its dragnet. Beforehand, the Center for Responsible Lending had worried publicly about the impact of such standards on the work of Self-Help.

In the final rule, however, two groups were exempted from the full requirements: (1) "People with subprime adjustable-rate mortgages or other risky loans who are refinancing," and (2) "mortgages issued by certain non-profits for low-income homebuyers."[45] Hmm, does the Center for Responsible Lending or Self-Help come to mind?

THE JOB OF BUREAUCRACY

Now if, as Timothy Geithner has argued, the Consumer Financial Protection Bureau is needed to simplify regulation, why haven't all those older, messy bureaus been dissolved after CFPB was granted their territory? Probably for the same reason so many other agencies continue to live long past politicians' pledges to dismantle them. Public-choice economists have shown that the chief incentive of a government bureaucracy is to perpetuate itself.[46] Charles Dickens anticipated the insight in his novel *Bleak House*, where the narrator observes that "the one great principle of the English law is, to make business for itself."

This tendency has everything to do with incentives and how the budget process works. If a regulatory agency has a $500 million budget (the Consumer Bureau's budget, circa 2012) and shows that it can fulfill its mandate by spending only $100 million, it will get its budget cut. An agency's fear is that once it stops growing, like any life-form, it will start to die. This fear, combined with the natural human desire to grow and thrive, means that bureaucracies, once started, are hard to contain, much less dissolve. "A government bureau," said Ronald Reagan, "is the nearest thing to eternal life we'll ever see on this earth."[47]

The nasty result is that a bureaucracy will survive and thrive even when it is clearly doing more harm than good.[48] The House Committee on Oversight and Government Reform summarized on December 14, 2012, what their research had turned up after the Consumer Bureau's first official year of work:

> Under the regulatory burden of the Dodd-Frank Act, financial products and services are costing more and small community banks are closing up shop at a pace of hundreds per year. . . . These effects have been felt most keenly by those borrowers at the margins, creating an economic divide in the United States between those with access to credit and those without.
>
> Yet the CFPB's unprecedented structure and vague mandate threatens to restrict credit access even further. The regulator has refused to add certainty to its nebulous and overly burdensome regulatory authority, causing banks and credit unions to restrict certain credit products

and services for fear of litigation and enforcement actions. The heavy-handed regulations proposed by the CFPB have proven costly for financial institutions, making borrowing more expensive and credit less available. . . .

Already, according to estimates, the CFPB has increased the cost of consumer credit by a total of $17 billion and depressed job creation by about 150,000 jobs.

Despite this toll, the Consumer Financial Protection Bureau "shows no signs of letting up," concludes the executive summary of the staff report. "If the Bureau is not careful to add clarity and much-needed certainty to the financial sector, the CFPB may continue to drastically affect credit access for millions of American families and small businesses."[49]

CHAPTER 11

THE GROUND
ASSAULT

So, now that Dodd-Frank has birthed the Consumer Financial Protection Bureau, and American consumers are safe from their own financial decisions, has the Center for Responsible Lending closed up camp? Hardly. With the Consumer Bureau now providing air cover and artillery, the infantry—that is, the Center and its scores of affiliated groups— has moved into a new phase of their work. Their basic approach is quite simple: in states with friendly legislators, they lobby for rules and regulations that will hinder, if not prohibit, whatever lending they don't like—which means all small-dollar loans. To do so, they employ a proverbial silver bullet: a cap on the annual percentage rate (APR), typically 36 percent. This may sound reasonable, but as we'll see, the bullet is financially lethal.

Their cap strategy has already worked in some states to eradicate private lending for the everyday citizen. The activists don't reveal their true intent because they don't need to. They understand a fact many legislators and ordinary citizens do not—that few, if any, small-dollar lenders can actually survive with such a rate cap, for reasons we'll explore in a moment. The real effect of rate caps is not to lower borrowing costs for consumers. Rather, it is to prevent consumers from getting small loans *at all* outside activist-supported—and, more important, taxpayer-supported—credit unions (like Martin Eakes's Self-Help) or banks. Banks are being coerced by consumer groups and even their federal regulators into making loans that they are generally ill equipped to handle. Caps also benefit a black market for loans as well as online lenders, some of which are offshore companies not subject to U.S. regulations. The legal businesses to which consumers have traditionally turned—and which provide loans at a significantly lower total cost—will have been bankrupted or driven out of business by the new regulations.

The disappearance of these small-dollar lenders can spell dire consequences for the people whom Eakes and the Center for Responsible Lending claim they wish to help. For instance, the single mother short on cash or credit who has a sudden issue with her car and needs it fixed today may have virtually nowhere to turn. Critics would say that she was being robbed by her potential lenders and should be more disciplined in the first place; but, if asked, the consumer herself would say she paid a reasonable amount to the lender; had fast, convenient service; and was able to pay off her loan. Yet Martin Eakes would legislate away her ability to get that loan. Instead, he'd most likely—and happily—give her one of his Self-Help loans (taxpayer subsidized and chock-full of stipulations), even though a regular installment loan costs just a few pennies more a day.

We might assume that Eakes and the Center for Responsible Lending are just trying to drive customers to their own credit union, but we'd be wrong. Although Self-Help is expanding rapidly, it simply couldn't handle all the business or sustain its model, dependent as it is on taxpayer subsidies. And many people would not want to go through the hassle—long applications, forced education, and waiting—or burden others by using a taxpayer-subsidized product. Instead, Eakes and his pals seemingly want to eliminate for-profit, small-dollar lending as part of a bigger strategy—quite simply, to hand over the consumer finance system in America to noble overseers like themselves.

In states where not enough legislators cooperate with the rate-cap strategy already mentioned, activists take their campaign directly to the public with ballot initiatives. This may include the usual community agitation, such as mob protests at lending offices and state capitols. These actions are intended to build public support for ballot initiatives to drive the lenders out.

All the shouts about high APR remind me of a story that a friend shared with me. While on a trip in Nigeria she was negotiating in a market stall for a garment, passionately arguing about the price the vendor wanted. In the local currency, there was a vast difference between his asking price and what she wanted to pay. But after a minute or two, my friend's husband leaned in and whispered in her ear, "You're arguing over a nickel." That nickel was trivial to her, but it might just help to keep the vendor in business. As soon as she understood the relative insignificance of her battle, she relented sweetly, and the vendor graciously accepted her payment. A nice ending. It calls to mind the relatively minor difference in small-dollar loan rates charged by a for-profit private community lender and a nonprofit, taxpayer-subsidized lender. It can be just pennies a day for the consumer, but multiplied by millions of borrowers, it becomes an enormous burden to taxpayers and our economy. Most borrowers don't want to be a burden on their neighbors; they just want the ability to get a small-dollar loan if and when they need one.

Here's how the consumer activists' strategy for banning these loans works. Outright bans on legal small-dollar loans might strike voters as heavy-handed and also offend the lenders' happy customers. So, instead, activists typically use ballot initiatives to push for some version of the interest-rate cap noted above. Getting an initiative on a ballot usually means first getting signatures on a petition. Among other tactics, local religious leaders are recruited for the crusade to gather signatures and often to serve as the first troops to land on the beach.

This has already happened in some states. In 2010, Montana voters approved a ballot measure to cap rates at 36 percent by a wide margin—78 percent for to 22 percent against—although the legislators and even the regulators had opposed the proposition. No doubt, Montanans thought they were choosing lower rates for themselves and the poor. The result, however, was that most small-dollar lenders could no longer afford to stay in business and simply left the state. This has left Montanans with fewer safe options than they had before, with a high cost to the state and local economies.

Banks, which rarely handle small loans, were exempted from Montana's 36 percent rate cap.[1] Although most banks have assumed they can't make a profit on small-dollar loans, some are exploring ways to get into these markets, especially at the urging of the FDIC. The FDIC has admitted that it is willing to change laws to make this happen and to use Community Reinvestment Act credits to induce banks into participating—in effect, to encourage and, if necessary, to coerce them to do so.

The Center for Responsible Lending and other consumer activist groups also want banks to enter this market. This was demonstrated in the meeting of the FDIC Advisory Committee on Economic Inclusion (ComE-IN) on December 7, 2010. Martin Eakes, a member of the committee, was in attendance. (In fact, over half the people on the committee are from consumer advocacy groups.)[2]

But why would consumer activists *want* banks to handle these loans at a higher interest rate and with taxpayer support when consumers have been well served by private lenders, such as installment loan companies, for over 100 years? Perhaps they believe that profits are ill-gotten gain and, as with home mortgages, feel a small loan made at rates lower than the market price is something people are entitled to.

The large banks, they presume, can be cajoled and manipulated into activities that may make no economic sense on their own but will please regulators whose ranks have been filled with consumer activists. One thing is clear: Eakes and others haven't learned the lesson from what happened the last time banks were forced into this Faustian bargain.

THE BASIC STRATEGY

The local tactics are legion, but the basic strategy will likely replicate the 2012 campaign in Missouri that was designed to restrict small-dollar loans (which generally range from $500 to $5,000). In Missouri, State Representative Mary Still had tried and failed to get a bill passed in her state. She couldn't even get a hearing in the state House. So a group named Missourians for Responsible Lending—sound familiar?—sponsored a ballot initiative to cap rates at 36 percent. Other groups endorsed it, including Grass Roots Organizing (GRO). GRO is an ACORN-like group that in 2011 descended on the headquarters of the largest payday lender in Missouri. Over 160 Grass Roots organizers entered the office with bullhorns to explain their concerns. And while GRO was bullying lenders, the kinder face of the activist movement was organizing field hearings around the state to increase public sentiment for their cause and to get signatures at participating churches.[3] "Sign here to help the poor and minorities" was the theme of their campaign, despite the evidence to the contrary.

One obstacle the campaign faced was the fact that many Missourians obviously *wanted* these loans—otherwise, the lenders wouldn't have stayed in business. Sure, we allow silly people to fight in wars, vote, marry whom they will, and even bear and raise children. But make their own financial decisions? No way. Not when we can give the government the coercive power to make the decisions for them. It is this "we know best what's best for you" assumption that allowed Al Ripley of the North Carolina Justice Center to shout down a consumer while spitting in her face (as mentioned in Chapter 1).

In February 2012, over 400 people rallied at the courthouse in Jefferson City, Missouri, to oppose the rate-cap ballot initiative. Meanwhile, the activists and compliant media falsely claimed the participants were hired guns for the "payday industry," which the activists had already vilified around the state.[4] That's a generally effective, if highly unethical, strategy for whipping up public outrage: paint your opponents with a broad, dirty brush of your own making.

Most of the time, however, activists choose a decoy for their activities, as they did in Missouri: if the people don't want to give up their loans, we will entice them with something they *do* want, and they'll never know what hit 'em. The activists quickly paired the rate-cap initiative with one to raise the state minimum wage (and thus get on board the labor unions and even more churches). Many people support minimum wage legislation, since they assume that they, or at least the less fortunate, will get paid more.[5] The minimum wage initiative thus became the sugarcoating on a pill intended to poison small-dollar lenders.[6] This strategy worked well enough to get an estimated 180,000 signatures in Missouri, which the campaign delivered to Jefferson City on May 6, 2012. It's a certainty that activists will use the minimum wage tactic in other states and that, if such laws pass, the poor will be worse rather than better off.

Opponents, for their part, hotly opposed the initiative. Two groups, Stand Up Missouri and Missourians for Responsible Government, ran ads and met with church leaders, business owners, and the press to educate the public and community leaders about what the loss of small-dollar loans would mean to consumers and the state.

The public debate and legal and public relations battles raged for months, and ultimately the ballot campaign failed. In August, three months before the 2012 election, courts determined that the organizers had not gathered enough legitimate signatures to qualify for the November ballot. It was a stunning defeat for the activist campaign, which had seemed headed for certain victory. However, with some tweaks to the signature-gathering operation, the campaign tested in Missouri will be returning there. If it hasn't already done so, soon it may also be coming to a city and state near you.

Even if statewide campaigns hit a wall, the activists are also seeking to change ordinances in individual cities and counties. This has already worked in some places, including major cities in Texas—Dallas, Austin, San Antonio, and El Paso—one of the reddest of states.[7] In Chicago, Mayor Rahm "Don't-Let-a-Serious-Crisis-Go-to-Waste" Emanuel has formed a "partnership" with the Consumer Financial Protection Bureau to eradicate "predatory lending" from the Windy City.[8] Expect more such partnerships in the future.

AIR COVER

These ground offensives enjoy protective fire from the Consumer Financial Protection Bureau, which conducts high-profile hearings around the country. The bureau clearly has its sights on payday lenders. Activists are hoping it will tackle all other forms of small-dollar lending while they're at it.

To this end, in May 2012 the Consumer Bureau hired University of Utah professor Chris Peterson, a dismissive critic of free markets, mortgage securitization, and payday lending.[9] One of his recent law review articles sums up his views. In the piece, he argues that city and county municipalities should force any lender who charges a rate over 45 percent to post big signs on their buildings that say, "Warning, Predatory Lender."[10] This seems far-fetched, but what is all too real and present is that Professor Chris Peterson is now ensconced in a powerful federal bureau, manning the regulatory equivalent of a squadron of fully armed aerial drones ready to protect consumers from their own freedom of choice.

The Center for Responsible Lending and its many allies are also providing air cover at the national level. The 2006 Military Lending Act, for instance, puts a 36 percent APR cap on loans to active-duty service members, though the Pentagon has interpreted the act to apply only to payday, refund anticipation, and car title loans. Significantly, the act exempts small-dollar installment lenders it considers beneficial in an effort "to balance protection with access to credit."[11] Jean Ann Fox, former financial services director of the Consumer Federation of America, an activist and lobbyist group that works closely with the Center for Responsible Lending, opposes the Pentagon's interpretation.[12] As it happens, much of the act's content came from Fox and other consumer activists who, according to a follow-up review by the Government Accountability Office,[13] heavily influenced the shaping of the act. Although it has been argued that imposing a 36 percent cap would create a hardship, activists are working to have caps placed on other financial transactions involving military service members.[14]

Finally, these efforts are getting fuel support from the Consumer Financial Protection Bureau. The agency has hired Holly Petraeus, the wife of General David Petraeus, as assistant director of its Office of Servicemember Affairs. Although she holds a powerful position, most Americans had not heard her name until late 2012, when her husband was forced to resign as CIA director after news of his extramarital affair with his biographer, Paula Broadwell, had leaked out. Insiders have told me that Petraeus is a compassionate woman, and, although her experience in consumer finance is limited, she understands the needs of military families. She is, however, working for the Consumer Bureau, and enforcing its agenda is her job.

Holly Petraeus had helped implement the bureau's plan in 2011 while it was being created. "In her role at the new agency, Holly will continue her work to strengthen consumer financial protection for servicemembers," wrote Elizabeth Warren on the White House blog when Petraeus first started working at the bureau.[15] Ms. Petraeus no doubt has good intentions, and the military deserve our best support. However, the campaign by the bureau—and the Center for Responsible Lending and its cohorts—to protect military consumers from small-dollar "predators" is built on fallacies and falsehoods.

FIRST, DO NO HARM

You might think that a small loan is just like a large loan, only smaller. But you'd be mistaken. Imagine Jan, a widowed mother who lives in Detroit. It's December 20 when her car breaks down, so she takes it to a garage to get it fixed. The bill is $1,000. She needs the car to get to her job at Applebee's. Applebee's health insurance is a real godsend, because her daughter has severe asthma. It's a new job, however, so she's still waiting for her first paycheck. The garage is sympathetic and agrees to let her pay in installments, but they require $500 up front, which is exactly $500 more than she has on hand. What should she do? What *can* she do?

In this case, she goes to Statewide Installment Loans, one of several lenders in her area, to apply for a $500 loan. She sits down and discusses her financial needs and reviews her household budget with the installment loan officer. To ensure that Jan can successfully pay back this loan, the loan officer works with her to verify her ability to repay. (Consumer installment lenders often do more detailed underwriting than banks or credit unions do.) She is approved for the loan and receives a check for $500, which she must repay in equal monthly payments. If she gets a loan with an eight-month term and a $25 application fee, her payments would be $83 per month, which she and the lender have determined is well within her budget. The total amount of interest she will pay each month is $20.50. Compared to a mortgage loan, this is simplicity itself.

The fact that she is getting this loan may imply that she does not have a credit card or has already maxed it out. Or she may actually prefer not to use a credit card. Certainly, banks would not normally make a loan this small, except perhaps as an overdraft on an otherwise healthy checking account. A small-dollar loan may seem unthinkable to those who don't need them, but they can make perfect sense to someone in a crisis. In Jan's case, it's the difference between keeping or losing a job. In such moments of need, people are willing to do what it takes to find the money. Compared to other options—hocking her old wedding ring, borrowing from an illegal loan shark, or bouncing a check—Jan's process of getting a loan is simple and legal. This loan keeps her moving in the right direction as long as she is responsible and pays it back in a timely way.

The cost of an installment or other small loan may seem steep, but such borrowers decide that it's better than paying a more costly overdraft fee for a bounced check or a stiff charge to reconnect their heat after shivering in the cold for several weeks. A small loan may be a quick patch for one leak rather than a long-term solution to financial problems. But it is a patch that can be the most feasible way to meet an immediate need. An installment loan can also help the borrower build her credit score and have time to get a handle on her finances and her life. Many seem to prefer this route rather than using a credit card and making seemingly endless minimum payments.

All of this goes to show that we can only evaluate someone else's choices by looking at his or her real options, not our own. We may wish that no one would ever need a small loan. But before converting that aspiration into legislation, we should think through the real consequences for the person we're hoping to help.

Sure, I suspect some people get an installment loan or even a quick payday loan, not for a dire emergency, but to compensate for previous bad decisions. But no one monitors our loans or yells "cycle of debt" each time we use a credit card. If we're going to criminalize everything that can be misused, we're going to need a lot of cops and prisons. Occasional misuse does not disprove proper use.

WHY PEOPLE GET SMALL-DOLLAR LOANS

The advocacy literature[16] of the Center for Responsible Lending and other groups often mentions the customer who takes out a payday loan and then follows it with a series of similar loans from other shops. The Center sees this as evidence of payday lenders being abusive. But the situation is similar to a patient duplicating a prescription and getting it filled at multiple pharmacies. That is abuse of the pharmacy, not the customer. Besides, the harmful effects from prohibition can be much greater than the problems we are trying to solve. If we want to help people, we must first avoid doing them harm.

Fortunately, we can do better than *guessing* what people do with small-dollar loans. In the last decade there have been several solid studies on the question. What these studies show is that, in many cases, borrowers use small loans to help out in an emergency, such as when a car breaks down, as in the scenario above, or when a heating bill is higher than expected. One such study from the Center for Financial Services Innovation showed that the highest percentage (17 percent) of respondents did indeed borrow money to pay a utility bill, and that 11 percent took out a loan for a vehicle repair.[17] The study also shows that nearly half of the respondents borrowed only once in a year and have money in savings. This indicates that some borrowers who have savings or credit cards feel better about paying for a small loan than drawing down those savings or adding to their credit card balance. Depending on their card's interest rate, the loan may or may not cost more, but a loan with a set payoff date can make good psychological sense for people who have a habit of running up credit card bills. It can also make sense for people who have given themselves strict rules about using their savings.

Some borrowers like the convenience and ease of getting a small-dollar loan. Some like the fact that they can get an installment loan or even a payday loan without involving friends and family.[18] In cases in which families, churches, or communities are close-knit and understanding, some may get help from loved ones when faced with a financial crisis. Legislating away the legal alternatives, however, doesn't magically mean that better options will be there for people who want or need small loans. Besides, Aunt Minnie may not actually like it when you ask her for money.

Unlike payday lenders, many installment loan companies have been around for generations, fully underwrite their loans, and interview borrowers to make sure they can repay the loan in a fixed number of installments. Activists from the Center for Responsible Lending and elsewhere, however, focus their campaign rhetoric almost entirely on the newer "payday" rather than other types of small-dollar loans. "Payday lending" is a handy catchall term for activists' purposes, since it creates confusion in the media and the public. Nonetheless, these legislative initiatives target all small-dollar lending. Because of the small size and relatively short terms of payday loans, any rate cap that blocks payday lending will almost surely do the same to small-dollar installment lending.

BOURGEOIS PREJUDICE

Part of the target audience for the activists' campaigns against small-dollar lending is the general public. People who haven't used installment loans themselves may vaguely remember when their parents or grandparents had one, back in the day before credit cards. If they don't know much about these loans, but someone is disparaging them, they're pretty sure these loans must be bad.

Most upper- and upper-middle-class people have a set of life experiences that makes it hard for them to imagine needing such a loan. Armed with their own small-loan arsenal of multiple credit cards, they don't grasp the limited options of some lower-income people in financial emergencies. Many of us have never known the fear of bouncing a check, not out of absentmindedness, but out of desperation. We also may not know what it feels like to have the utilities shut off five days before a paycheck is due. If this naive prejudice against small lenders is combined with a high view of government's ability to "help the little guy," then it isn't hard to convert such an outlook into a powerful impulse to legislate small-dollar lenders into oblivion.

How do I know this? Because, until I studied the subject carefully, I nurtured the same opinions. It was easy to feel a sense of indignation at small-dollar lenders while imagining poor people with bad financial management skills getting stuck in a debt trap. Digging into the particulars and thinking hard about economic realities and the unintended consequences of regulation was much less easy. It doesn't take a PhD in economics or finance, however, to understand it. What it does require is for us to step back, turn on the lights, and take in the bigger picture.

USURY?

The most common objection to small-dollar loans is that they cost too much. Compared to the larger loans available to people with more money and better credit, the cost for small loans, whether in interest or fees, may look sky-high. In fact, small-dollar lenders are often accused of "usury," even when the consumer's actual cost for the loan is slight. This is a perennial theme of the state-level campaigns of the Center for Responsible Lending. When activists shout "Stop triple-digit rates!" it gets a reaction. They fail to mention that the dollar cost of paying the minimum balance on a credit card each month can far exceed that of an installment loan or even a typical payday loan.

Professor Chris Peterson, now at the Consumer Financial Protection Bureau, was once on a panel with Billy Webster, then-CEO of the country's largest payday lender, Advance America. During the discussion, Peterson told Webster that since the Bible condemns usury, he was pretty sure that Webster was going to hell. A joke perhaps, but a telling one.

One of the Center's go-to methods for building local support is to recruit leaders of what the activists call the "faith community." Through their "Faith & Credit" program, the Center for Responsible Lending works to rally "clergy and faith leaders" to their cause. Some of these are self-appointed faith leaders, but others are credentialed and sincere and have been approached on the premise that they are helping the poor and minorities.

Infusing your political cause with spiritual resonances and having religious leaders carry your message has obvious advantages. Among other things, religious figures can go where secular leaders may fear to tread. In February 2013, the Center for Responsible Lending supported the "National Day of Action: An Emancipation Proclamation," highlighting Reverend DeForest Soaries Jr., one of the event chairs. Soaries led the attack for the Center: "I am as committed to protesting the allowance of predatory lending as my forebears were committed to fighting against segregation. If Dr. King were alive today, he would confront the predatory payday industry. We must do no less."[19]

A few months earlier in Missouri, in an online video interview, a young African American professor from a local university had spoken out *in support* of a consumer installment lender who had helped her build her credit score. She also mentioned Dr. King, saying she was inspired by his message encouraging people to stand up for and speak out about things they believe in. For her efforts, activists and their media allies vehemently criticized her on the grounds that she had implied Dr. King would support these loans. "Critics need to understand that there are . . . great places doing a great service for people like me," the professor had said in her interview. "A lot of times politicians forget about the people they may be affecting."

Although the pastors, priests, and citizens who are recruited for the "grassroots" campaigns are local, the messaging is packaged at the national level. The Center for Responsible Lending provides a detailed toolkit for local advocates, giving advice on everything from how to work with the media, to how to manage a letter-writing campaign, write press releases and letters to the editor, and testify in hearings.[20]

The Center for Responsible Lending has even produced a church discussion guide that connects modern payday loans with the ancient condemnations of "usury"—an incitement if there ever was one. The guide is filled with quotations from Scripture to give the campaign a patina of biblical authority.[21] It packs a wallop for the pastor who skims it. Only careful scrutiny reveals that the guide is filled with misleading claims about usury.

Those who call on Old Testament bans against usury will misunderstand those bans unless they know that the word now has a different meaning. Nowadays, *usury* is used to refer to charging *too much* interest on a loan. But there isn't a single black line on the interest-rate scale where usury starts. Without factoring in market considerations, any number you pick will be arbitrary. Say, 36 percent? What relevant moral principle makes 35 percent okay, but 37 percent usurious? We could play the same game all up and down the number line.

Precisely because the "usury starting line" is arbitrary, the fact that so many different groups in different states have pushed a 36 percent rate is not a coincidence but evidence of a conspiracy. If these campaigns were really spontaneous and local, rather than orchestrated by central sources, the campaigns would undoubtedly pick different numbers.

To think there is a single, fixed rate beyond which usury begins is to misunderstand the historical meaning of usury—and to misunderstand the function of prices in a market economy.

Again, let's shine a little economic light on things. Think of a price as a little packet of information. The price of a product or service in a free, competitive market communicates not only information about the product or service itself but also something about an underlying economic reality. The price of milk in such a market will tell you about the supply and demand for milk at that time: how much it costs to extract it from cows, produce it, ship it, pasteurize and package it, and just as important, how much other people want the milk. These concepts—supply, demand, and price function—are so important that they're often the first and most useful things you learn in an economics course.

Now keep in mind what you just read while you think about small loans. Typically, critics such as the Center for Responsible Lending compare these loans to the much larger loans familiar to those of us with good credit: car and home loans. When the White House released its paper defending its installation of a Consumer Financial Protection Bureau director, it pulled language straight from one of the Center's studies on payday loans: "Payday loans offer short-term funds at very high rates of interest (on average 400 percent according to some studies)."[22]

The issue is the phrase "high rates of interest." In fact, small-dollar lenders are required by law to post their fees in terms of an *annual* percentage rate (APR), even though their loans may last only 2, 12, or 24 weeks, rather than 52. Herein lies the rub—and why capping APR as a way to protect consumers is nonsensical, unfair to lenders, and harmful to consumers.

Borrowers often find APR confusing. In the case of payday loans, the lender tells borrowers they will pay a $15 fee per $100 borrowed. Good enough. But then the borrowers see this enormous annual charge in bold numbers on the contract—the annual percentage rate, or APR—*as if the loan lasts for a year.* Borrowers aren't confused because they're stupid. They're confused because translating the cost of a short-term, small-dollar loan into an *annual* percentage rate is intended by regulators to frighten borrowers.

For any lender to make loans without going broke, it will need to charge enough not only to cover the costs in acquiring the money but also to offset the costs for processing the loan, as well its fixed costs of doing business—rent, electricity, insurance, and so on—and the risk of providing the loan.

The cost of underwriting and processing any loan may seem trivial, but it's not. Let's say GMC must take 150 minutes to investigate (or, underwrite) a $10,000 loan for a car, while an installment lender has to take at least 30 minutes to investigate/underwrite a $100 loan.[23] Do you see the imbalance if they charge the same APR? (Remember, APR includes interest and fees.) The auto loan company took five times as long to investigate the borrower but is making a loan 100 times as large. Or, to put it the other way, the small-dollar installment lender invested one-fifth the labor costs to investigate his borrower, but would stand to receive only one-hundredth the return on that investment. *This difference in the ratios between fixed costs and profits make small- and large-dollar loans completely different.*

Suppose Joanna buys a house for $250,000. She takes out a $200,000 mortgage and puts $50,000 in as a down payment. If it's a fixed-rate, 30-year mortgage, the straight interest rate may be 4 percent; however, by law, the bank must include in its calculation of APR the up-front fees to cover the bank's costs to process the loan. Thus, Joanna might have an effective APR of 4.1 percent. The loan is very large, the bank gets a hefty down payment and monthly payments for 30 years, and there's a house to serve as collateral. Even if it takes 20 person-hours to process the mortgage, that and other fixed costs are tiny *compared to the size of the loan.* So the lender doesn't need to set the APR much above the straight interest on the loan—4.1 percent APR will do.

Now back to Jan. When Jan received her $500 installment loan, she did not provide the lender with any collateral at all, and her rate was far below the triple digits that the activists yell about. The loan was convenient and economical, and most likely it helped build her credit score.

But because payday loans are the ones we hear so much about, let's also look at the true cost of a payday loan. Let's say Jan experiences another unexpected need—this time to pay out of pocket for a drug for her daughter—an expense for which she knows she will later be reimbursed. She has paid all her bills for the month and knows the expensive drug will leave her short. So she goes to the payday loan company near her workplace to take out a $100 loan. She provides the lender with a postdated check. Now, this check could bounce and is not really collateral, so the lender is assuming more risk in giving her this loan than it would if it were giving her a mortgage or car loan. Even if we ignore the other fixed costs, it still takes, say, 20 minutes (one-third of a person-hour) to process the loan. The $15 fee barely covers the lender's processing cost and the risk of lending Jan $100 for two weeks. Nonetheless, when we think of the $15 fee in terms of *rates*, the lender is setting a 15 percent charge to cover all those costs and risks. It sounds fairly reasonable when you look at it in that light. But when you extrapolate the rate out over a full year, the APR is a whopping 391.07 percent.

Do you see the problem? Using APR to express the *consumer's cost* for any small-dollar loan is misleading and virtually useless. It is like comparing the price per mile on taxi service in Manhattan with the price per mile on a roundtrip flight between New York and Los Angeles. The flight costs $70 per 1,000 miles. The taxi will run you over $2,000 for the same distance, and that's if you don't catch any red lights. Thieving taxi drivers! This way of measuring the consumer's cost makes the cab ride look like a huge rip-off, when it could very well be your best way to get from Battery Park to Eighty-Fifth Street for a job interview. That's why Dr. Harold Black, Professor of Financial Institutions at the University of Tennessee and an expert on APR policy, says that for small, short-term loans, APR is a "terrible metric to use to measure lending costs."[24]

Meanwhile, Jan paid her loan back out of her next paycheck and was grateful to get that loan right when she needed it.

DON'T FORGET COMPETITION

I'm not saying every small-dollar lender is a St. Francis. As with professionals in other fields, no doubt they come in many varieties. So as not to bias the discussion in favor of lenders, however, let's assume for the moment that they're interested only in making as much money as they can. Even if this were the case, small-dollar lenders face fierce competition for the same customers. In fact, there are often many small-dollar competitors crowded into the same part of a city. If one lender is charging more and treats its customers rudely, then the customer will go down the street to another lender who charges less and treats customers with respect.

And in most places, small-dollar lenders have dozens of competitors, ranging from large national chains to various local mom-and-pop companies. The effect of all this market competition is to drive down costs and improve service for customers. This is simple economic logic, but the conclusion is also confirmed by empirical studies.[25]

PROFITS WITHOUT HONOR

Another common complaint about payday lenders is that they make a profit from people in need. "Payday lending sinks borrowers in debt with $4.2 billion in predatory fees every year" is the title of one CRL study quoted by the White House paper.[26]

Karl Marx had exactly the same view. If you think the market is a zero-sum game where one person wins and another must lose, then profits are, as Marx called them, a "surplus value" that you have extracted either from employees or customers. But this argument, if taken to its logical conclusion, would mean that all profit is bad and *no* business—not Starbucks, Microsoft, Home Depot, or Apple—could justly earn a profit.

If this sounds like a ludicrously reductive argument, there are a couple of things to keep in mind. One, it's actually just following a bad assumption (profit is inherently predatory) to its logical conclusion. Two, some profoundly socialist economies, such as the Soviet Union in the years after the 1917 Bolshevik Revolution, actually followed this way of viewing profit to its logical, destructive conclusion, while claiming that they were protecting the people. These socialists nationalized all companies and farms that were making a nefarious profit, so that the workers, rather than all those fiendish investors and fat-cat managers, could enjoy the fruits of their labors. These socialist experiments were based on bad assumptions taken to their logical conclusions and led to tens of millions of deaths, long ago exposing the danger of vilifying profits. Do we really want to apply that bad assumption to American consumer finance, which frees up funds and offers lifelines to millions of people every year?

To avoid falling for the false assumption, you just need to reflect for a few moments on human nature and the power of incentives. Most people don't tend to work hard—to offer costly goods and service for others, to improve manufacturing and delivery methods, to enhance quality and service—if there's no prospect for personal gain. This is why a society in which no one has any prospects of making a profit is one whose future is dim. "To the economically illiterate, if some company makes a million dollars in profit, this means that their products cost a million dollars more than they would have without profits," said economist Thomas Sowell. "It never occurs to such people that these products might cost several million dollars more without the incentives to be efficiently created by the prospect of profits."[27]

Attacking small-dollar lending companies because some make a profit should elicit disdain, not new legislation.

PRICE-FIXING

Capping interest rates for small-dollar lenders is a form of price-fixing. Millions of well-meaning people think that price-fixing across a variety of industries helps the poor. It doesn't. Fixing prices by political fiat normally makes things worse, not better, for the very people who are already bad off. Again, this is due to economic realities that no politician has the power to change. We can put the point thus: *prices need to be sensitive to reality; otherwise they will confuse rather than communicate.*

Let's return to our previous illustration. Even if your community lender is the most competitive in the area, it would go broke if it charged only a $5 monthly fee on a $300 loan, since that amount would not even cover its fixed costs. Fixed costs are what they are. They don't change just because a regulatory office in the state capital sets a price ceiling on small loans.

Imagine that the governor of Michigan signs a law called the "Responsible Lending Act" that prohibits all loans with an APR greater than 36 percent.[28] (This, in fact, is exactly what activists tried to do in Missouri via the ballot initiative.) Come December, if Jan finds herself in a situation similar to last year—running short of cash but needing to pay an unexpected bill—what is she going to do? Has the price ceiling on small loans improved the weather in Detroit so she can bicycle to work the week before Christmas? Has it increased Jan's income? Has it lowered the cost of car repairs? No, no, and no.

One thing has changed: Jan's legal options. She won't be able to get a loan from her local lender or their competitors because the law has effectively prevented them from doing business in her state. The law has the same effect as if it had made small loans illegal. Jan, however, still has a need; the law didn't change that. She's just lost her legal lender of last resort.

The Center for Responsible Lending has tried to insist that rate-capping policies don't have perverse effects, but economic common sense and dispassionate research say otherwise. "All of the research shows that these sorts of caps actually decrease the wealth and well-being of the people who you are intending to protect," argues Professor Harold Black in discussing the effects of interest-rate caps. "The research shows that there are higher bankruptcies. It shows that people become worse off financially. It shows strife within families, increases in divorce, increase in debt burdens. And the ironic thing is that the research also shows that when those caps are lifted, that people become better off and actually reduce their debt. And those are things that need to seriously be considered by the public—that legislation with the intent of helping people actually turns out to hurt them and make them worse off."[29]

Price-fixing creates shortages as if by an invisible hand. The point is obvious for other goods. What would happen in Manhattan if the mayor imposed a five-cent-per-mile price cap on taxi service because that's close to the cost per mile of a cross-country flight? You can be sure that you would never find a cab to take you from Wall Street to Forty-Second Street during rush hour—or ever.

Of course, a less drastic price cap would have less dire consequences, but only because the less that price-fixing distorts the way the market naturally sets a price (remember our example with milk), the less destructive are its effects.[30] A million-dollar-per-mile cap on taxi rates would do no harm precisely because it would have no effect.

None of this is rocket science. Yet you can read a hundred stories about consumer credit, and you'll never hear about the many historical examples of price caps backfiring. And you'll never learn the obvious and important differences between small- and large-dollar loans—namely, the fixed costs relative to the size of the loans.

One example among many: in *Broke, USA*, Gary Rivlin tells the story of Tim Thomas, the owner of Daddy'$ Money Pawnshop in Wichita, Kansas (which also gives payday loans). Rivlin, who portrays Thomas as filthy rich, describes Thomas taking "a relatively small portion (2 percent) when a customer presents a payroll check but a relatively high one (10 percent) if it's a handwritten personal one." Rivlin admits that "on the surface, this makes sense. Taking a handwritten check for collateral is surely far riskier than taking one issued by an established business." But according to the author, "Thomas has removed almost all the risk inherent in the transaction before a clerk slides over any money. By that point, one of Thomas's employees has spoken to both the person who has written the check, and to the bank, to make sure the funds are available." Rivlin asks, "Why then does he still take one-tenth of the face value of the check given the improbability that it will bounce?" Rivlin quotes Thomas for the answer: "Because I can." That is, Thomas charges 10 percent simply because the state of Kansas allows him to do so.

Can you spot Rivlin's mistake? Actually, there are three. First, he seems to forget that Thomas surely has competitors, so the lender can't charge whatever he wants. Second, just because the money is in the bank when the borrower gives him the check doesn't mean it will be there when Thomas goes to cash it in two weeks. In fact, since the person is taking out a payday loan, the borrower presumably knows that he doesn't have enough to cover the following two weeks.

Third, and more significantly, Rivlin talks as if risk is the only factor determining the price of a loan. But there is also the cost of underwriting the loan. A loan officer at Daddy'$ Money has had to call the borrower's employer and his bank to verify that there's enough money in the account to cover the check. That takes time and labor. The loan officer has probably also had to explain some of the loan basics to the customer and help him fill out the paperwork. And the phone itself and the loan officer's computer and desk, as well as the office in which he is making and servicing the loan, all cost Daddy'$ Money, well, money. The more time and labor involved in processing a loan, the higher the fee or interest rate must be to cover the cost. It's hard to know how a business writer like Gary Rivlin could miss such an elementary point.

FORETASTE OF INTIMIDATION

Daddy'$ Money—with its "because I can" owner—is hardly the only face of payday lending. Moneytree is one of the oldest payday lenders in the country (and only glancingly mentioned by Rivlin). In Seattle, it "has received 27 civic and corporate awards," according to *Seattle Business Magazine*, which reports on the company's devoted base of customers and employees. By 2011, Moneytree had won first place in the magazine's "Best Companies to Work For" competition for three years in a row. The team of husband, wife, and brother running the company credits its success to the golden rule. The stories employees tell seem to support what could be a clichéd claim: from the company president holding her umbrella over a worker unloading boxes in a downpour, to an employee's claim that "Moneytree saved my life emotionally and financially and I will never forget that."[31] In every field, some companies are better than others.

The campaign to eradicate legal small-dollar loans may be well motivated at some levels. The volunteers who stand in parking lots asking folks to sign their petition "to help the poor" surely mean well. But eradicating such loans will not end well for the middle class and the poor and for every American who prizes freedom. State campaigns are of course simply the leading edge of a much larger national campaign to control the consumer financial sector of our economy. It has troops on the ground, a massive communications network, uniformly compliant media, lavish funding from public and private sources, and the protective shield of a new, largely unaccountable, and perhaps unconstitutional government bureaucracy. Martin Eakes called these insiders and activists "financial terrorists," and now we see why. The intimidation of marine Jim Everhardt, serving in Afghanistan, and his wife, Annie, mentioned in Chapter 1, is just a foretaste of what we can expect if these activists are not stopped.

CHAPTER 12

THE WAR
AGAINST FREE
ENTERPRISE

*Of all tyrannies, a tyranny sincerely exercised for the good
of its victims may be the most oppressive.*
—C. S. Lewis

On a rainy day in October 2012, the Consumer Financial Protection Bureau held a hearing on debt collectors at the Seattle Public Library, an angular, gravity-defying profusion of glass and steel just four blocks from my office. I was one of a few hundred people who attended. The hearing was organized as a panel discussion, with a long table crossing the floor at the front of the room. Five representatives of collection agencies sat on the right side; five consumer activists on the left. In the middle of the long table sat Consumer Bureau director Richard Cordray and, to his left, then–deputy director Raj Date.

Seattle mayor Michael McGinn welcomed the participants and said he was very interested in pursuing predatory lending in the Emerald City. Then Congressman Jim McDermott came to the lectern. McDermott is Seattle's contribution to the U.S. House of Representatives. As a Democrat in a die-hard Democratic district, he tends to speak his mind. "I've been looking at this issue of consumer protection for a very long time," he announced, explaining that he was in Congress during the savings and loan crisis a quarter of a century earlier. Then, referring to the Consumer Bureau, he said, "It took the collapse of 2007 for Congress to take this seriously and put something like this in place."

Warming up, he turned to the economy. "Free enterprise is simple: make money any way you can."

The importance of regulatory agencies is to "protect people from the excesses of the free enterprise system." And the job of the Consumer Bureau, he concluded, is "to stand against the entire free enterprise system."

Richard Cordray and Raj Date, who, to this audience member, came off as reasonable and articulate, did their best to ignore the firebrand who had welcomed them. But they said nothing to contradict McDermott's summary of their mandate. Indeed, the hearing seemed to confirm it.

The debt collection industry representatives had a few minutes to explain the purpose and standards that guide their work. All agencies, for instance, are subject to the Fair Debt Collection Practices Act (2009).[1] Some speakers described the many ways debt collection had improved for everyone over the years.

Then the activists on the left did their best to paint collection agencies as barely legalized thugs who harass poor people unjustly for minor credit infractions. Lawyer Richard Rubin, flushed and agitated, claimed that the problem wasn't just one or two bad apples. The *culture* of debt collectors requires them to come as close to illegality as possible, and not to comply with the law when they think they can get away with it. (No evidence was presented to establish this sweeping claim, but none was apparently needed.)

After the panelists made their official statements, preselected members of the audience were called on to give personal testimony. A number of women described bad experiences they had had with collection agencies. One woman in her early thirties lamented that she had been badgered by a collection agency for debts incurred by her deadbeat husband.

The Consumer Financial Protection Bureau wished to appear balanced, of course, so individuals in the audience on the other side were also called on to speak. These appeared to be small business owners who had their own stories of customers who had been only too happy to receive their goods and services but not pay for them, and of how debt collectors had helped their businesses avoid firing staff and going under. I'm just speculating, though, because when these people (mostly men) were called on, they all declined to make a statement. It was easy to understand why. The hostility to debt collectors became so thick in the room you could almost see it. Only a very hardy soul would dare to defend debt collectors in such an atmosphere.

The Seattle hearing was a microcosm of what now besets us. Under the guise of protecting defenseless consumers against giant rapacious corporations, the federal government—the only real monopoly in this game, with its regulatory tanks and artillery—is standing against the entire free enterprise system. It's refreshing to hear a member of Congress admit that unreservedly. Of course, Jim McDermott defines free enterprise in the same way Martin Eakes does—as a lawless, amoral jungle, saved from itself only by a few brave federal agencies, a pitiless system in which a few giant corporate beasts prey on the majority of defenseless consumers. *Consumers are consumed.* If that's what the term "free enterprise" means, then of course, as Jim McDermott said, people need to be protected from it.

But we should recognize this as an old rhetorical trick used by those who are hostile to economic freedom. It's actually a logical fallacy called "false dilemma." Its purveyors present two extremes. One is the failed strategy of Soviet-style communism; the other, lawless, predatory capitalism, or an unnamed anarchy in which the strong consume the weak. What's needed, they suggest, is a system in which large, robust federal agencies turn the ruthless jungle of free enterprise into something like a well-ordered zoo. While they are usually careful not to say so explicitly, what they seem to be describing and aiming for is something like the socialist corporatism of present-day Europe—in which national governments and the

European Union collude with a few giant corporations to control the economy.[2] In presenting this "third way," however, these advocates are increasingly eager to keep any mention of Europe out of the discussion, since much of Europe's economy has been moribund for years.

But the deception in their rhetorical sleight of hand runs deeper than this. The picture painted of such a dichotomy of extremes is itself misleading. The real extremes are not capitalism and Soviet-style communism; they are anarchy on one side and centralized, authoritarian rule on the other. Giant predators consuming prey with impunity is the absence of law—where the powerful few can "make money any way they can" at everyone else's expense. If you've seen the old Mel Gibson dystopian film *Mad Max* and its sequels, you get some sense of what this might look like.

Free enterprise, in contrast, refers to an economic system founded on the rule of law—including stable property and titling rights—and widespread trust (sufficient, for instance, to buy and sell things on eBay). It's a system with institutions to allocate capital for investments, and the opportunity for individuals and firms to enter into contracts or trades *freely*, which they will only do if they see some mutual benefit. It is the only system that historically has lifted societies out of widespread poverty and into economic and political stability.

Think about it. You probably have a relationship with at least one of two of the largest corporate entities in history—Apple or Microsoft. Do you really perceive yourself as prey in that relationship? When I go into an Apple Store, I don't feel like a bunny staring into the fangs of a jaguar. Quite the contrary. The employees are eager to meet my needs because they have competitors and want to keep getting my business. The minute they started treating me like dinner, I would leave and switch back to Dell.

Market competition strongly discourages predatory behavior. So too does the existence of police officers and courts guided by the rule of law. In fact, widespread freedom in society exists only where there is rule of law. It's hard to get your mind around this fact at first, but to enjoy real freedom in this life, there must be laws that prevent actors from doing certain things—stealing, defrauding, murdering, and so forth. This is what the American Founders thought of as *ordered* liberty, as opposed to libertinism where everybody does what he or she wants. Indeed, only when a social setting is ordered by law can it preserve liberty. Only then can ordinary people and great entrepreneurs participate in and contribute to a wealth-creating economy; only then can they compete, cooperate, and pursue their own legitimate self-interests while also serving others.

Free enterprise requires a free market, but more than this, it is the system in which human beings can exercise their freedom to take risks, to build a better mousetrap, invent a technology that no one has imagined before, deliver a good or service better than before, or to boldly go where no entrepreneur has gone before. It is the social space in which we can best exercise our freedom to *create*.

At one extreme, in a truly lawless economy, the strong prey on the weak, since the weak have no recourse to the police or the courts. At the other, everyone is coerced by the state and a few corporate toadies. History has proven that both ways lead to poverty, bondage, and despair for the masses. *Free enterprise is the golden mean between these extremes—a lawful system that provides everyone the freedom to engage, exchange, cooperate, compete, and create.*

But since free enterprise requires the rule of law, don't we need laws to protect people from the excesses of the free enterprise system? No. Certainly we need laws to protect people from *criminality* and unjust coercion. Yet, as we've discussed throughout this book, in a free and competitive market—where people aren't allowed to defraud or steal from their neighbors—the prices for auto repair, haircuts, papayas, and other economic goods and services will vary based on the supply and demand for these things. These prices allow people in the marketplace to make decisions based on accurate information about underlying realities.

Perhaps the best way to understand this is to think of an economy as a vast communications network. In the worldwide telecommunications network, there are transmitters, receivers, and information being passed through fiber-optic cables, cell phone towers, wireless routers, and radio towers. A free market (with a stable rule of law) is like a predictable channel that allows signals within an economic network to be accurately transmitted, received, and responded to.[3] To convert this to a more old-school example, imagine what would happen if ink responded to paper randomly and unpredictably—if sometimes it formed lines, sometimes it disappeared 24 hours after it dried, sometimes it just formed a glob. This would make it impossible to write meaningful letters with ink and paper.

When a government manipulates prices, it creates the same problem. Recall the shortages and long lines when gasoline prices were capped in the 1970s—or, as we've just seen, the destructive housing bubble that was inflated by the Fed setting artificially low interest rates for years and, especially, by the federal policies that degraded the underwriting standards on home loans. These and other artificial manipulations of prices, such as caps on interest rates for small loans, don't magically create more prosperity. Just the opposite: they add noise to the transmission of price signals. The more the signals are distorted, the harder it is for individuals and companies to respond realistically to fulfill their economic objectives, and the greater the destructive consequences for everyone in the long run.

THE GREATEST REGULATOR OF ALL

But don't businesses need to be regulated? Of course, every business, as well as every government agency, is made up of less-than-perfect human beings. The question is: what is the *best* way to regulate firms so they won't act in destructive ways? Straightforward laws against stealing and defrauding are an essential part of the equation. But once our laws have met this minimum threshold, the best regulators of economic behavior are clear market signals themselves.

Take Goldman Sachs. We can assume that executives of this Wall Street investment bank know what is in their own and their company's best interests, or at least they know this better than a

random bystander or a regulator at the SEC. Almost by definition, a regulator can't have more and better information about a
bank's work than does an expert inside a bank's operations, even if
that regulator has an office in the bank. So what is the best way to
discourage Goldman Sachs from taking foolish risks that will lead
to its bankruptcy? Two main alternatives: (1) the federal government could write rules of incomprehensible detail and complexity
to try to account for every possible eventuality and so prevent collapse at Goldman Sachs or rescue it before it collapses; or, (2) the
government could clearly and consistently maintain the policy that
the companies and executives that take risks in the hope of future
benefit get to enjoy those benefits if they succeed, but must bear
the weight of the consequences if they fail. The first option would
almost certainly destroy the institution being regulated. The second
option, however, would create market discipline, which is *the greatest regulator, because it aligns incentives correctly*. It strengthens and
clarifies the key market signal. Any secondary regulations imposed
by government should strengthen that key signal—namely, that you
gain when your risks pan out, and you pay the consequences if they
fail. At the very least, it should not interfere with it. Unfortunately,
this commonsense market regulator has been mostly scrambled and
subverted by a government preference for option number 1—our
old friend, the moral hazard.

INFILTRATED

This moral hazard grows more severe every day because of activists
who have infiltrated public institutions at both the state and national
levels. The infiltration is even more extensive than I've described
here—in fact, far more.

Though in public the Consumer Financial Protection Bureau's
work may appear moderate and reasonable, just below the surface a
growing army of activists has infiltrated not just the bureau but also
the FDIC, Treasury Department, and other regulatory agencies. In
keeping with its covert strategy, however, the Consumer Bureau has

been careful to avoid public associations with known ideologues and extremists. Thus, its Consumer Advisory Board includes "external experts, industry representatives, consumers, community leaders and advocates,"[4] but it doesn't include representatives from any of the big consumer activist groups, such as the National Consumer Law Center, National Community Reinvestment Coalition, Consumer Federation of America, and Center for Responsible Lending. But based on confidential interviews with eyewitnesses, I can report that after their public hearings around the country, Consumer Financial Protection Bureau representatives privately meet, coordinate, and plan with the very ideologues they avoid in public. There may have been hundreds, if not thousands, of such meetings.

To prevent these "financial terrorists" from consolidating their control over the entire financial sector of our economy, millions of Americans must wake up, understand what is happening, and help stop them in their tracks. Because of the inroads they have already made, it's a very tall order, fraught with danger and uncertainty, but the alternative is a gray and darkening twilight for the United States of America.

WHAT MUST BE DONE

Because of the federal government's current War on Economic Reality, we can anticipate that every major financial event in the next few years, good or bad, will be a pretense to increase government control over the economy. If a large bank enjoys windfall profits one quarter, that will provide a pretense for government action. If the bank loses billions of dollars on a bad investment, that too will provide a pretense for action. All of this will be camouflaged with crackdowns on some genuinely bad actors. But if you know what to look for, you will see an inexorable tightening of the bureaucratic ratchet at every opportunity.

The good news is that we still have a system that can respond, though with increasing difficulty, to the efforts of individual citizens. If we're going to stop an authoritarian juggernaut centered in the District of Columbia, with outposts from the Atlantic to the Pacific, millions of Americans will need to do something.

What actions could really restore economic freedom and the long-term prospects for the American Experiment? Here are a few suggestions.

GET INFORMED

As we've seen, an elite army of activists, philanthropists, and political insiders not only contributed to the 2008 crisis but also were able to blame others and use the fallout to greatly increase their own power. If we don't prepare ourselves, it's safe to assume that the same deception and cynicism will prevail during the next crisis. And on the present course, there will be a next crisis. The only way to prevent it is for a critical mass of ordinary and influential citizens to figure out what's going on—to get informed and outraged enough to do whatever they can to change our fiscal and regulatory trajectory.

When I say we need to get outraged, I'm not calling for mindless peasants with pitchforks. To be channeled productively, our indignation and concern must be combined with knowledge, prudence, and intelligent action. If you're reading this, you are already ahead of the learning curve. As we've seen, the campaign of infiltration and control relies on and enjoys the support of most of the influential media. We need a countercampaign of well-informed citizens, able to think clearly and accurately about the world—especially the economy. When you're well informed, you can help inform others; you're equipped to help your friends, neighbors, and associates see through the misinformation campaign and to find the real solution. (See "Additional Resources" at the end of the book for ways to do that.)

EVANGELIZE AND RECRUIT

If you have kids or grandkids, pass this knowledge on to them. They're getting plenty of the contrary arguments everywhere else. Online video shorts are probably the best place to start. I recommend a 15-week course for high-schoolers, called "Economics in a Box," that includes some good books as well as a documentary film, *The Call of the Entrepreneur*.[1] Check out the course at: http://www.economicsinabox.com.

Next, make a list of your neighbors, friends, family members, rabbi, pastor, and so on who would share your views if they had the information you now have. Talk to them, give them this book, and make sure that every one of them gets up to speed on what is happening. If you know some especially influential people, focus on them first. If they're not book readers, then ply them with DVDs, online video shorts, valuable websites, and audio or video lectures that communicate the essentials. I've included a list of some of the best of these resources in "Additional Resources."

KNOW YOUR LOCAL, STATE, AND NATIONAL REPRESENTATIVES

Although many politicians are hopelessly compromised, there are others who are open to reason when it comes to financial regulations. Some are also skeptical of the Center for Responsible Lending and local shakedown groups. Others have expressed concern about the unprecedented and unchecked power of the Consumer Financial Protection Bureau.

But all of these representatives are busy and may not know they have constituents who are also concerned about the Consumer Bureau and the activist campaigns in their own backyard and who want something done about these threats to our freedom. Use the power of your support—and your vote. These politicians are under pressure, since even those who oppose what is happening assume that most of the public supports what now masquerades as "consumer protection." Your representatives need to know that they have ordinary constituents (and not just industry representatives and lobbyists) who support them in this battle. Call them, write them, and visit them in their offices. Doing so will give them stiffer backbones when the opposition accuses them of catering to lobbyists and "robber barons."

As for center-left or liberal politicians who may support the Consumer Financial Protection Bureau, they also need to know that you are well informed on this matter—and that you will campaign against them relentlessly if they vote to increase the power of the state over the economy.

What should you ask of these politicians?

- **First, tell them that you're worried.** For local and state politicians, try to get their commitment to resist all the local agitators and activists gathered under the soothing and deceptive banner of "responsible lending." If you can find evidence in your state that the activists' campaign has put down roots, provide politicians with that information.

- **With members of the U.S. Congress, ask them to state publicly (if they haven't already done so) that they oppose Dodd-Frank and its bureaucratic spawn, the Consumer Financial Protection Bureau.** Ask them to say that they want Dodd-Frank *repealed and replaced* with policies that strengthen rather than undermine the regulatory power of market incentives. And again, demonstrate your views with your vote.

- **Encourage politicians to work to get the government out of the business of manipulating the mortgage market**, which was a well-meaning but destructive policy from the beginning. Tell them you'd like to see them call for the federal government to sell off Fannie Mae and Freddie Mac, which continue to distort the mortgage market and put taxpayers at risk. This is not a radical idea. In her recent book, *Bull by the Horns*, Sheila Bair, former head of the FDIC, calls for precisely this. "The hybrid nature of Fannie and Freddie led to disastrous consequences," she writes. "Ultimately, both institutions need to be liquidated."[2] Currently, both are strapped to U.S. Treasury feeding tubes and are undermining private firms. With reforms, they could be sold and run more efficiently in the private sector and eliminate the very real threat to taxpayers.[3]

Given the current makeup of the federal government, this advice may seem quixotic—both idealistic *and* seemingly impossible. But there are signs of hope.

In March 2012, the House Financial Services Committee held a hearing. One of the people questioned was the new Consumer Financial Protection Bureau director Richard Cordray. His position was hugely controversial, since President Obama had appointed Cordray during what the president said—incorrectly—was a legislative recess. This angered some of the committee, and some members seemed equally concerned about other personnel being hired by the new agency.

There were rumors that Martin Eakes would be appointed to the bureau's new Consumer Advisory Board. However, Representative Blaine Luetkemeyer, Republican committee member from Missouri, had just viewed a videotape of Martin Eakes giving his infamous "financial terrorist" speech at Duke in 2010. Luetkemeyer raised the speech in the hearing and asked Cordray to comment on whether he thought it was appropriate for people with such views to be responsible for regulating financial industries. Cordray deflected the questions, but they were enough to quash Eakes's likely appointment to the committee. Publicly, Cordray and the Consumer Bureau have kept their distance from Eakes since then.

This doesn't mean that Eakes's ambitions were stopped that day. Quite the contrary. He's now working, perhaps even more effectively, behind the scenes, while less visible activists acquire official government positions. Still, the incident shows that it is possible to fight back and to win small battles, especially when the activists' real aims are publicly revealed.

There are also major battles that can be won. Dodd-Frank and its Consumer Financial Protection Bureau, in particular, could very well be struck down as unconstitutional. Several states, such as Oklahoma, South Carolina, and Michigan, as well as the Competitive Enterprise Institute, the 60 Plus Association, and private organizations have already joined a complaint in federal court by the State National Bank of Big Spring (Texas).[4] The bank argues in its complaint that the structure of the Consumer Bureau contradicts the separation of powers inherent in constitutional government.[5] That's a plausible criticism,[6] and there's some reason to be optimistic about the complaint's prospects in court, especially if more parties join or file their own.

More encouraging news: in January 2013, a three-judge panel of the U.S. Court of Appeals in Washington, D.C., ruled unanimously that President Obama overstepped his constitutional bounds in making supposed "recess" appointments when Congress wasn't in recess. Chief Judge David B. Sentelle observed that if the appointments were constitutionally legit, then the president would have "free rein to appoint his desired nominees at any time he pleases, whether that time be a weekend, lunch, or even when the Senate is in session and he is merely displeased with its inaction."[7] Although the case did not involve the president's appointment of Consumer Bureau director Richard Cordray, if the court's ruling is upheld, it will mean that Obama's appointment of Cordray was invalid. We should hope that the Supreme Court uses the same common sense exercised by the circuit court of appeals. If it does, it could not only void Cordray's position but also all the rules and regulations made by the bureau since he began his tenure in January 2012.

We can be encouraged that something similar has happened before. In 1935, President Franklin Delano Roosevelt was busy growing government and increasing its control over the economy. One part of his agenda was the National Industry Recovery Act, a public works program that allowed the president to set up cartels in industry, supposedly to reduce unemployment. The Supreme Court ruled unanimously against the act, which it judged was in violation of the Constitution's Commerce Clause.[8]

The fate of the complaints against Dodd-Frank and the Consumer Financial Protection Bureau in federal court is uncertain, but the courts will be more likely to rule the right way if they witness widespread public protests. Although we always hope that the courts are impartial, in reality, they have been known to reflect public opinion on certain issues.

SUPPORT ORGANIZATIONS IN YOUR COMMUNITY THAT REALLY HELP THE POOR AND NEEDY

Many of the destructive policies we discussed here come from genuine concern for the poor, wedded to a faulty understanding of the economy and human nature. Caring for the poor is a moral responsibility we should all take seriously. The question is: how are the poor best helped? Answering that question would require another book, but there are thousands of private charities helping people every day in countless places. These can and should be a social safety net for those who fall between the cracks.

For many decades, unfortunately, U.S. citizens have believed that the government should be providing and holding the net. This attitude has given rise to a large class dependent on government as well as an unsustainable entitlement machine that in many ways does more harm than good. With the decrease in federal entitlements, however, there will be many *more* people who need care. Those of us most concerned about the future should be the first to grow and support effective, local organizations that provide a real safety net for the destitute. I won't endorse any specific charities here, but, if you're looking for ideas, check out PovertyCure online, at www.povertycure.org.

Though government hasn't ended poverty with its welfare programs, government *does* have the capacity to exacerbate poverty by undermining families, churches, and neighborhood communities. It does so by taking over more and more of the functions traditionally filled by charities, churches, parents, adult children, and neighborhoods, something it has aggressively pursued since at least the Great Society programs of the 1960s. Unfortunately, we know it just doesn't work. The rapid expansion of government into civil society had a disastrous effect on the health of lower-income families and communities.[9]

This bad news has a silver lining, however. If government overreach has undermined the ties that bind families and communities, then a concerted effort by political leaders to turn community care work back over to families, churches, and private neighborhood groups could have the happy effect of gradually reinvigorating such ties. Unfortunately, rather than take that approach, too many insiders and activists have decided that the answer is more government intervention in the private sector—one of the very things that helped fray lower income communities in the first place.

CARE ABOUT THE FUTURE

The *greatest debtor in the history of the human race*—the U.S. government—has deigned to take over private industries and even dictate the terms under which Americans can freely use consumer credit, often while running roughshod over preexisting state and federal regulations. And when I say consumer credit, I mean everything from large home mortgages to credit cards to the lending and borrowing of a few hundred dollars. This is the same government that spends over a trillion dollars more than it takes in *every year*, that has racked up $17 trillion in debt, most of it in the last decade, and that has absolutely no working plan to cut deficits, let alone pay back its accumulated debt.

At its current pace, by 2020 the federal government will spend more annually on interest on its debt than on national defense—four times what it paid in 2012.[10] And keep in mind that the United States spends almost as much on defense as all other countries combined—around $700 billion per year. To finance our national debt, we'll need what amounts to almost a fifth of the rest of the world's gross domestic product.[11]

From the founding of the United States to 2004, the federal government racked up a total debt of about $7 trillion. Just seven years later, in early 2011, we had doubled that number and still were adding far more than a cool trillion dollars per year—over $4 billion every single day.[12] Bill Gross, head of PIMCO, which runs the world's largest bond fund, has said that the United States "is a serial offender, an addict whose habit extends beyond weed or cocaine and who frequently pleasures itself with budgetary crystal meth."[13]

In theory, a government can borrow as long as the economy is growing faster than the borrowing. But spending has outstripped that pace for years. (Some states, like California, are on a debt binge as well.) On top of that, our government has made all sorts of promises it can't keep. According to the government's own estimates, just *two* of our federal entitlements, Medicare and Social Security, have "unfunded liabilities" of $46.2 trillion.[14] Total liabilities are something like $86.8 trillion.[15] These future obligations will become present obligations if the structure of entitlements isn't overhauled soon.[16] To make the point personal, this means that you—one American—will soon have a $200,000 debt on your balance sheet.

The deductions from your paycheck won't cover these liabilities. The money we're paying into Social Security is passed on to current retirees. When the program was started in 1935, it worked because the average life expectancy was 62 and folks had a lot of kids; so there were 42 workers paying in for every retiree receiving benefits. Now average life expectancy is around 78, and with fewer kids per family. As a result, there are fewer than three workers for every retiree, and, if nothing is done to overhaul the system, this ratio is on its way to becoming two workers for every one retiree. The Social Security watering hole is drying up, even as more and more retirees arrive at its edge for a drink.

It is such nondiscretionary entitlement spending that should infuriate every American who cares about the future. Because of the way entitlements are set up, Congress doesn't even debate them as part of the budget. Their budget is determined by how many recipients there are, not by how much revenue government takes in. They even have automatic increases every year. (Ironically, the basic functions of government, such as national defense and a legal system, are considered "discretionary," and can be cut.)

Entitlements and other mandatory spending—spending that is required by law—will burden more and more of the federal budget in the coming years. Already in 2011, all revenue went to pay for mandatory spending. The rest—defense, homeland security, and so on—was paid for with borrowed money![17] "We have now gotten to the point," writes Jeffrey Anderson, "where if national defense, interstate highways, national parks, homeland security, and all other discretionary programs somehow became absolutely free, we'd still have a budget deficit."[18] Our total debt is now larger than our economy.[19] In 2012, 31 cents of every dollar spent by the government was borrowed. Economist Robert Samuelson calls it "suicidal government."[20]

Government borrows trillions of dollars for current consumption, and we will suffer some of the consequences. Much of the burden of the debt, however, will be borne by other people—our children, our neighbors' grandchildren, and their children. Whatever the morality of borrowing for personal consumption, normally when a consumer borrows, she or he alone bears the debt. When government spends for our supposed short-term benefit, somebody else will be expected to foot some, or all, of the bill. This is obviously immoral, and no fancy economic theory can change that.

You might think that the problem can be fixed by raising taxes. At the rate the debt is now growing, however, it will accumulate beyond what any realistic amount of taxes can cover. To even attempt to fix it that way, taxes would get so high that government would consume most of our economy's output but would provide no services, since all taxes would go to pay interest on previous debts. This would so retard economic growth that it would probably make the debt larger, not smaller.

That scenario isn't the real threat, though. Long before this happens, something will have to give. The United States could default on its loans like a banana republic. That's unlikely, since, unlike U.S. states or private citizens, the federal government can simply print the money it needs to pay the bills.[21] In fact, a lot of politicians know this and are more or less counting on this strategy to get us out of the fix when the time comes. And, hey, why not? Printing money sounds like a free lunch, a sort of get-out-of-debt-free card. But there's a catch, and it's a doozy: printing money fuels price inflation. Printing enough money to service the kind of debt we're accumulating would devalue every dollar in circulation and trigger hyperinflation. This has happened elsewhere—such as in Germany after World War I.[22] It didn't just lead to starvation, riots, and massive unemployment. It so debased the population that even many well-meaning and well-informed Germans fell for the promises and conspiracy theories of a murderous tyrant.

"There is no subtler, no surer means of overturning the existing basis of society than to debauch the currency," said economist John Maynard Keynes. "The process engages all the hidden forces of economic law on the side of destruction, and does it in a manner which not one man in a million is able to diagnose."[23] The simple truth is that if we can't solve our spiraling debt crisis by reducing spending and restructuring the entitlement programs—especially Social Security, Medicare, and Medicaid—the best-case scenario is probably hyperinflation.

Politicians in Washington know these programs are going to collapse. They don't do anything about it because they know that most voters don't understand the problem, and besides, they assume the catastrophe is still farther away than the next election. So they have precious little political incentive to reform these costly but popular entitlement programs.

RECOGNIZE AND RESIST SOFT TYRANNY

The rule of law refers to general rules laid down ahead of time, not to ad hoc and ever-expanding regulations that eventually turn ordinary people into criminals. Rule of law must apply both to individuals and to the government charged with enforcing it. Hence the paradox that we need a state strong enough to enforce the rule of law but not so strong as to violate it. The American Founders sought to resolve the paradox by separating powers between the executive, legislative, and judicial branches of government, as well as between the national and state governments, and balanced by citizens with certain guaranteed rights. That way, the power and ambition of the Congress would be checked by the president, and vice versa. A slightly detached Senate and more detached Supreme Court would check the madness of crowds and Congressmen, while an informed and voting citizenry would check the ambitions of government. Unfortunately, the centralizing impulses of progressivism, which in the twentieth century overwhelmed every political institution and both major political parties, have eroded these original checks and balances beyond recognition.

We all know that the greatest threat to rule of law in the twentieth century was not random gangs of anarchists but unconstrained governments. We recognize the obvious examples of this: the Nazis (National Socialists), Stalinist Russia, Mao's China, and other brutal Communist experiments.

As keepers of such knowledge, we think we're mentally prepared. If government-authorized militias in brown shirts take to the streets and start barking out orders like villains in a World War II movie and rounding up targeted groups, we'll be ready. If the government tries to collectivize the farms and send the owners packing to very cold places, we'll rise up. We are *not* ready, however, for what is already happening: the slow, creeping ratchet of the bureaucratic state, which rarely engages in large, overtly violent actions but instead extends its tentacles bit by quiet bit until it has everything in its grip.

In his book *Democracy in America*, the nineteenth-century writer Alexis de Tocqueville recorded his mostly admiring observations of the early American Experiment. At the same time, he conjured up an eerily prophetic image of the future of democratic societies like the United States: a soft despotism that he feared would eventually beset "the nations of Christendom" and "degrade men without tormenting them." It employs no thumbscrews or gulags but instead works much more subtly. His unsettling portrait continues:

> But every day it renders the exercise of the free agency of man less useful and less frequent; it circumscribes the will within a narrower range and gradually robs a man of all the uses of himself. . . . After having thus successively taken each member of the community in its powerful grasp and fashioned him at will, the supreme power then extends its arm over the whole community. It covers the surface of society with a network of small complicated rules, minute and uniform, through which the most original minds and the most

energetic characters cannot penetrate, to rise above the crowd. The will of man is not shattered, but softened, bent, and guided; men are seldom forced by it to act, but they are constantly restrained from acting. Such a power does not destroy, but it prevents existence; it does not tyrannize, but it compresses, enervates, extinguishes, and stupefies a people, till each nation is reduced to nothing better than a flock of timid and industrious animals, of which the government is the shepherd.[24]

Such soft tyranny is not led by misanthropic maniacs in black boots, red armbands, and a fondness for firelit nighttime rallies. The coming soft tyranny is led by mostly mild-mannered men and women, genteel, educated, earnest, and well meaning in their own way. While a few are simply cynical and power hungry, most have complex motivations. They believe they are on the side of the angels and that their critics are not. Many of them are guided partially by a noble concern for justice and fairness. They seek to protect consumers, stamp out fraud and exploitation, and ensure that the poor and downtrodden get a fair shake—but by restricting freedom and personal responsibility. Few really understand the destructive long-term effect of their actions, and some would be horrified if they did.

It is their actions, however, and not their motivations that will harm us. If we fail to resist their efforts, it is to *such* men and women, and not to the mustachioed despots of the last century, that we will lose our liberty. "It may be that freedom sows the seeds of its own destruction," wrote the great economist F. A. Hayek. "We value freedom only when it has been lost." Let us hope that he was wrong.

ADDITIONAL
RESOURCES

I f you haven't studied economics or finance, you might think you don't have the time or ability to understand these subjects. The good news is that you don't need a PhD from the London School of Economics to learn what you need to stay informed—and to be able to spot misinformation when you see it. You just need to be exposed to some of the books and articles that translate sound economic thinking for the ordinary person.

For simple financial literacy—for example, how to maintain a budget, how to use credit cards responsibly, and how to avoid a debt trap—there are too many resources to list here. To get started, especially for young people, check out the online MoneySKILL course sponsored by the American Financial Services Association, which represents traditional installment and other lenders. A "free online comprehensive personal finance course, MoneySKILL educates high school students on money management fundamentals in the content areas of income, expenses, saving and investing, credit and insurance."[1]

To understand the most important economic concepts, you don't need a 10-pound $120 economics textbook; read *Common Sense Economics*, by James D. Gwartney, Richard L. Stroup, Dwight R. Lee, and Tawni H. Ferrarini.[2] To learn to recognize confused ideas about the economy, I'd suggest my own *Money, Greed, and God: Why Capitalism Is the Solution and Not the Problem*,[3] and *Economics in*

One Lesson, by Henry Hazlitt.[4] You won't find any math or supply/demand charts anywhere in these books.

For recent moral defenses of free enterprise, check out *The Road to Freedom*, by Arthur C. Brooks,[5] and *Defending the Free Market*, by Rev. Robert Sirico.[6] For extra credit, read the classic *Wealth and Poverty*, by George Gilder,[7] which will transform how you see entrepreneurs, and his new sequel, *Knowledge and Power*.[8]

If you want all the details about the financial crisis and its lawless aftermath, read Peter Wallison's book on the financial crisis: *Bad History, Worse Policy: How a False Narrative About the Financial Crisis Led to the Dodd-Frank Act*.[9] If you like gory details, Wallison does not disappoint.

To learn what can happen when government spending gets out of control, read *When Money Dies: The Nightmare of Deficit Spending, Devaluation, and Hyperinflation in Weimar Germany*.[10] The book was originally published in 1975 and was rereleased in 2010. In the book, Fergusson argues that no two hyperinflationary cycles are exactly alike, but the similarities between German spending policies then and American spending policies now is disquieting.

Imbibe even a few of these books, and I *promise* that you will be equipped to slice through 95 percent of the economic balderdash thrown in your face by the mainstream media. In fact, if you are a member of the media, please open a few of these books for a whole new perspective. (And please accept my apologies if you don't fit the stereotype I have cast here of the biased journalist.)

There are also lots of good video sources. *The Call of the Entrepreneur* and *The Birth of Freedom* are hour-long documentaries available on DVD. For free online videos, Economic Freedom (http://www.economicfreedom.org/videos/) has a growing portfolio of excellent video shorts demonstrating the superiority of free economies for human flourishing.

For an inspiring look at the wonders of global economic freedom, check out the "I, Smartphone" short at: http://tifwe.org/smartphone/.

For a quick lesson on "How Not to Help the Poor," see http://www.youtube.com/watch?v=4MGYzhbKPDg. For DVDs and online videos, see PovertyCure (http://www.povertycure.org/dvd-series/). See also respective YouTube channels and iTunes lists of online video lectures about economics from scholars at the Institute for Faith, Work & Economics, Discovery Institute, Acton Institute, American Enterprise Institute, and the Heritage Foundation.

If you got this far in the Additional Resources, you should congratulate yourself. I know you'll find this further exploration well worth your time and energy.

ACRONYMS
AND NICKNAMES

ACORN	Association of Community Organizations for Reform Now
ARM	Adjustable-rate mortgage
APR	Annual percentage rate
CDFI	Community Development Financial Institutions
CDO	Collateralized debt obligation
CDS	Credit default swap
CFPB	Consumer Financial Protection Bureau
CFTC	Commodity Futures Trading Commission
CPSD	Consumer Product Safety Commission
CRA	Community Reinvestment Act
CRL	Center for Responsible Lending
Fannie Mae	Federal National Mortgage Association
FCIC	Financial Crisis Inquiry Commission
FDIC	Federal Deposit Insurance Corporation
FHA	Federal Housing Administration

FICO   Fair Isaac Corporation (now uses "FICO" as its corporate identity)

Freddie Mac Federal Home Loan Mortgage Association

FSOC   Financial Stability Oversight Council

GSE   Government sponsored enterprise (such as Fannie Mae, Freddie Mac, and Federal Home Loan Banks)

HUD   Department of Housing and Urban Development

LMI   Low- and moderate-income (as in: low- and moderate-income borrower)

MBS   Mortgage-backed security

OLA   Orderly Liquidation Authority

OTC   Over the counter (as in: over-the-counter derivatives)

SEC   Securities and Exchange Commission

SIFI   Systemically important financial institution

SOS   The distress signal normal people want to send out when surrounded by so many acronyms

NOTES

PROLOGUE

1. See "Country Rankings," at: http://www.heritage.org/index/ranking. See also the separate Economic Freedom of the World Report, at: http://www.freetheworld.com/.
2. Ayn Rand, *Atlas Shrugged* (New York: Random House, 1957), Appendix.
3. Rand said things along these lines in many places, but these quotes are from a lecture she gave in 1960, entitled "Faith and Force: The Destroyers of the Modern World." It is posted online at: http://freedomkeys.com/faithandforce.htm.
4. Robin Wilson, "Liberal 'Group Think' Puts Professors at Odds with Most Americans," *The Chronicle of Higher Education* (October 19, 2006).
5. Jay W. Richards, *Money, Greed, and God: Why Capitalism Is the Solution and Not the Problem* (San Francisco: HarperOne, 2009).

CHAPTER 1

1. The U.S. military has identified traditional installment loans as a beneficial form of credit for military service members. The Department of Defense specifically exempted traditional installment loans from the rate cap limits in the 2007 John Warner Defense Authorization Act, Section 670, which in its final rule notes the need to "isolate detrimental credit products without impeding the availability of favorable installment loans."
2. Hilary Lewis, "Bailout Sketch 'Didn't Meet Our Standards, So We Took It Down,'" *Business Insider* (October 7, 2008), at: http://www.business insider.com/2008/10/nbc-snl-bailout-sketch-didn-t-meet-our-standards-so-we-took-it-down.
3. Other details of the bill included permission to slightly increase the rate schedule on their loans. It also made some incremental adjustments to the blended rate schedule for consumer loans, although it ultimately lowered the state's maximum rate set in 1983. Currently, the top rate for over 98 percent of loans made in the state is 30 percent up to $1,000, after which

the rate then declines for each incremental increase in the loan amount. The essence of the original HB 810 was passed into law in June 2013 as NC Senate Bill 489 and was signed by Governor Pat McCrory.

4. "Military Group Opposes Rate Hike for Consumer Finance Loans," *Stanly News & Press* (Albemarle, NC) (April 27, 2011), at: http://thesnaponline.com/servicenews/x1250115285/Military-groups-oppose-rate-hike-for-consumer-finance-loans/print.

5. See the rules for the North Carolina Assembly at: http://ftp.legislature.state.nc.us/NCGAInfo/buildingrules.html?bPrintable=true&.

6. Daniel Wagner, "How the Consumer Protection Bureau Raided One Business," Associated Press (September 12, 2012), at: http://bigstory.ap.org/article/how-consumer-protection-bureau-raided-one-firm.

7. Heather Anderson, "CFPB Legal Action Halts Two Alleged California Mortgage Scammers," *Credit Union Times* (December 11, 2012), at: http://www.cutimes.com/2012/12/11/cfpb-legal-action-halts-two-alleged-california-mor.

8. "CFPB Orders American Express to Pay $85 Million Refund to Consumers Harmed by Illegal Credit Card Practices," CFPB press release (October 1, 2012), at: http://www.consumerfinance.gov/pressreleases/cfpb-orders-american-express-to-pay-85-million-refund-to-consumers-harmed-by-illegal-credit-card-practices/.

9. "2012 U.S. Credit Card Satisfaction Study," J.D. Power & Associates press release (August 23, 2012), at: http://www.jdpower.com/content/press-release/xdTqU1T/2012-u-s-credit-card-satisfaction-study.htm.

10. Ronald L. Rubin, "The Identity Crisis at the Consumer Financial Protection Bureau," BNA's Banking Report 100, no. 4 (January 22, 2013), at: http://www.hunton.com/files/Publication/a1756099-61d1-47c2-b99f-e96b5507ec4c/Presentation/Publication Attachment/824b1003-7cdb-478c-9e5b-ec5c52602db9/Identity_Crisis_at_the_Consumer_Financial_Protection_Bureau.pdf.

11. Ibid.

12. Michael S. Greve, "Kill Dodd-Frank (II)," *Library of Law & Liberty* (October 6, 2012), at: http://www.libertylawsite.org/2012/10/06/kill-dodd-frank-ii/.

13. Joel Gehrke, "Report—CFPB Stifles 150,000 Jobs after Controversial 'Recess' Appointment," *Washington Examiner* (December 14, 2012), at: http://washingtonexaminer.com/report-cfpb-stifles-150000-jobs-after-controversial-recess-appointment/article/2515968#.UMuQUbYh0ik. The report is "The Consumer Financial Protection Bureau's Threat to Credit Access in the United States," Staff Report, U.S. House of Representatives 112th Congress (December 14, 2012), at: http://oversight.house.gov/wp-content/uploads/2012/12/Access-to-Credit-Report-12.14.12.pdf.

CHAPTER 2

1. Quoted in Jack Cashill, *Popes and Bankers: A Cultural History of Credit and Debt, from Aristotle to AIG* (Nashville, TN: Thomas Nelson, 2010), p. 94.
2. Ibid., p. 96.
3. Ibid., p. 19.
4. Exodus 22:25.
5. Leviticus 25:35–37.
6. Deuteronomy 23:19–20.
7. Luke 6:34–35.
8. See Andrea Peyser, "The Hate in Zuccotti," *New York Post* (October 24, 2011), at: http://www.nypost.com/p/news/local/the_hate_in_zuccotti _KyGNaMM6eLBirVJN24fEEP.
9. This doesn't mean that basic economic realities like supply and demand didn't exist for them. But typically there are lower "transaction costs" when trading with family members than when trading with someone you don't know in another country. See Edd S. Noell, "A 'Marketless' World: An Examination of Wealth and Exchange in the Gospels and First Century Palestine," *Journal of Markets & Morality* 10, no. 1 (2007): 85–114.
10. St. Thomas argued, "If a man wanted to sell wine separately from the use of the wine, he would be selling the same thing twice, or he would be selling what does not exist." *Summa Theologica* II.2, Question 78, parts 1–4. Quoted in Cashill, p. 30.
11. There were rudimentary "banks" during the New Testament era and earlier, but they were much less significant economically than the banks we know today.
12. Rodney Stark, *The Victory of Reason: How Christianity Led to Freedom, Capitalism, and Western Success* (New York: Random House, 2005), pp. 112–113. I'm indebted in this section to Stark's lucid account.
13. Ibid., p. 45.
14. This quote is from Aristotle's *Physics*, quoted in Cashill, p. 29.
15. Cashill, *Popes and Bankers*, p. 26.
16. Quoted in Lendol Calder, *Financing the American Dream: A Cultural History of Consumer Credit* (Princeton: Princeton University Press, 1999), p. 113.
17. For a detailed study of the Reformer's views of usury, see David W. Jones, *Reforming the Morality of Usury: A Study of the Differences that Separated the Protestant Reformers* (Lanham, MD: University Press of America, 2004).
18. For more, see John T. Noonan Jr., *The Scholastic Analysis of Usury* (Cambridge, MA: Harvard University Press, 1957), p. 399; Samuel Gregg, *Banking, Justice and the Common Good* (Lanham, MD: Lexington Books, 2004), p. 38. The earlier reason for the near complete ban on charging interest dissolved and, with it, the ban itself. The classic rule here is *Cessante ratione, cessat ipsa lex*: "When the reason for the law ceases, the law itself ceases." John T. Noonan Jr. uses this reference in *A Church*

That Can and Cannot Change (South Bend, IN: University of Notre Dame Press, 2005), p. 205. Quoted in Cashill, p. 30. Of course, there can still be situations where the *moral* concerns regarding usury still exist. For instance, imagine that a wealthy man could charge his reliable, hardworking brother 500 percent interest for a loan for lifesaving emergency surgery and ruthlessly demand full payment after the recovery process was slower than expected. Most of us would judge the wealthy man harshly in such a circumstance.

19. Exodus 22:25–27; Leviticus 25:35–38; Deuteronomy 23:19–20.
20. Luke 6:34–35.
21. John 2:13–22; see George Beasley-Murray, *John, Word Biblical Commentary* (Waco, TX: Word Books, 1987), p. 39. He may also have been protesting collusion between these merchants and the political authorities who gave the merchants a monopoly, allowing them to charge exorbitant prices for the priest-approved animals the worshippers were required to purchase. If so, their commerce was unjust, no matter where it was located. Noell, p. 102. Most biblical scholars think Jesus's action is meant to be a "prophecy of the temple's impending destruction." See Craig L. Blomberg, *Neither Poverty Nor Riches* (Downers Grove, IL: InterVarsity Press, 1999), pp. 142–143.
22. Matthew 6:19–20a.
23. Matthew 25:14–30.
24. Here I am drawing on the more detailed discussion from Chapter 6, Jay W. Richards, *Money, Greed, and God: Why Capitalism Is the Solution and Not the Problem* (San Francisco: HarperOne, 2009).
25. Noonan, *Scholastic Analysis*, p. 2.
26. This is based on a true story, but I have simplified the details.
27. Quoted in Calder, *Financing the American Dream*, p. 99.
28. Ibid., p. 100.
29. Ibid., p. 101.
30. Ibid., p. 158.
31. Ibid, p. 38.
32. Ibid., p. 160.
33. See discussion in Calder, *Financing the American Dream*, pp. 98–104.
34. Ibid., p. 162.
35. Ibid., p. 184.
36. Ibid, pp. 107–108.

CHAPTER 3

1. The word *philanthrocapitalist* was coined by Matthew Bishop of *The Economist*. Joe Nocera uses it to refer to the Sandlers in his profile, "Self-Made Philanthropists," *New York Times* (March 9, 2008), at: http://www.nytimes.com/2008/03/09/magazine/09Sandlers-t.html?pagewanted=all.
2. As Joe Nocera puts it in "Self-Made Philanthropists."

3. Michael Moss and Geraldine Fabrikant, "Once Trusted Mortgage Pioneers, Now Scrutinized," *New York Times* (December 24, 2008), at: http://www.nytimes.com/2008/12/25/business/25sandler.html?page wanted=all.
4. See Herb Sandler's official website at: http://www.herbsandler.com/.
5. Kathleen McKay, "The Osher Family's Credo: Giving Is a Way of Life," *Maine* (November/December 2011), at: http://www.themainemag.com /people/profiles/1734-the-osher-family.html.
6. See Marion Sandler's official website at: http://www.marionsandler.com.
7. Ibid.
8. Richard W. Stevenson, "Inside the Nation's Best-Run S.&L.," *New York Times* (September 9, 1990), at: http://www.nytimes.com/1990/09/09/ business/inside-the-nation-s-best-run-s-l.html?pagewanted=all&src=pm.
9. McKay, "The Osher Family's Credo."
10. Charles McCoy, "If Only All the S&Ls Had Been Managed Like Golden West," *Wall Street Journal* (June 29, 1990), at: http://www.golden westworld.com/wp-content/themes/goldenwest/docs/press/062990_If _only_GDW_McCoy_WallStreetJournal.pdf.
11. Moss and Fabrikant, "Once Trusted Mortgage Pioneers, Now Scrutinized," supra note 3.
12. This is from the description at Herb Sandler's official website, at: http:// www.herbsandler.com/.content/themes/goldenwest/docs/press/062990 _If_only_GDW_McCoy_WallStreetJournal.pdf .
13. Herb Sandler and Marion Sandler, "Don't Pin the Blame on Us," *Time* (April 2010), at: http://www.time.com/time/magazine/pdf /SandlerResponse.pdf.
14. Moss and Fabrikant, "Once Trusted Mortgage Pioneers, Now Scrutinized," supra note 3.
15. This is how A. F. Ehrbar characterized them in "The Mysteriously Profitable S&L," *Fortune* (June 29, 1981), pp. 94–99.
16. Heidi N. Moore, "Wachovia-Golden West: Another Deal from Hell?," *Wall Street Journal* (July 22, 2008), at: http://blogs.wsj.com /deals/2008/07/22/wachovia-golden-west-another-deal-from-hell/.
17. "Focused 527 Organizations, 2004 Election Cycle," OpenSecrets.org, at: http://www.opensecrets.org/527s/527indivs.php?cycle=2004.
18. Ed Lasky, "How Allies of George Soros Helped Bring Down Wachovia Bank," *American Thinker* (September 29, 2008), at: http://www .americanthinker.com/2008/09/how_allies_of_george_soros_hel.html.
19. For a detailed treatment of ACORN, see Matthew Vadum, *Subversion, Inc.* (Nashville: WND Books, 2011).
20. "Golden West Financial Corporation History," *Funding Universe*, at: http:// www.fundinguniverse.com/company-histories/golden-west-financial -corporation-history/.

21. Moss and Fabrikant, "Once Trusted Mortgage Pioneers, Now Scrutinized," supra note 3.

22. Laurence Arnold, "Marion Sandler, Home Lender Who Made Billions, Dies at 81," *Bloomberg* (June 4, 2012), at: http://www.bloomberg.com /news/2012-06-04/marion-sandler-home-lender-who-made-billions -dies-at-81.html.

23. Seth Lubove, "Stick to your Knitting," *Forbes* (March 1, 2004), at: http:// www.forbes.com/global/2004/0301/036.html.

24. According to the Form 10-K, submitted to the SEC from Golden West Financial Corporation, for the Fiscal Year Ended December 31, 2005.

25. Ibid.

26. Moss and Fabrikant, "Once Trusted Mortgage Pioneers, Now Scrutinized," supra note 3.

27. The standard for the Office of the Comptroller of the Currency is 660. For years, however, Fannie and Freddie counted loans they bought from originators as subprime only if they were "self-denominated" as subprime by the originators. This was a serious mistake.

28. Dean Foust, "Pick-A-Pay Goes Away..." *Bloomberg Businessweek* (June 29, 2008), at: http://www.businessweek.com/printer/articles/360538-pick-a -pay-goes-away?type=old_article.

29. Ibid.

30. According to Moss and Fabrikant, "Once Trusted Mortgage Pioneers, Now Scrutinized," supra note 3.

31. Ibid.

32. From "Myths and Facts," on the website that Herb Sandler started to counter the negative press they received, last updated June 25, 2010, at: http://www.goldenwestworld.com/myths-and-facts/.

33. Foust, "Pick-A-Pay Goes Away. . ."

34. Arnold, "Marion Sandler, Home Lender Who Made Billions, Dies at 81."

35. "The heart of both stories," according to a largely sympathetic report in the *Columbia Journalism Review*, "was that Golden West had intentionally sacrificed its lending standards to boost sales of a predatory product." Jeff Horwitz, "The Education of Herb and Marion Sandler," *Columbia Journalism Review* (March/April 2010), at: http://www.cjr.org/feature /the_education_of_herb_and_marion.php?page=all.

36. The transcript of the story "World of Trouble" was published on the CBS website on August 19, 2010, at: http://www.cbsnews.com /stories/2009/02/13/60minutes/main4801309.shtml. The video segment can be viewed at: http://www.cbsnews.com/video/watch/?id=4803928n& tag=contentBody;storyMediaBox.

37. The "Special" is a short gallery or slide show, at: http://www.time.com/time /specials/packages/article/0,28804,1877351_1877350_1877339,00.html.

38. Moss and Fabrikant, "Once Trusted Mortgage Pioneers, Now Scrutinized," supra note 3.

39. Quoted in Arnold, "Marion Sandler, Home Lender Who Made Billions, Dies at 81."

40. Brian Stelter, "NBC Edits 'Saturday Night Live' Skit," *New York Times Media Decoder Blog* (October 8, 2008), at: http://mediadecoder.blogs .nytimes.com/2008/10/08/nbc-edits-saturday-night-live-sketch/.

41. At: http://guestofaguest.com/new-york/finance/the-forbidden-snl -economic-bailout-skit.

42. At: http://www.moonbattery.com/archives/2008/10/saturday_night_2.html.

43. Jeff Horwitz, "The Education of Herb and Marion Sandler," *Columbia Journalism Review* (March 18, 2010), at: http://www.cjr.org/feature/the _education_of_herb_and_marion.php?page=all.

44. "Letter from Herb Sandler to CBS" (April 29, 2010), at: http://www .cbsnews.com/htdocs/pdf/Sandler_Letter_to_CBS_4-26-10.pdf?tag =contentMain;contentBody.

45. *60 Minutes* posted the update on its website (June 3, 2010), at: http://www .cbsnews.com/stories/2010/06/03/60minutes/main6545387.shtml.

46. This quote is from a presentation by T2 Partners LLC, posted as part of an online discussion at DoctorHousingBubble.com.

47. Quote from Sandler and Sandler, "Don't Pin the Blame on Us."

48. http://www.goldenwestworld.com/wp-content/uploads/history-of -the-option-arm-and-structural-features-of-the-gw-option-arm2.pdf.

49. Moss and Fabrikant, "Once Trusted Mortgage Pioneers, Now Scrutinized," *The New York Times*, supra note 3.

50. Sandler and Sandler, "Myths and Facts."

51. According to the Form 10-K, submitted to the SEC from Golden West Financial Corporation, for the Fiscal Year Ended December 31, 2005, Golden West assets totaled $124.6 billion.

52. The following are excerpts from their Form 10-K filing to the SEC for year ending December 31, 2005.

Securitization Activity

We often securitize our portfolio loans into mortgage-backed securities. We do this because MBS are a more valuable form of collateral for borrowings than whole loans. Because we have retained all of the beneficial interests in these MBS securitizations to date, the accounting rules require that securities formed after March 31, 2001 be classified as securitized loans and included in our loans receivable. Securitization activity for the years ended December 31, 2005, 2004, and 2003, amounted to $34.3 billion, $24.5 billion, and $13.7 billion, respectively. The volume of securitization activity fluctuates depending on the amount of collateral needed for borrowings and liquidity risk management.

. . .

Borrowings. We also borrow money from a variety of sources to fund our loan origination activities. Borrowings include taking "advances" from the Federal Home Loan Bank (FHLB) system, entering into reverse repurchase agreements with selected dealers, and issuing unsecured debt securities. FHLB advances and reverse repurchase agreements require us to pledge collateral to the lenders, sometimes in the form of whole loans and sometimes in the form of securitized pools of loans. We regularly securitize loans from our portfolio into MBS and Real Estate Mortgage Investment Conduit securities (MBS-REMICs) to create collateral for our secured borrowings. *Additional information about our borrowings and securitization activity can be found in the MD&A under "The Loan Portfolio – Securitization Activity" and "Borrowings," and detailed borrowing Tables 16 and 17.*

. . .

At December 31, 2005 and 2004, the Company had $83 million and $52 million, respectively, in loans held for sale, all of which were carried at the lower of cost or fair value. At December 31, 2005, the Company had $49.9 billion of loans that were securitized after March 31, 2001 that are securities classified as loans receivable in accordance with SFAS 140. The outstanding balances of securitizations created prior to April 1, 2001 are included in MBS with recourse.

. . .

Loans totaling $57.8 billion and $52.5 billion at December 31, 2005 and 2004 were pledged to secure advances from the FHLBs and securities sold under agreements to repurchase.

53. The opening paragraph of World Savings Bank REMIC 12 reads:

This is a Pooling and Servicing Agreement, effective as of June 21, 2002, among WORLD SAVINGS BANK, FSB, as the depositor (in such capacity, together with its permitted successors and assigns, the "Depositor") and as the master servicer (in such capacity, together with its permitted successors and assigns, the "Master Servicer"), and Deutsche Bank National Trust Company, as Trustee (together with its permitted successors and assigns, the "Trustee").

Though we know that World Savings securitized its loans even as it referred to them as "portfolio" loans, the details and discussion about the Sandlers' securitization methods is chaotic and uncertain at the moment. Some online discussion boards provide clues but shouldn't be treated as decisive evidence. See, for instance, the discussion in "World Savings Bank

Loans Were Securitized—Pooling and Servicing Agreement Uncovered,"
DTC Systems (March 15, 2011), at: http://dtc-systems.net/2011/03/world
-savings-bank-loans-were-securitizated/. The document is posted online,
at: http://www.scribd.com/doc/76668823/World-Savings-Bank-REMIC
-12-PSA.

54. Sandler and Sandler, "Don't Pin the Blame on Us."
55. "The Giving Pledge is an effort to help address society's most pressing
problems by inviting the world's wealthiest individuals and families to
commit to giving more than half their wealth to philanthropy or charitable causes either during their lifetime or after their death," at: http://
givingpledge.org/.
56. Jane Mayer, "The Money Man," *New Yorker* (October 18, 2004), at: http://
www.newyorker.com/archive/2004/10/18/041018fa_fact3.

CHAPTER 4

1. It seems likely that this program is designed to produce more Martin Eakeses.
2. "Day in Durham 2010 Keynote Address," at: http://www.youtube.com
/watch?v=QuY25_FNpA0&feature=edu&list=PL847FB15F14D14C5F.
3. Originally published in 2007. Leslie R. Crutchfield and Heather McLeod
Grant, *Forces for Good: The Six Practices of High Impact Nonprofits* (San
Francisco: Jossey-Bass, 2012).
4. James R. Haggerty, "When Martin Eakes Speaks, Citigroup Listens,"
Wall Street Journal (July 12, 2005), at: http://online.wsj.com/article
/0,,SB112112308799082755,00.html.
5. Since this was the mid-1970s, a '65 Buick wasn't all that old. But when
referenced in a story told in 2010, it sounds ancient.
6. I supplemented the details here from an article by Jim Nesbitt, "2005 Tar
Heel of the Year: Self-Help's Martin Eakes," *News Observer* (December
18, 2005), at: http://www.newsobserver.com/2005/12/18/51568/2005-tar
-heel-of-the-year-self.html. For more of the Self-Help organization, see
its website at: http://www.self-help.org.
7. See "Day in Durham 2010 Keynote Address," at: http://www.youtube
.com/watch?v=QuY25_FNpA0&feature=edu&list=PL847FB15F14D14
C5F.
8. Eric Nee, "15 Minutes with Martin Eakes," *Stanford Social Innovation
Review* (Summer 2008), at: http://www.ssireview.org/articles/entry/15
_minutes_with_martin_eakes.
9. "Martin Daniel Eakes '76 and Bonnie Marie Wright '79," *Davidson News
& Events* (October 30, 2001), at: http://www2.davidson.edu/news/news
_archives/archives_imgs/0110_convocation/0110convo-citation1.html.
10. Ibid.
11. "Martin Eakes, Self Help, Durham, North Carolina." Interview by Lynn
Adler and Jim Mayer for *Faith, Hope and Capital*, at: http://www.pbs.org
/capital/stories/martin-eakes-print.html.

12. Nesbitt, "2005 Tar Heel of the Year."
13. Haggerty, "When Martin Eakes Speaks, Citigroup Listens."
14. Martin Eakes, Self Help, Durham, North Carolina," interviewed by Lynn Adler and Jim Mayer, *Faith, Hope, and Capital*, at: http://www.pbs.org/capital/stories/martin-eakes-print.html.
15. The quotes from Eakes in this section are from the interview for *Faith, Hope and Capital*.
16. At: http://www.pbs.org/capital/stories/martin-eakes-print.html.
17. Described by Eakes in "Self Help, Durham, North Carolina."
18. "Ford Foundation Grant of $50 Million Will Generate $2 Billion in Affordable Mortgages for 35,000 Low-Wealth Home Buyers," Ford Foundation (July 23, 1998), at: http://www.fordfoundation.org/newsroom/news-from-ford/7.
19. Ibid.
20. Quote in Ibid.
21. The details here are complicated, but Self-Help didn't bear the full risk of these loans over the long haul, because Self-Help *sold* them to Fannie Mae. And the loans from private banks would be either on the banks' books or sold on the secondary market. Self-Help wouldn't hold them indefinitely.
22. "Self-Help, Ford Foundation, Bank of America, Chevy Chase Bank and Fannie Mae Announce Successful Completion of $2 Billion Homeownership Initiative," Ford Foundation (October 28, 2003), at: http://www.fordfoundation.org/newsroom/news-from-ford/83.
23. Nesbitt, "2005 Tar Heel of the Year."
24. Quoted in Nesbitt, "2005 Tarheel of the Year."
25. For a historical treatment, see Alyssa Katz, *Our Lot: How Real Estate Came to Own Us* (New York: Bloomsbury USA, 2010).
26. Quoted in Thomas Sowell, *The Housing Boom and Bust* (New York: Basic Books, 2009), p. 103. See discussion in Steven Malanga, "Obsessive Housing Disorder," *City Journal* 19, no. 2 (Spring 2009), at: http://www.city-journal.org/2009/19_2_homeownership.html; and Jack Cashill, *Popes and Bankers: A Cultural History of Credit and Debt, from Aristotle to AIG* (Nashville: Thomas Nelson, 2010), p. 204.
27. John Allison, the former CEO of BB&T Bank, discusses this in *The Financial Crisis and the Free Market Cure: Why Pure Capitalism Is the World Economy's Only Hope* (New York: McGraw-Hill, 2013), p. 42. The practice of "redlining" was a concern. Redlining referred to the practice of some lenders to distinguish some communities from others in developing their lending criteria. Some of this seems perfectly reasonable. After all, if lenders can't distinguish low-crime areas from high-crime ones in their lending policy, then they can't adequately price risk. But in some cases, redlining seemed to result from racial discrimination, so the practice is now prohibited.

28. Housing and Community Development Act of 1977—Title VIII (Community Reinvestment), at: http://www.fdic.gov/regulations/laws /rules/6500-2515.html.

29. See discussion in Housing and Community Development Act of 1977, pp. 42–43.

30. Otherwise known as the Federal Housing Enterprises Financial Safety and Soundness Act of 1992.

31. Peter Wallison, in his Dissent, *The Financial Crisis Inquiry Report, Official Government Edition* (revised February 25, 2011), p. 453, at: http://www .gpo.gov/fdsys/pkg/GPO-FCIC/pdf/GPO-FCIC.pdf.

32. The FHA was originally set up in 1934, but HUD had absorbed it in 1965 when President Lyndon Johnson created the department as part of his Great Society initiative.

33. "Community Development Financial Institutions Fund," at: http://www .cdfifund.gov/who_we_are/about_us.asp.

34. Ibid. There were two legislative initiatives in 1994–1995 as part of this effort. The first revised and strengthened the mandates of the 1977 Community Reinvestment Act. The second was the Riegle-Neal Act. It created the CDFI Fund and also made the provisions of the Community Reinvestment Act a prerequisite for banks to expand, merge, make acquisitions, or work in more than one state. This shift in policy transformed the job of federal regulators. "Since The Great Depression the goal of bank regulation had been to ensure the solvency of lending institutions. After 1994 regulators were tasked also with implementing and enforcing the NHS's social agenda. Extending loan access to the uncreditworthy was in direct opposition to bank solvency." In "Origin of the Housing Bubble: 'The National Home Ownership Strategy,'" *The Affordable Mortgage Depression*, at: http://theaffordablemortgagedepression.com/2010/03/11 /origin-of-the-housing-bubble-the-national-homeownership-strategy .aspx.

35. See the Community Development Financial Institutions Fund website for updated information, at: http://www.cdfifund.gov/awardees/db /basicSearchResults.asp?programName=%25&yearOfAward=%25&sort =yearOfAward&mailingState=NC. As of 2011, Self-Help Credit Union in North Carolina had 14 offices and 40,000 such members. Its Federal Credit Union in California had 18 branches and 50,000 members. "Self-Help Annual Report 2011," at: http://www.self-help.org/custom/fi/self -help/fb/disclosure/Self-Help-AnnualReport-20111.pdf.

36. In the United States, credit unions such as Self-Help are insured by the National Credit Union Administration (NCUA), at: http://www.ncua .gov/.

37. Nesbitt, "Tarheel of the Year."

38. James Hagerty refers to "a 1992 Chevrolet Corsica with a cracked windshield" in "When Martin Eakes Speaks, Citigroup Listens,"

Wall Street Journal (July 12, 2005), at: http://online.wsj.com/article /0,,SB112112308799082755,00.html.

39. Nesbitt, "Tarheel of the Year."

40. For instance, see Hagerty, "When Martin Eakes Speaks, Citigroup Listens." Note the similarities to his 2010 speech at Duke. Compare also the interview with Eakes conducted by Lynn Adler and Jim Mayer for the PBS documentary *Faith, Hope, and Capital*, aired in 2000, at: http://www .pbs.org/capital/stories/martin-eakes-print.html.

41. "Man Arrested in Attack on Self-Help Founder," *WRAL.com* (January 14, 2009), at: http://www.wral.com/news/news_briefs/story/4317222/.

42. Jay W. Richards, *Money, Greed, and God: Why Capitalism Is the Solution and Not the Problem* (San Francisco: HarperOne, 2009).

43. Adam Smith, *An Inquiry into the Nature and Causes of the Wealth of Nations*, edited by Edwin Cannan (New York: Modern Library, 1994), p. 15.

44. Ibid., p. 485.

45. The problem of cronyism is especially a problem for socialism (think of modern Russia), because socialism limits the opportunities for greedy people to gain wealth through constructive enterprise. It also creates a myriad of opportunities for government officials to gain wealth by abusing their authority, since they are entangled in so many different aspects of the market.

CHAPTER 5

1. Joe Nocera, "Self-Made Philanthropists," *New York Times* (March 9, 2008), at: http://www.nytimes.com/2008/03/09/magazine/09Sandlers-t .html?pagewanted=all.

2. Seth Lubove, "Stick to Your Knitting," *Forbes* (March 1, 2004), at: http:// www.forbes.com/global/2004/0301/036_print.html.

3. Mary Walton, "The Nonprofit Explosion," *American Journalism Review* (September 2010), at: http://www.ajr.org/article.asp?id=4906.

4. On her personal blog, Tucker describes herself this way: "Journalist. Professor. Progressive." At: http://cynthiatucker.com/.

5. Arthur Brisbane, "Success and Risk as the *Times* Transforms," *New York Times* (August 25, 2012), at: http://www.nytimes.com/2012/08/26 /opinion/sunday/success-and-risk-as-the-times-transforms.html?_r=1.

6. Dylan Byers, "NYT's Abramson Rebuts Brisbane Charge," *Politico* (August 25, 2012), at: http://www.politico.com/blogs/media/2012/08 /nyts-abramson-rebuts-brisbane-charge-133211.html.

7. See discussion in Jeff Horwitz, "The Education of Herb and Marion Sandler," *Columbia Journalism Review* (March/April 2010), at: http://www .cjr.org/feature/the_education_of_herb_and_marion.php?page=all.

8. This was during his testimony to the Financial Crisis Inquiry Commission, which we discuss in Chapter 8.

9. Cora Currier, "Mitt Romney's Tax Mysteries: A Reading Guide," *ProPublica* (August 28, 2012), at: http://www.propublica.org/article /romneys-tax-mysteries-a-reading-guide.

10. View the entire series at: http://www.propublica.org/series/the-wall
-street-money-machine.

11. Amy Chozick, "Steiger to Step Down as ProPublica's Editor," *New
York Times* (May 14, 2012), at: http://mediadecoder.blogs.nytimes
.com/2012/05/14/steiger-to-step-down-as-propublicas-editor/?hp.

12. Quote is from the summary of the article at: http://www.propublica.org
/series/freddie-mac. The article is by Jesse Eisinger and Chris Arnold,
"Freddie Mac Bets Against American Homeowners" (January 30, 2012), at:
http://www.propublica.org/article/freddy-mac-mortgage-eisinger-arnold.

13. Frontline, "Programs by Year: 2009," at: http://www.pbs.org/wgbh/pages
/frontline/programs/2009.html.

14. At: http://www.pbs.org/wgbh/pages/frontline/money-power-wall-street/.

15. At: http://www.pbs.org/wgbh/pages/frontline/untouchables/.

16. See his interview, "Phil Angelides: Enforcement of Wall St. Is 'Woefully
Broken,'" *Frontline* (January 22, 2013), at: http://www.pbs.org/wgbh
/pages/frontline/business-economy-financial-crisis/untouchables/phil
-angelides-enforcement-of-wall-st-is-woefully-broken/.

17. "Breaking the Bank," *Frontline*, PBS.org, at: http://www.pbs.org/wgbh
/pages/frontline/breakingthebank/etc/script.html.

18. At: http://www.pbs.org/wgbh/pages/frontline/creditcards/.

19. The phrasing is borrowed from Alexis de Tocqueville's description of
the nanny state he feared would grow from the soil of democracy. See
Democracy in America (1835, 1840), Trans. Gerald E. Bevan (New York:
Penguin, 2003), pp. 805–806.

20. James Davison Hunter, *To Change the World: The Irony, Tragedy, and
Possibility of Christianity in the Late Modern World* (New York: Oxford
University Press, 2010), p. 41.

21. "Wachovia Acquires Golden West Financial," Associated Press (May
8, 2006), at: http://www.msnbc.msn.com/id/12680868/from/RSS/#
UFdo046yrao.

22. Herb Sandler and Marion Sandler, "Don't Pin the Blame on Us" (April
2010), at: http://www.time.com/time/magazine/pdf/SandlerResponse.pdf.
The *Time* story put the Sandlers as number 10 out of 25. This is what *Time*
wrote:

> In the early 1980s, the Sandlers' World Savings Bank became
> the first to sell a tricky home loan called the option ARM. And
> they pushed the mortgage, which offered several ways to back-
> load your loan and thereby reduce your early payments, with
> increasing zeal and misleading advertisements over the next
> two decades. The couple pocketed $2.3 billion when they sold
> their bank to Wachovia in 2006. But losses on World Savings'
> loan portfolio led to the implosion of Wachovia, which was sold
> under duress late last year to Wells Fargo.

"25 People to Blame for the Financial Crisis," at: http://www.time.com/time /specials/packages/article/0,28804,1877351_1877350_1877343,00.html.

23. Horwitz, "The Education of Herb and Marion Sandler."

24. Dan Gainor, "Why Is Soros Spending Over $48 Million Funding Media Organizations?" FoxNews.com (May 18, 2011), at: http://www.foxnews .com/opinion/2011/05/18/soros-spending-48-million-funding-media -organizations/.

25. See "2004 Top Donors to Outside Spending Groups," OpenSecrets .org, at: http://www.opensecrets.org/outsidespending/summ.php?cycle= 2004&disp=D.

26. Jane Mayer, "The Money Man," *New Yorker* (October 18, 2004), at: http:// www.newyorker.com/archive/2004/10/18/041018fa_fact3.

27. From Matthew Vadum, "ACORN: Who Funds the Weather Underground's Little Brother?," *Capital Research Center Foundation Watch* (November 1, 2008), at: http://www.capitalresearch.org/2008/11/acorn -who-funds-the-weather-undergrounds-little-brother-2/:

> By using philanthropy databases and nonprofit tax returns (IRS Form 990) Capital Research Center has gathered a wealth of information on money that flows into and out of ACORN network coffers.
>
> Project Vote (Voting for America Inc.) discloses on its 990s that it received $23,658,487 in donations from 1994 through 2005. The American Institute for Social Justice Inc. reports that it took in $32,497,575 in donations from 1993 through 2005. ACORN Housing Corp. Inc. reports it took in $48,666,179 in donations from 1993 through 2004. ACORN Institute Inc. took in donations of $2,074,409 from 2001 through 2005.
>
> This means the four ACORN affiliates took in a total of at least $106,896,650 in donations from foundations and individuals since 1993.

28. Ibid.

29. For example, Eric Shawn, "Four Indiana Dems Charged with Election Fraud in 2008 Presidential Race," FoxNews.com (April 3, 2012), at: http://www.foxnews.com/politics/2012/04/02/4-indiana-dems-charged -with-election-fraud-in-2008/#ixzz1qzJKfcoE.

30. For instance, Drew Griffin and Kathleen Johnston, "Thousands of Voter Registration Forms Faked, Officials Say," CNN.com (October 9, 2008), at: http://articles.cnn.com/2008-10-09/politics/acorn.fraud.claims_1 _acorn-officials-voter-fraud-voter-registration?_s=PM:POLITICS.

31. Vadum, "ACORN: Who Funds the Weather Underground's Little Brother?"

32. Bill Tucker, Chris Murphey, and Steve Turnham, "ACORN Workers Caught on Tape Allegedly Advising on Prostitution," CNN.com

(September 11, 2009), at: http://www.cnn.com/2009/POLITICS/09/10/acorn.prostitution/.

33. Though Wikipedia is an unreliable source for political topics, its article on the controversy provides an accurate and detailed timeline of events, as of September 16, 2012, at: http://en.wikipedia.org/wiki/ACORN_2009 _undercover_videos_controversy.

34. Eric Shawn, "ACORN Pleads Guilty to Voter Fraud in Nevada," FoxNews.com (April 6, 2011), at: http://www.foxnews.com/politics /2011/04/06/acorn-pleads-guilty-voter-registration-fraud-nevada/; Matthew Vadum, "ACORN Leader Avoids Prison for Voter Fraud Conspiracy," *Daily Caller* (January 12, 2011), at: http://dailycaller .com/2011/01/12/acorn-leader-avoids-prison-for-voter-fraud -conspiracy/.

35. As John Fund described them just two months before the financial crisis in "Obama's Liberal Shock Troops," *Wall Street Journal* (July 12, 2008), at: http://professional.wsj.com/article/SB121581650524447373 .html?mg=reno64-wsj.

36. Matthew Vadum, *Subversion, Inc.: How Obama's ACORN Red Shirts Are Still Terrorizing and Ripping Off American Taxpayers* (Los Angeles: WND Books, 2011), p. 202.

37. Ibid., loc. 3466. Vadum is quoting from an interview on the Glenn Beck television program, which aired on CNN on June 3, 2009.

38. Dennis Domrzalski, "ACORN Files 14 Complaints Against Wells Fargo Financial," *New Mexico Business Weekly* (November 3, 2003), at: http://www.bizjournals.com/albuquerque/stories/2003/12/01/story8 .html?page=all.

39. Vadum, *Subversion, Inc.*, p. 203.

40. "ACORN Announces Class Action Lawsuit against Wells Fargo" (June 28, 2004), at: http://www.businesswire.com/news/home/20040628005656 /en/ACORN-Announces-Class-Action-Lawsuit-Wells-Fargo.

41. "ACORN's New Target: Wells Fargo," *St. Petersberg Times* (May 5, 2003), at: http://www.sptimes.com/2003/05/05/Business/ACORN_s_new _target__W.shtml.

42. Vadum gives details of these activities in *Subversion, Inc.*

43. Both are quoted in Vadum, *Subversion, Inc.*, p. 233.

44. Saul Alinsky, *Rules for Radicals* (New York: Vintage Books, 1989), pp. 130, 132.

45. Matthew Vadum, "ACORN Exposed: Stealing Democracy," *Townhall* (September 10, 2009), at: http://townhall.com/columnists/matthew vadum/2009/09/10/acorn_exposed_stealing_democracy/page/full.

46. Kevin Mooney, "Liberty Tax CEO Recalls ACORN's 'Mongolian Horde,'" *Washington Examiner* (July 6, 2009), at: http://washingtonexaminer .com/article/36983#.UEoqe46yrao.

47. Quoted in Vadum, *Subversion, Inc.*, p. 225.

48. Ibid., p. 227.
49. Vadum gives more examples in *Subversion, Inc.*, pp. 225–229.
50. "ACORN Announces Class Action Lawsuit against Wells Fargo," *Business Wire* (June 28, 2004), at: http://www.businesswire.com/news /home/20040628005656/en/ACORN-Announces-Class-Action-Lawsuit -Wells-Fargo.
51. "Wells Fargo Financial Settles California Class Action Lawsuit," PRNewswire (April 26, 2007), at: http://www.prnewswire.com/news -releases-test/wells-fargo-financial-settles-california-class-action-lawsuit -58814302.html.
52. See the list of grantees at: http://www.sandlerfoundation.org/grants.
53. R.A. Dyer, "ACORN Activists Re-emerge Here with a Determined Voice," *Houston Chronicle* (January 17, 1997). Quoted in Vadum, *Subversion*, Inc., p. 230.
54. Michael A. Memoli, "ACORN Filing for Chapter 7 Bankruptcy," *Los Angeles Times* (November 2, 2010), at: http://articles.latimes.com/2010 /nov/02/news/la-pn-acorn-bankruptcy-20101103.
55. Sol Stern, "ACORN's Nutty Regime for Cities," *City Journal* (Spring 2003), at: http://www.city-journal.org/html/13_2_acorns_nutty_regime .html.
56. One example is the Clergy and Laity United for Economic Justice (CLUE), in Los Angeles, which ACORN set up with local churches to help push through a "living wage" law. In Stern, "ACORN's Nutty Regime for Cities," p. 238.

CHAPTER 6

1. Quoted in Gary Rivlin, *Broke, USA* (New York: HarperBusiness, 2010), p. 106.
2. This is from Eakes's own account in his 2010 speech at Duke University. "Day in Durham 2010 Keynote Address," at: http://www.youtube.com /watch?v=QuY25_FNpA0&feature=edu&list=PL847FB15F14D14C5F.
3. From his 2010 speech at Duke University:

   > I sat down and did a calculation that if he had had a Self-Help loan during those ten years that he paid, he would have completely paid off the loan and built up $10,000.00 of savings with the payments that he had made. Instead, he was in my office with his loan I foreclosure and the balance still owed was $43,500.00. And so I was—you know, you can't tell it from now but I used to have really long, curly red hair and a really hot temper, and so I started to boil. I mean I was really getting mad, and I said, "Well, let me call this company and we'll see what we can find out."

4. Rivlin, *Broke, USA*, p. 112.
5. Ibid., p. 113.

6. Ibid., p. 114.
7. Ibid., p. 144.
8. Julie Flaherty, "Five Questions for Martin Eakes; An Advocate for the Poor and a Thorn for Citigroup," *New York Times* (November 12, 2000), at: http://www.nytimes.com/2000/11/12/business/five-questions-for -martin-eakes-advocate-for-poor-thorn-for-citigroup.html.
9. Rivlin, *Broke, USA*, p. 159.
10. Ibid., p. 163; Tania Padgett, "Shareholders Find Fault with Citigroup," *Newsday* (April 17, 2001), at: http://www.newsday.com/business/ technology/shareholders-find-fault-with-citigroup-1.307614.
11. "Citigroup Settles FTC Charges against the Associates Record-Setting $215 Million for Subprime Lending Victims" (September 19, 2002), at: http://www.ftc.gov/opa/2002/09/associates.shtm.
12. The Community Reinvestment Association of North Carolina, The Center for Community Capitalism, Frank Hawkins Kenan Institute of Private Enterprise, and The University of North Carolina at Chapel Hill, *Too Much Month at the End of the Paycheck* (January 2001), p. v, archived at: http://www.ccc.unc.edu/documents/CC_2MuchMonth.PaydayNC.pdf.
13. Gary Rivlin describes these events in *Broke, USA*, pp. 165–167.
14. Quoted in Rivlin, *Broke, USA*, p. 235.
15. The foundation is expert at turning grants into "awards" that give the recipient free PR. The CRL grant was an "Award for Creative and Effective Institutions." From the MacArthur Foundation website, at: http://www.macfound.org/press/from-field/center-responsible-lending -2012-macarthur-award-creative-effective-institutions/.
16. In *The Big Short* (New York: W.W. Norton & Company, 2010), Michael Lewis tells the story of a few individuals who anticipated the housing crisis and got rich as a result. Greg Zuckerman tells the story of Paulson in *The Greatest Trade Ever: The Behind-the-Scenes Story of How John Paulson Defied Wall Street and Made Financial History* (New York: Crown Business, 2010).
17. A *cramdown* refers to a court imposing a reorganization of a financial contract, such as a mortgage, on creditors such as banks. A *clawback* refers to a situation in which money is given and then at least some is taken back, perhaps opportunistically, based on a change of terms or circumstances. In at least some cases, these actions weaken the certainty of lenders that authorities will uphold their contracts.
18. "Statement of Eric Stein, Center for Responsible Lending: Straightening Out the Mortgage Mess: How Can We Protect Home Ownership and Provide Relief to Consumers in Financial Distress—Part 2" (October 30, 2007), at: http://judiciary.house.gov/hearings/printers/110th/38638.PDF.
19. John Murawski, "Advocate for Poor Picked for D.C. Post," *Charlotte News and Observer* (June 30, 2009), at: http://archive.is/3ZaU.

20. Stein identifies himself with both titles in his 2012 testimony to the House Financial Services Committee, online at: http://financialservices.house .gov/uploadedfiles/hhrg-112-ba15-wstate-estein-20120711.pdf. However, he is not identified as such on the CRL website at the time of this writing.

21. "Husband's Suicide Yesterday, Wells Fargo to Evict Wife Tomorrow Anyway," *Mandelman Matters* (May 15, 2012), at: http://mandelman .ml-implode.com/2012/05/husbands-suicide-yesterday-wells-fargo-to -evict-wife-tomorrow-anyway/#.T7HDX8Iw28Y.twitter. The loan, like so many others, ended up being a public relations nightmare for Wells Fargo, which, you'll recall, had bought World Savings from Wachovia in 2008. Many of these loans, made before the Sandlers sold World Savings, didn't reset until after Wells Fargo acquired them.

22. Uriah King, Wei Li, Delvin Davis, and Keith Ernst, "Race Matters: The Concentration of Payday Lenders in African-American Neighborhoods in North Carolina," Research Report for the Center for Responsible Lending (March 22, 2005), at: http://www.responsiblelending.org/north -carolina/nc-payday/research-analysis/racematters/rr006-Race_Matters _Payday_in_NC-0305.pdf.

23. Ozlem Tanik, "Payday Lenders Target the Military: Evidence Lies in Industry's Own Data," *CRL Issue Paper 11* (September 29, 2005).

24. Uriah King, Leslie Parrish, and Ozlem Tanik, "Financial Quicksand: Payday Lending Sinks Borrowers in Debt with $4.2 Billion in Predatory Fees Every Year," Research Report for the Center for Responsible Lending (November 30, 2006), at: http://www.responsiblelending.org /payday-lending/research-analysis/rr012-Financial_Quicksand-1106.pdf. The prejudicial language of this paper is typical for CRL "research."

25. Donald P. Morgan and Michael Strain, "Payday Holiday: How Households Fare After Payday Credit Bans," *Federal Reserve Bank of New York Staff Reports* (revised February 2008), at: http://www.newyorkfed .org/research/staff_reports/sr309.html.

26. Kelly D. Edmiston, "Could Restrictions on Payday Lending Hurt Customers?" *Federal Reserve Bank of Kansas City Economic Review* (First Quarter 2011), p. 64.

27. This is one of the details that was corrected in the *New York Times* story by Michael Moss and Geraldine Fabrikant, "Once Trusted Mortgage Pioneers."

28. "Gramm Says Regulators' Responses Underscore Need for Defining 'Predatory Lending,'" Senate Banking Committee press release (August 24, 2000), at: http://www.banking.senate.gov/prel00/0823pred.htm.

29. In 2007, Donald Morgan of the New York Federal Reserve published an important analysis of the concept of predatory lending, as well as a response to CRL's claim that payday lending is predatory. Donald Morgan, "Defining and Detecting Predatory Lending," *Federal Reserve Bank of New York Staff Reports* no. 273 (January 2007).

30. Arthur Delaney, "Center for Responsible Lending in Fight with Front Group," *Huffington Post* (March 18, 2010), at: http://www.huffingtonpost .com/2009/10/20/center-for-responsible-le_n_327003.html.

31. Thomas Lehman, "In Defense of Payday Lending," *The Free Market* 23, no. 9 (September 2003). The article he references is M.A. Stegman and R. Faris, "Payday Lending: A Business Model That Encourages Chronic Borrowing," *Economic Development Quarterly* 17, no. 1: pp. 8–32. Lehman's main article, published under the auspices of the Coalition for Financial Choice, was "Payday Lending and Public Policy: What Elected Officials Should Know" (August 2006), at: http://www.coalitionforfinancial choice.org/pdf/Payday%20Lending%20Public%20Policy.PDF. See research articles by Lehman and others at the Consumer Credit Research Foundation, at: http://www.creditresearch.org/default.php?id=2.

32. Quoted in John Grady, "Of Wealth and Responsibility" (May 9, 2011), at: http://blog.pallspera.com/2011/05/of-wealth-responsibility/. In *Broke, USA*, his fawning 2010 book on Eakes and other like-minded activists, journalist Gary Rivlin offered the similar explanation that banks decided to get into the subprime business because of the "spread"—the difference between how much it cost them to borrow money and how much they could charge when they lent it out. There was big money in subprime, and so the banks got into the market. Nowhere in his 350-page book does Rivlin ask why, if subprime loans were so lucrative, lenders hadn't been making truckloads of subprime loans for decades. If he pursued that question, he might have figured out what caused the subprime crisis. But then he would have had to write an entirely different book. Rivlin, *Broke, USA*, pp. 153–154.

CHAPTER 7

1. Among the CEOs in attendance were Lloyd Blankfein of Goldman Sachs, Jamie Dimon of JPMorgan Chase, John Mack of Morgan Stanley, Vikram Pandit of Citigroup, and John Thain of Merrill Lynch. Eric Dash, "U.S. Gives Banks Urgent Warning to Solve Crisis," *New York Times* (September 13, 2008), at: http://www.nytimes.com/2008/09/13/business/13rescue .html?_r=1&hp.

2. Ronald D. Orol, "Dimon: We Did Fed 'Favor' to Buy Bear Stearns," *Wall Street Journal MarketWatch* (October 10, 2012), at: http://articles .marketwatch.com/2012-10-10/economy/34356386_1_bear-stearns -morgan-ceo-jamie-dimon-credit-derivatives.

3. Alex Berenson, "Wall St.'s Turmoil Sends Stocks Reeling," *New York Times* (September 15, 2008), at: http://www.nytimes.com/2008/09/16/business /worldbusiness/16markets.html?_r=0.

4. The participants were Richard Kovacevich of Wells Fargo, Vikram Pandit of Citigroup, Jamie Dimon of JPMorgan Chase, John Thain of Merrill Lynch, John Mack of Morgan Stanley, Lloyd Blankfein of Goldman

Sachs, Robert Kelly of the Bank of New York Mellon, and Ronald Logue of State Street Bank.

5. Justin Fox, "Runners-Up: Henry Paulson," *Time* (December 17, 2008), at: http://www.time.com/time/specials/packages/article /0,28804,1861543_1865103_1865105,00.html.

6. "More than 1.2 Million Foreclosure Filings in 2006," *RealtyTrac* (February 8, 2007), at: http://www.realtytrac.com/content/press-releases/more -than-12-million-foreclosure-filings-reported-in-2006-2234.

7. "US Foreclosure Activity Increases 75 Percent in 2007," *RealtyTrac* (January 30, 2008), at: http://www.realtytrac.com/content/press-releases /us-foreclosure-activity-increases-75-percent-in-2007-3604.

8. Adam Michaelson, *The Foreclosure of America: The Inside Story of the Rise and Fall of Countrywide Homes, the Mortgage Crisis, and the Default of the American Dream* (New York: Berkley Books, 2009), p. 136, quoted in Jack Cashill, *Popes and Bankers*, p. 214.

9. Mary Kane, "Quiet Countrywide Bailout Serves as Warning for Congress," *Washington Independent* (February 9, 2009), at: http://washington independent.com/29414/countrywide-indymac.

10. Gretchen Morgenson and Eric Dash, "Bank of America to Buy Countrywide," *New York Times* (January 11, 2008), at: http://www.nytimes .com/2008/01/11/business/worldbusiness/11iht-bofa.3.9157464.html.

11. Eric Dash, "Wells Fargo to Buy Wachovia for $15.1 Billion," *New York Times* (October 3, 2008), at: http://www.nytimes.com/2008/10/03 /business/worldbusiness/03iht-03bank.16664809.html?pagewanted=all.

12. A bond pays a fixed interest rate either at a specific date when it matures or at fixed intervals over a specific amount of time as well as when it matures.

13. Also called *REMIC* (Real Estate Mortgage Investment Conduit). A collateralized mortgage obligation is a type of mortgage-backed security, but the terms are often used synonymously. Collateralized *debt* obligations (CDOs) are related but are not the same thing. If you can memorize these distinctions, you'll really be able to impress people, bore them to tears, or maybe both.

14. I assume this is done to confuse 99 percent of the population, but if you're reading closely, you're now part of the lucky 1 percent.

15. A CDO could even be made up of other CDOs, like the set of all sets in set theory.

16. See, for example, the CNBC documentary, *Goldman Sachs: Power and Peril* (2010), at: http://www.cnbc.com/id/37274104.

17. Ian Wilhelm, "Ford Foundation Links Parents of Obama and Treasury Secretary Nominee," *The Chronicle of Philanthropy* (December 3, 2008), at: http://philanthropy.com/blogs/government-and-politics/ford -foundation-links-parents-of-obamatreasury-secretary-nominee/10851.

18. Ben Protess, "Barney Frank, Financial Overhaul's Defender in Chief," *New York Times* (July 20, 2011), at: http://dealbook.nytimes.com/2011/07/20 /barney-frank-financial-overhauls-defender-in-chief/.

CHAPTER 8

1. See the CFTC document on over-the-counter derivatives at: http://www .cftc.gov/opa/press98/opamntn.htm.

2. See online, at: http://www.pbs.org/wgbh/pages/frontline/money-power -wall-street/#a.

3. "The Warning," *Frontline*, transcript, at: http://www.pbs.org/wgbh/pages /frontline/warning/etc/script.html.

4. Ibid.

5. For example, a year later, at a conference in Jekyll Island, Georgia (where the plans for the Fed were originally dreamed up), Greenspan complained about the problems created by moral hazard and "rampant fraud." "Fraud creates very considerable instability in competitive markets," the former Fed chairman said. "If you cannot trust your counterparties, it would not work." Scott Lanman and Steve Matthews, "US Fed Boss Rejects 'Super-Normal' Inflation," *BusinessDay* (November 8, 2010), at: http://www .bdlive.co.za/articles/2010/11/08/us-fed-boss-rejects-super-normal -inflation.

6. *The Financial Crisis Inquiry Report, Official Government Edition* (Revised February 25, 2011), p. 546, at: http://www.gpo.gov/fdsys/pkg/GPO -FCIC/pdf/GPO-FCIC.pdf.

7. Ibid.

8. "California State Treasurer Angelides' *Green Wave* Initiative" (December 7, 2005), at: http://www.treasurer.ca.gov/greenwave/update.pdf.

9. "Double Bottom Line Investment Initiative: Five Years Later: Delivering on Both Bottom Lines" (October 1, 2005), at: http://www.treasurer .ca.gov/publications/dbl/five_years.pdf.

10. See, for instance, Joe Nation, "Pension Math: How California's Retirement Spending Is Squeezing the State Budget," Stanford Institute for Economic Policy Research (December 13, 2011), at: http://siepr .stanford.edu/system/files/shared/Nation%20Statewide%20Report%20 v081.pdf.

11. *The Financial Crisis Inquiry Report* (January 2011), p. xvii, available at: http://www.gpo.gov/fdsys/pkg/GPO-FCIC/pdf/GPO-FCIC.pdf.

12. Ibid., pp. xviii– xxv.

13. Ibid., p. xviii.

14. Ibid., p. 323.

15. Jeff Madrick, "The Wall Street Leviathan," *New York Review of Books* (April 28, 2011), at: http://www.nybooks.com/articles/archives/2011/apr/28 /wall-street-leviathan/.

16. *The Financial Crisis Inquiry Report*, p. 414.

17. Ibid., p. xviii.

18. They offer a spot-on diagnosis of the symptoms at one point:

In effect, many of the largest financial institutions in the world, along with hundreds of smaller ones, bet the survival of their institutions on housing prices. Some did this knowingly; others not.

Many investors made three bad assumptions about U.S. housing prices. They assumed:

- A low probability that housing prices would decline significantly;
- Prices were largely uncorrelated across different regions, so that a local housing bubble bursting in Nevada would not happen at the same time as one bursting in Florida; and
- A relatively low level of strategic defaults, in which an underwater homeowner voluntarily defaults on a non-recourse mortgage.

When housing prices declined nationally and quite severely in certain areas, these flawed assumptions, magnified by other problems described in previous steps, created enormous financial losses for firms exposed to housing investments.

An essential cause of the financial and economic crisis was appallingly bad risk management by the leaders of some of the largest financial institutions in the United States and Europe. Each failed firm that the Commission examined failed in part because its leaders poorly managed risk.

Ibid., p. 424.

19. A few of these are described in A. Mechele Dickerson, "The Myth of Home Ownership and Why Home Ownership Is Not Always a Good Thing," *Indiana Law Journal* 84, no. 1 (January 1, 2009), pp. 193–194.

20. In fact, charges of Wall Street greed are often a distraction. Obviously, private banks played a role in the crisis, but if those nine bank CEOs came to Washington on October 13, 2008, begging for a bailout from Washington, why did Hank Paulson have to *compel* them to accept the money? Only Dick Fuld at Lehman Brothers had really wanted a bailout, and he was never invited to the party.

21. *The Financial Crisis Inquiry Report*, p. xviii.

22. Peter J. Wallison, *Dissent: The Financial Crisis Inquiry Report, Official Government Edition* (revised February 25, 2011), p. 470.

23. http://www.factcheck.org/2008/10/who-caused-the-economic-crisis/.

24. The details are complicated. For a thorough treatment of the subject, see Peter J. Wallison, "Deregulation and the Financial Crisis: Another Urban Myth," *AEI Financial Services Outlook* (October 2009), at: http://www.aei.org/files/2009/10/31/10-FSO-October-g.pdf.

25. The explanation at FactCheck.org is quite balanced and well informed. Joe Miller and Brooks Jackson, "Who Caused the Financial Crisis?"

FactCheck.org (October 1, 2008), at: http://www.factcheck.org/2008/10/who-caused-the-economic-crisis/.

26. Andrew Ross Sorkin and Vikas Bajaj, "Shift for Goldman and Morgan Marks the End of an Era," *New York Times* (September 21, 2008), at: http://www.nytimes.com/2008/09/22/business/22bank.html?em.

27. There has been a lot of loose talk about the many trillions of dollars of CDSs held by different firms, such as the $2.7 trillion worth of CDSs on AIG's books, or $62 trillion in the total global market, but these are misleading numbers. It's akin to speaking of the $25 trillion of U.S. life insurance policies or $75 trillion of other types of insurance. See George Gilder, *Knowledge and Power* (Washington, DC: Regnery, 2013), Chapter 14.

28. This is because of an accounting rule called "mark-to-market," which some argued made the financial crisis *more severe.*

29. Peter J. Wallison, "Everything You Wanted to Know About Credit Default Swaps—but Were Never Told," *AEI Financial Services Outlook* (December 2008), at: http://www.aei.org/files/2008/12/31/20090107_12DecFSOg.pdf. See also Peter J. Wallison, "Deregulation and the Financial Crisis," *AEI Financial Services Outlook* (October 2009), at: http://www.aei.org/files/2009/10/31/10-FSO-October-g.pdf.

30. Robert O'Harrow Jr. and Brady Dennis, "Downgrades and Downfall," *Washington Post* (December 31, 2008), at: http://www.washingtonpost.com/wp-dyn/content/article/2008/12/30/AR2008123003431.html.

31. Of course, the majority preferred to use sweeping and vague terms such as "shadow banking."

32. Chris Arnold, "Forcing Banks to Put More 'Skin in the Game,'" National Public Radio (June 18, 2009), at: http://www.npr.org/templates/story/story.php?storyId=105558991.

33. *Financial Crisis Inquiry Report*, p. xxv.

34. Of course, a smaller percentage of a CDO would get the highest rating, compared to the CDO or mortgage-backed securities from which it is built. That is, if 95 percent of the collateral mortgage-backed securities received AAA to A ratings, only 90 percent of the CDO made up of the mezzanine tranches of underlying mortgage-backed securities might get the top ratings. In theory and in practice, this sort of thing could be done again and again, with a smaller percentage of each new derivative CDO containing top ratings. If this doesn't make sense, see the diagram "When Is AAA Not a AAA?" *Global Financial Stability Report: Containing Systemic Risks and Restoring Financial Soundness*, International Monetary Fund (April 2008), pp. 59–62, at: http://www.imf.org/External/Pubs/FT/GFSR/2008/01/pdf/text.pdf.

35. John Allison, the former CEO of BB&T Bank, discusses this in *The Financial Crisis and the Free Market Cure: Why Pure Capitalism Is the World Economy's Only Hope* (New York: McGraw-Hill, 2013), pp. 83–84.

36. As Michael Lewis puts it in *The Big Short: Inside the Doomsday Machine* (New York: W.W. Norton, 2011), p. 73.

37. The video short "I, Smartphone" illustrates this point nicely. Check it out at: http://www.youtube.com/watch?v=V1Ze_wpS_o0.

38. Peter J. Wallison, *Dissent: The Financial Crisis Inquiry Report, Official Government Edition* (revised February 25, 2011), p. 2.

CHAPTER 9

1. Quoted in *Social Benefits of Homeownership and Stable Housing*, by the National Association of Realtors (January 2006). The document is no longer on the NAR website, but it is online at: http://www.randytempleman .com/files/370198/Social%20Benefits%20of%20Stable%20Housing.pdf.

2. Robert Stowe England, *Black Box Casino: How Wall Street's Risky Shadow Banking Crashed Global Finance* (Westport, CN: Praeger, 2011), p. 42.

3. Peter Wallison, in his *Dissent: The Financial Crisis Inquiry Report, Official Government Edition* (revised February 25, 2011), p. 453, at: http://www .gpo.gov/fdsys/pkg/GPO-FCIC/pdf/GPO-FCIC.pdf.

4. John Allison, *The Financial Crisis and the Free Market Cure: Why Pure Capitalism Is the World Economy's Only Hope* (New York: McGraw-Hill, 2013), p. 58.

5. See Table 10 in Wallison, *Dissent*, p. 510.

6. Ibid., p., 73.

7. Quoted in Wallison, *Dissent*, p. 514. The quote is from Fannie Mae's 2006 10-K, p. 146.

8. Gretchen Morgenson and Joshua Rosner, *Reckless Endangerment: How Outsized Greed, Ambition, and Corruption Created the Worst Financial Crisis of Our Time* (New York: Times Press, 2011), p. 3.

9. Wallison, *Dissent*, p. 454.

10. Ibid., pp. 454–455.

11. Peter Wallison, "The True Story of the Financial Crisis," *American Spectator* (May 2011), at: http://spectator.org/archives/2011/05/13/the -true-story-of-the-financia.

12. Of course, some people have down payments because of financial gifts or inherited wealth. But banks treat this money differently than down payments from earned savings, since it reflects less on a homebuyer's financial habits.

13. In some urban areas, land use restrictions increased prices even above the surge created by federal policies. In other words, local, state, and federal policies conspired to create a housing bubble.

14. See John B. Taylor, "Monetary Policy and the Next Crisis," *Wall Street Journal* (July 4, 2012), at: http://online.wsj.com/article/SB100014240527 023042118045775011903492448440.html.

15. Ibid.

16. Wallison, *Dissent*, p. 456.

17. Pinto originally estimated that there were 25 million nontraditional mortgages in the system. He later revised the number up to 27 million. See Edward Pinto, "Triggers of the Financial Crisis" (March 15, 2010, revised and updated), at: http://www.aei.org/files/2010/03/15 /PintoFCICTriggers.pdf; and Edward Pinto, "Government Housing Policies in the Lead-up to the Financial Crisis: A Forensic Study" (which was updated February 11, 2011), at: http://www.aei.org/files/2011/02/05 /Pinto-Government-Housing-Policies-in-the-Lead-up-to-the-Financial -Crisis-Word-2003-2.5.11.pdf.

18. Strictly speaking, Wallison showed in his dissent that government housing policy was the crisis's necessary condition: "*but for* the government's housing policy, there wouldn't have been a financial crisis." Wallison puts the point this way in an interview with Anthony Randazzo, "The Financial Crisis Was the Result of Government Housing Policy," *Reason* (June 2012), at: http://reason.com/archives/2012/05/17/the-financial-crisis -was-the-result-of-g.

19. From a private interview, October 2, 2012.

20. See John B. Taylor, "How Government Created the Financial Crisis," *Wall Street Journal* (February 9, 2009), at: http://online.wsj.com/article /SB123414310280561945.html.

21. "Too big to fail" refers to the idea that some institutions are so integral to the national or international financial system that they cannot be allowed to go bankrupt. The problem with the policy, obviously, is that any company that suspects it is too big to fail will also suspect that, if it gets into financial trouble, the government will bail it out. So the policy actually *encourages* risky behavior, since a company will enjoy the benefits of good decisions but won't directly suffer the consequences of bad decisions. Nicole Gelinas describes this aspect of the crisis in *After the Fall: Saving Capitalism from Wall Street and Washington* (New York: Encounter Books, 2009). For a short article by Gelinas summarizing the details, see Nicole Gelinas, "'Too Big to Fail' Must Die," *City Journal* 19, no. 3 (Summer 2009), at: http://www .city-journal.org/2009/19_3_financial-institutions.html.

22. David Skeel argues, on the basis of solid empirical evidence, that if Bear Stearns had been handled like a normal bankruptcy rather than a bailout, subsequent events might have been quite different. In *The New Financial Deal: Understanding the Dodd-Frank Act and Its (Unintended) Consequences* (New York: John Wiley & Sons, 2011).

23. The obvious exception was the investment bank Lehman Brothers, which had to declare bankruptcy.

24. Thanks to my colleague Eric Garcia for suggesting an example something like this.

25. Peruvian economist Hernando de Soto refers to this as the "destruction of economics facts" in his interpretation of the financial crisis. See Hernando de Soto, "The Destruction of Economic Facts," *Bloomberg*

Businessweek (April 28, 2011), at: http://www.businessweek.com/magazine/content/11_19/b4227060634112.htm.

26. See it online, with additional resources and interviews, at: http://www.pbs.org/wgbh/pages/frontline/meltdown/.

27. Andrew Ross Sorkin, *Too Big to Fail* (New York: Viking, 2009). Sorkin does discuss the role of Fannie Mae and Freddie Mac in more detail in his book, but key players, such as Fannie Mae CEO Franklin Raines, play no role in the drama.

28. Joe Nocera, "Inquiry Is Missing Bottom Line," *New York Times* (January 28, 2011), at: http://www.nytimes.com/2011/01/29/business/29nocera.html.

29. Bethany McLean and Joe Nocera, *All the Devils Are Here: The Hidden History of the Financial Crisis* (New York: Portfolio/Penguin, 2010).

30. David Min, "Faulty Conclusions Based on Shoddy Foundations" (Center for American Progress, February 2011), at: http://www.americanprogress.org/wp-content/uploads/issues/2011/02/pdf/pinto.pdf.

31. Peter Wallison (Joseph Lawler, ed.), "The True Story of the Financial Crisis—Responding to Criticism," *The Spectacle Blog*, May 24, 2011, at: http://spectator.org/blog/2011/05/24/the-true-story-of-the-financia#commentcontainer.

32. Asam Ahmed and Ben Protess, "S.E.C. Accuses Former Chiefs of Freddie and Fannie of Deception," *New York Times* (December 16, 2011), at: http://dealbook.nytimes.com/2011/12/16/s-e-c-sues-6-former-top-fannie-and-freddie-executives/.

33. Joe Nocera, "An Inconvenient Truth," *New York Times* (December 19, 2011), at: http://www.nytimes.com/2011/12/20/opinion/nocera-an-inconvenient-truth.html?ref=opinion.

34. The quote is from the news story to which Nocera was responding. Ahmed and Protess, "S.E.C. Accuses Former Chiefs of Freddie and Fannie of Deception."

35. Peter J. Wallison, "Where No Mortgage News Is Fit to Print," *The American* (December 20, 2011), at: http://www.american.com/archive/2011/december/where-no-mortgage-news-is-fit-to-print/. Wallison also discussed the SEC complaint in "The Financial Crisis on Trial," *Wall Street Journal* (December 2011), at: http://online.wsj.com/article/SB10001424052970204791104577108183677635076.html.

36. Peter J. Wallison and Edward Pinto, "Why the Left Is Losing the Debate over the Financial Crisis," *The American* (December 27, 2011), at: http://www.american.com/archive/2011/december/why-the-left-is-losing-the-argument-over-the-financial-crisis.

37. Wallison, "The True Story of the Financial Crisis."

38. Dan Murphy, "Obama's November Surprise," *National Review Online* (October 4, 2012), at: http://www.nationalreview.com/articles/329370/obama-s-november-surprise-dan-murphy.

39. Ibid.

CHAPTER 10

1. For a general presentation of the organizational structure of the government agencies Dodd-Frank mandated, see "Too Big Not to Fail," *The Economist* (February 18, 2012), at: http://www.economist.com /node/21547784.

2. Stephen Labaton, "New Agency Proposed to Oversee Fannie Mae and Freddie Mac," *New York Times* (September 11, 2003), at: http://www .nytimes.com/2003/09/11/business/new-agency-proposed-to-oversee -freddie-mac-and-fannie-mae.html.

3. Terry Ponick, "Barney Frank Flees the Scene of His Fiscal Crimes," *Washington Times* (November 29, 2011), at: http://communities. washingtontimes.com/neighborhood/prudent-man/2011/nov/29/barney -frank-flees-scene-his-fiscal-crimes/.

4. Bill Sammon, "Lawmaker Accused of Fannie Mae Conflict of Interest," FoxNews.com (October 3, 2008), at: http://www.foxnews.com /story/0,2933,432501,00.html.

5. For instance, "Top Ten Barney Frank Offenses," *Human Events* (December 3, 2011), at: http://www.humanevents.com/2011/12/03/top-10-barney -frank-offenses-2/.

6. Ross Kaminsky, "Democratic Coverup for Fannie and Freddie Led to 2008 Meltdown," *Human Events* (September 30, 2008), at: http://www .humanevents.com/2008/09/30/democratic-coverup-for-fannie-and -freddie-led-to-2008-meltdown/.

7. Larry Margasak, "Countrywide Financial Corporation Won Influence with Discount Loans," Associated Press (July 5, 2012). The SEC made Mozilo pay a $22.5 million penalty in 2010 for misleading investors and another $45 million for similar infractions.

8. Quoted in Ronald D. Orol, "Dodd Retirement May Help Pass Bank Reform: Analysts," *Wall Street Journal Market Watch* (January 6, 2010), at: http://articles.marketwatch.com/2010-01-06/economy/30796536_1 _dodd-retirement-bank-reform-connecticut-senator.

9. See the complete list at the FSOC website, at: http://www.treasury.gov /initiatives/fsoc/about/council/Pages/default.aspx.

10. As Peter Wallison argues in "Dodd-Frank's Threat to Financial Stability," *Wall Street Journal* (March 25, 2011), at: http://professional .wsj.com/article/SB10001424052748703858404576214193957527406 .html?mg=reno64-wsj.

11. The criteria for being designated a SIFI include size; lack of adequate substitutes in the market; the interconnectedness of a firm with other firms; risk factors such as leverage, liquidity risk, and maturity mismatch; and the existing regulatory framework for the company. See "Authority to Require Supervision and Regulation of Certain Nonbank Financial Companies," *Federal Register* (April 11, 2012), at: https://www.federalregister.gov

/articles/2012/04/11/2012-8627/authority-to-require-supervision-and
-regulation-of-certain-nonbank-financial-companies.

12. The banks on the G20 list are Bank of America, Bank of New York Mellon,
Citigroup, Goldman Sachs, JPMorgan, Morgan Stanley, State Street, and
Wells Fargo. The G20 charged its own Financial Stability Board (FSB)
to designate certain banks outside the United States as G-SIFIs (global
systemically important financial institutions). Twenty-nine banks are now
on the elite list, 17 in Europe, 8 in the United States, 3 in Japan, and 1 in
China. The FSB was set up as a part of the Third Basel Accord, often called
Basel III. See the complete list at "FSB Publishes List of Systemically
Important Banks," *Wall Street Journal Market Watch* (November 4, 2011),
at: http://www.marketwatch.com/story/fsb-publishes-list-of-systemically
-important-banks-2011-11-04.

13. This list is from Peter Wallison, "The Election and Dodd-Frank,"
National Review Online (October 8, 2012), at: http://www.nationalreview
.com/articles/329626/election-and-dodd-frank-peter-j-wallison.

14. There were a few good things in the reform package, such as requiring government sponsored enterprises to keep more capital in reserves.
Unfortunately, the reform doesn't solve the big problem—political manip-
ulation of the mortgage market. See Kevin Williamson, "Fannie Times
Five," *National Review* (May 13, 2011), at: http://www.nationalreview.com
/exchequer/267124/fannie-times-five.

15. C. Boyden Gray and Adam J. White, "The Biggest Kiss," *Weekly Standard*
18, no. 7 (October 29, 2012), at: https://www.weeklystandard.com/articles
/biggest-kiss_655091.html.

16. David Skeel, *The New Financial Deal: Understanding the Dodd-Frank Act and
Its (Unintended) Consequences* (New York: John Wiley & Sons, 2010).

17. See "Scenes from a Nationalization" on the *Free Exchange* blog at *The
Economist* (April 8, 2009), at: http://www.economist.com/blogs/free
exchange/2009/04/scenes_from_a_nationalisation.

18. "Sens. Sherrod, David Vitter Press Fed Chairman Bernanke on
Capital Standards" (August 7, 2012), at: http://www.brown.senate.gov
/newsroom/press/release/sens-sherrod-brown-david-vitter-press-fed
-chairman-bernanke-on-capital-standards-.

19. Ammon Simon, "Dodd-Frank in the News," *National Review Online*
(October 11, 2012), at: http://www.nationalreview.com/bench-memos
/330085/dodd-frank-news-ammon-simon.

20. Peter Wallison, "Dodd-Frank's Threat to Financial Stability," *Wall Street
Journal* (March 25, 2011), at: http://professional.wsj.com/article/SB1000
14240527487038584045762141939575227406.html?mg=reno64-wsj.

21. Wallison, "The Election and Dodd-Frank."

22. The numbers and the quote are from the "Dodd-Frank Burden Tracker"
maintained by the U.S. House Financial Services Committee, at: http://
financialservices.house.gov/burdentracker/.

23. Peter Wallison, "Dodd-Frank's Too-Big-To-Fail Dystopia," *Wall Street Journal* (May 23, 2012), at: http://professional.wsj.com/article/SB10001 424052702303610504577420234053483326.html?mg=reno64-wsj.

24. The FHFA was created as a merger of some older agencies in the Federal Housing Finance Regulatory Reform Act of 2008, which was part of the Housing and Economic Recovery Act of 2008. President George W. Bush signed the bill on July 30, 2008. Less than two months later, Fannie Mae and Freddie Mac were put under the "conservatorship" of the FHFA.

25. Jim Millstein and Phillip Swagel, "It's Time to End the Bailout of Fannie and Freddie: Here's How," *Washington Post* (October 12, 2012), at: http://www.washingtonpost.com/opinions/its-time-to-end-government -control-of-fannie-and-freddie-heres-how/2012/10/12/49f7d9a2-123d -11e2-a16b-2c110031514a_story.html.

26. Quoted by Representative Spencer Bachus, "Protecting Taxpayers by Ending Bailouts" (May 31, 2012), at: http://financialservices.house.gov /news/documentsingle.aspx?DocumentID=297809.

27. In one funny episode, *Politico* discovered a 1997 article in the *Fordham University Law Review* with the stereotypically postmodern language so fashionable at the time, "Intersectionality and positionality: Situating women of color in the affirmative action dialogue." The author, Laura Padilla, told *Politico* that her source for the claim came from a phone conversation she had with then–Harvard Law spokesman, Mike Chmura. Maggie Haberman, "Fordham Piece Called Warren Harvard Law's 'First Woman of Color,'" *Politico* (May 15, 2012), at: http://www.politico.com /blogs/burns-haberman/2012/05/fordham-piece-called-warren-harvard -laws-first-woman-123526.html.

28. Jeffrey Toobin, "The Professor," *New Yorker* (September 17, 2012).

29. Elizabeth Warren, "Unsafe at Any Rate," *Democracy* 5 (summer 2007). She wrote a more technical article later, but the original article is more widely referenced.

30. Warren clearly wanted the agency to be outside of Congress's jurisdiction. She summarizes her proposal in one long paragraph:

> A commission would be able to collect data about which financial products are least understood, what kinds of disclosures are most effective, and which products are most likely to result in consumer default. Free of legislative micromanaging, it could develop nuanced regulatory responses; some terms might be banned altogether, while others might be permitted only with clearer disclosure. A Commission might promote uniform disclosures that make it easier to compare products from one issuer to another, and to discern conflicts of interest on the part of a mortgage broker or seller of a currently loosely regulated financial product. In the area of credit card regulation, for example,

an FPSC might want to review the following terms that appear in some—but not all—credit card agreements: universal clauses; unlimited and unexplained fees; interest rate increases that exceed 10 percentage points; and an issuer's claim that it can change the terms of cards after money has been borrowed. It would also promote such market-enhancing practices as a simple, easy-to-read paragraph that explains all interest charges; clear explanations of when fees will be imposed; a requirement that the terms of a credit card remain the same until the card expires; no marketing targeted at college students or people under age 21; and a statement showing how long it will take to pay off the balance, as well as how much interest will be paid if the customer makes the minimum monthly payments on the outstanding balance on a credit card.

31. In 2012, the MacArthur Foundation (again) gave the Center for Responsible Lending an award. The foundation's press release for the award, "Defending American Consumers" (February 16, 2012), credited CRL with anticipating the subprime mortgage crisis and contributing to the passage of Dodd-Frank. It also explicitly connected their award to CRL with the formation of the Consumer Financial Protection Bureau. At: http://www.macfound.org/press/from-field/center-responsible-lending-2012-macarthur-award-creative-effective-institutions/.

32. Michael Patrick Leahy, "Harvard Knew Elizabeth Warren Was a Poor Scholar When It Hired Her," *Breitbart* (August 6, 2012), at: http://www.breitbart.com/Big-Government/2012/08/04/Did-Harvard-Know-Of-and-Fully-Investigate-Elizabeth-Warren-Scientific-Misconduct-Charges-on-Hiring.

33. Ibid.

34. See Michael Patrick Leahy, "The Academic Scandal Elizabeth Warren and Harvard Don't Want You to Know About," *Breitbart* (June 11, 2012), at: http://www.breitbart.com/Big-Government/2012/06/11/The-Academic-Scandal-Elizabeth-Warren-and-Harvard-Dont-Want-You-to-Know-About.

35. The original charge came from a lengthy piece by Cornell Law professor William A. Jacobson, "Elizabeth Warren's Law License Problem," *Legal Insurrection* blog (September 24, 2012), at: http://legalinsurrection.com/2012/09/elizabeth-warrens-law-license-problem/.

36. Noah Bierman, "Elizabeth Warren Was Key in Asbestos Case," *Boston Globe* (May 1, 2012), at: http://www.bostonglobe.com/metro/2012/04/30/elizabeth-warren-had-key-role-travelers-asbestos-case-before-supreme-court/yf2idVzvhK6jhzV2isAvnL/story.html.

37. Toobin recounts the conversation between Frank and Obama in "The Professor."

38. "Fed Agency's All Grown Up," *Boston Herald* (October 12, 2012).

39. Stephan Richter, "President Elizabeth Warren: An Angela Merkel in the Making?" *Globalist* (December 11, 2012), at: http://www.theglobalist.com /StoryId.aspx?StoryId=9837.

40. "The Card Game," *Frontline*, at: http://www.pbs.org/wgbh/pages /frontline/creditcards/etc/script.html.

41. Jim Puzzanghera, "GOP Stalls Confirmation of Consumer Agency Nominee," *Los Angeles Times* (September 7, 2011), at: http://articles .latimes.com/2011/sep/07/business/la-fi-consumer-bureau-cordray -20110907.

42. "Improving Americans' Financial Security: The Importance of a CFPB Director" (The White House Press Office, December 2011), at: http:// www.whitehouse.gov/sites/default/files/cfpb_-_master_final_120411.pdf.

43. This authority is provided in Sec. 1031 of Dodd-Frank, entitled "Prohibiting Unfair, Deceptive, or Abusive Acts of Practices." See discussion in Michael S. Greve, "Kill Dodd-Frank, and Save the Constitution (I)," *Library of Law and Liberty* (October 5, 2012), at: http://libertylawsite .org/2012/10/05/kill-dodd-frank-and-save-the-constitution-i/.

44. Kate Berry, "Mortgage Lenders Brace for CFPB Exams; Fair Lending Is Top Concern," *American Banker* (October 3, 2012), at: http://www .americanbanker.com/issues/177_192/mortgage-lenders-brace-for-cfpb -exams-1053223-1.html?ET=americanbanker:e12586:2352326a:&st =email&utm_source=editorial&utm_medium=email&utm _campaign=AB_Washington_Regulatory_100412.

45. Les Christie, "New Rules Aim to Make Mortgages Safer," *CNNMoney* (January 10, 2013), at: http://money.cnn.com/2013/01/10/real_estate /qualified-mortgages-cfpb/index.html.

46. See, for instance, Chapter 16 of Dennis C. Miller, *Public Choice III* (Cambridge, UK: Cambridge University Press, 2003).

47. It doesn't follow that no bureaucracies should exist, just that politicians, activists, and voters rarely anticipate the bad and often counterproductive effects of creating new ones and rarely set things up to avoid perverse incentives. That's true even when a bureaucracy is created to try to fix a real problem.

48. Once a new bureaucracy is created, even its opponents assume it is here to stay. See, for instance, Barbara Rehm, "It's Time for Bankers to Make Peace with Dodd-Frank," *American Banker* (November 14, 2012) at: http://www.americanbanker.com/issues/177_220/its-time-for -bankers-to-make-peace-with-dodd-frank-1054356-1.html?ET =americanbanker:e13083:2352326a:&st=email&utm_source=editorial &utm_medium=email&utm_campaign=AB_Intraday_111412.

49. Joel Gehrke, "Report: CFPB Stifles 150,000 Jobs after Controversial 'Recess' Appointment," *Washington Examiner* (December 14, 2012), at: http://washingtonexaminer.com/report-cfpb-stifles-150000-jobs-after -controversial-recess-appointment/article/2515968#.UMuQUbYh0ik.

The report is "The Consumer Financial Protection Bureau's Threat to Credit Access in the United States," Staff Report, U.S. House of Representatives 112th Congress (December 14, 2012), at: http://oversight.house.gov/wp-content/uploads/2012/12/Access-to-Credit-Report-12.14.12.pdf.

CHAPTER 11

1. John Koppisch, "Montana Voters Approve Interest-Rate Cap on Small Loans," *Forbes* (November 3, 2010), at: http://www.forbes.com/sites/johnkoppisch/2010/11/03/montana-voters-approve-interest-rate-cap-on-small-loans/.

2. Read about the Advisory Committee at the FDIC website: http://www.fdic.gov/about/comein/. The origin of the committee is described in this way:

> The Advisory Committee on Economic Inclusion (ComE-IN) was established by Chairman Sheila C. Bair and the FDIC Board of Directors pursuant to the Federal Advisory Committee Act. The Committee was chartered in November 2006. The Committee is to provide the FDIC with advice and recommendations on important initiatives focused on expanding access to banking services by underserved populations. This may include reviewing basic retail financial services such as check cashing, money orders, remittances, stored value cards, short-term loans, savings accounts, and other services that promote asset accumulation by individuals and financial stability.

3. Jason Hancock, "Battle Looming Over Missouri Payday Loan Restrictions," *St. Louis Times-Dispatch* (November 25, 2011), at: http://www.stltoday.com/news/local/govt-and-politics/battle-looming-over-missouri-payday-loan-restrictions/article_e4db6fa6-c220-5837-805f-609d92212cd5.html. Although the Missouri campaign was organized and sponsored by the state affiliate of the Center for Responsible Lending, it was endorsed by some 44 groups:

- AARP Missouri
- American Association of University Women—Missouri
- American Federation of State, County, and Municipal Employees, Council 72
- Beyond Housing
- Catholic Charities of Central and Northern Missouri
- Church Women United in Missouri, Inc.
- Communities Creating Opportunity
- Consumers Council of Missouri
- Department of Human Rights, Diocese of Kansas City—St. Joseph

- Goodwill—Eastern Kansas and Western Missouri
- GRO—Grass Roots Organizing
- Ivanhoe Neighborhood Association
- Jewish Community Relations Council
- Jobs with Justice
- LIUNA Local 53
- M-SLICE
- Metro St. Louis Coalition for Inclusion and Equity
- Metropolitan Congregations United
- Missouri Alliance for Retired Americans Education Fund
- Missouri Alliance of Retired Americans
- Missouri Association of Social Welfare
- Missouri Faith Voices
- Missouri Immigrant and Refugee Advocates
- Missouri Rural Crisis Center
- National Alliance for the Mentally Ill Missouri
- National Association for the Advancement of Colored People
- National Council of Jewish Women—St. Louis
- National Women's Political Caucus—Metro St. Louis
- North County Labor Legislative Committee
- Northland Neighborhoods, Inc.
- Northwest Missouri Policy Network
- Operation Breakthrough
- Progress Missouri
- ProVote
- Rolla Area "Phelps County" NAACP
- Service Employees International Union
- Slough Connealy Irwin & Madden LLC
- Social Witness Action Team 4
- UAW Retirees
- UFCW 88
- United Media Guild
- Utility Workers Union of America Local 335
- Women's Voices Raised for Social Justice
- Women's International League for Peace and Justice

4. For example, see Iris Zhang, "Group Rallies Against Payday Loan Ballot Initiative," KOMU.com (February 8, 2012), at: http://www.komu.com /news/group-rallies-against-payday-loan-ballot-initiative/.

5. Even though minimum wage laws are popular, they are another form of price-fixing. In this case, they build a floor rather than a ceiling for hourly wages. For an explanation of why this is a problem, see James Robison and Jay Richards, *Indivisible: Restoring Faith, Family, and Freedom Before It's Too Late* (New York: FaithWords, 2012), pp. 252–253.

6. In fact, they printed the two ballot initiatives on one piece of paper, with the minimum wage increase on one side and the interest rate cap on the other. When speaking with potential petition signers, they would lead with the wage initiative and then flip the page over to sign for the rate cap initiative.

7. Aileen B. Flores, "El Paso City Council OKs Payday-, Car-Title Loan Rules," *El Paso Times* (January 9, 2013), at: http://www.elpasotimes.com /news/ci_22336426/council-oks-payday-car-title-loan-rules?source =most_emailed.

8. Peter Schroeder, "Consumer Bureau, Chicago Join Forces in Hunt for Predatory Lending," *The Hill* (December 5, 2012), at: http://thehill.com /blogs/on-the-money/banking-financial-institutions/271217-consumer -bureau-chicago-join-forces-in-hunt-for-predatory-lending.

9. Jeff Horwitz, "CFPB Hires Outspoken Critic of MERS and Payday Lending," *American Banker* (May 10, 2012), at: http://www.american banker.com/people/cfpb-MERS-payday-lending-Chris-Peterson-senior -counsel-1049205-1.html.

10. Chris Peterson, "'Warning, Predatory Lender,' A Proposal for Candid Predatory Small Loan Ordinances," *Washington and Lee Law Review* 69, no. 2 (2012), at: http://papers.ssrn.com/sol3/papers.cfm?abstract _id=1971971.

11. "Limitations on Terms of Consumer Credit Extended to Service Members and Dependents; Final Rule" (Department of Defense, Rules and Regulations), 72 Fed. Reg. 169 (August 31, 2007), p. 50583, and 32 C.F.R. 232.

12. See the extremely biased story from Karen Jowers, "Consumer Watch: Legal Installment Loans Can Still Rip You Off," *Army Times* (August 3, 2009), at: http://www.armytimes.com/money/financial_advice/offduty _consumerwatch_073109w/.

13. Government Accountability Office, *Military Personnel: DOD's Predatory Lending Report Addressed Mandated Issues, but Support Is Limited for Some Findings and Recommendations*, GAO-07-1148R (August 31, 2007).

14. Military service members often borrow before they deploy in order to get their households in order and have emergency cash on hand for their spouses and families. Because of permanent change-of-station moves, overseas assignments, and relocations, service members often say that they need funds in addition to what the military provides for moving costs, security deposits, and new appliances.

15. Elizabeth Warren, "Welcoming Holly Petraeus to the Consumer Financial Protection Bureau Implementation Team," *The White House* (blog, January 6, 2011), at: http://www.whitehouse.gov/blog/2011/01/06 /welcoming-holly-petraeus-consumer-financial-protection-bureau -implementation-team.

16. For example, "Easy Money, Impossible Debt: How Predatory Lending Traps Alabama's Poor," Southern Poverty Law Center (February 2013),

at: http://www.splcenter.org/sites/default/files/downloads/publication
/Payday_Lending_Report_web.pdf.

17. Center for Financial Services Innovation, "The CFSI Underbanked
Consumer Study: Underbanked Consumer Overseas and Market
Segments Fact Sheet" (June 8, 2008), at: http://www.cfsinnovation.com
/system/files/underbankedconsumerstudy_factsheet.pdf.

18. See discussion and references to academic studies in Thomas Lehman,
"Payday Lending and Public Policy: What Elected Officials Should
Know" (August 2006).

19. At: http://www.nationaldayofaction.org/. Progressive Christian magazine
Sojourners covered the campaign. See, for example, Elaina Ramsey, "Faith
Groups Take on Payday Lenders," *Sojourners* (January 2013), at: http://
sojo.net/magazine/2013/01/faith-groups-take-payday-lenders.

20. At: http://www.responsiblelending.org/allies/.

21. *Modern Day Usury: The Payday Loan Trap* (Center for Responsible
Lending, November 2010), at: http://www.responsiblelending.org/allies
/faith-and-credit/Modern-Day-Usury-The-Payday-Loan-Trap.pdf.

22. "Improving Americans' Financial Security: The Importance of a CFPB
Director" (The White House Press Office: December 2011), at: http://
www.whitehouse.gov/sites/default/files/cfpb_-_master_final_120411.pdf.

23. These numbers are not precise, of course, just illustrative.

24. This quote is from an interview with Black on Carolina Journal Radio on
June 10, 2011, at: http://www.carolinajournal.com/articles/display_story
.html?id=7862.

25. Donald P. Morgan, of the Federal Reserve Bank of New York, and Michael
Strain wrote a seminal critique of the Center for Responsible Lending's
sloppy use of "predatory" when it comes to payday lending. "Payday
Holiday: How Households Fare After Payday Credit Bans," *Federal
Reserve Bank of New York Staff Report No. 309* (February 1, 2008). One
part of the paper shows the effects of competition on payday lending.
Unfortunately, the authors had only a small sample size available, so more
research is needed to confirm what economic reasoning suggests—namely,
that competition among payday lenders lowers prices and improves service
for borrowers. "Using a small set of data," they argue, "we find that payday
loan rates and fees decline significantly as the number of payday lenders
and pawnshops increase. Despite their alleged naïveté, payday borrowers appear sophisticated enough to shop for lower prices. The problem
of high prices may reflect too few payday lenders rather than too many. If
scrutiny and prosecution risk limit entry into payday lending, the lack of
competition may drive rates higher. In the end, the simple fact that payday lenders have triumphed over pawnshops suggests that payday lending
raises household welfare by providing a preferable alternative."

26. Uriah King, Leslie Parrish, and Ozlem Tanik, *Financial Quicksand: Payday
Lending Sinks Borrowers in Debt with $4.2 Billion in Predatory Fees Every Year*

(Center for Responsible Lending, November 30, 2006), at: http://www
.responsiblelending.org/payday-lending/research-analysis/rr012exec
-Financial_Quicksand-1106.pdf.

27. Thomas Sowell, "Profits Without Honor," *Townhall.com* (December 23,
2003). I've used Sowell's title in the title of this section.

28. See, for instance, CRL's discussion of payday lending at: http://www
.responsiblelending.org/payday-lending/research-analysis/index
.jsp?page=2.

29. Carolina Journal Staff, "Consumer Loan Industry Explored," *Carolina
Journal Online* (June 10, 2011), at: http://www.carolinajournal.com
/exclusives/display_exclusive.html?id=7862.

30. As an aside, there is a way to lower cab fares in the Big Apple, but it would
require the mayor and the New York City government to break with the
culture of hyperregulation that has characterized the city's politics for
decades and allow real competition. Although cab companies are privately
owned in New York City, they are so regulated that they end up functioning much like a government monopoly from the perspective of customers.
Even without much competition, a cab is still better for getting across
town than is a commercial airliner. For details, see Samuel R. Staley, "Taxi
Regulation and the Failures of Progressivism," *The Freeman* (January 4,
2012), at: http://www.fee.org/the_freeman/detail/taxi-regulation-and
-the-failures-of-progressivism#axzz2HnpVc6PK.

31. Myke Folger, "Treating Them Right: The Golden Rule Stands as
MoneyTree's Core Principle," *Seattle Business Magazine* (July 2009), at:
http://www.seattlebusinessmag.com/article/treating-them-right; Myke
Folger, "Listening to MoneyTree: 2010's Hall of Fame Winner Has
Consistently Shown That Making Communication with Employees a
Priority Reaps Rewards," *Seattle Business Magazine* (July 2010), at: http://
seattlebusinessmag.com/article/listening-moneytree; and Sheila Bacon
Cain and Nick Horton, "Nice Work! Seattle Business Magazine's 100 Best
Companies to Work For," *Seattle Business Magazine* (July 2011), at: http://
seattlebusinessmag.com/article/nice-work.

CHAPTER 12

1. The Fair Debt Collection Practices Act is available online, at: http://www
.ftc.gov/os/statutes/fdcpa/fdcpact.shtm.

2. For a study of how the United States is beginning to resemble Europe,
see Samuel Gregg, *Becoming Europe: Economic Decline, Culture, and How
America Can Avoid a European Future* (New York: Encounter, 2013).

3. If a radio wave weren't the same on both the transmitting and receiving ends, it would be impossible to modulate the wave to encode it with
information.

4. Quoted on the CFPB webpage, "Advisory Groups," at: http://www
.consumerfinance.gov/advisory-groups/.

CONCLUSION

1. Full disclosure: I was the executive director. Available at: http://www
.calloftheentrepreneur.com/. The documentary first aired on PBS and
then later on Fox Business Channel, and has been translated into several
languages.

2. Sheila Bair, *Bull by the Horns: Fighting to Save Main Street from Wall Street
and Wall Street from Itself* (New York: Free Press, 2012), pp. 347–348.

3. See the suggestions in Jim Millstein and Phillip Swagel, "It's Time to End
the Bailout of Fannie and Freddie: Here's How," *Washington Post* (October
12, 2012), at: http://www.washingtonpost.com/opinions/its-time-to-end
-government-control-of-fannie-and-freddie-heres-how/2012/10/12/49f7
d9a2-123d-11e2-a16b-2c110031514a_story.html.

4. Iain Murray, "Dodd-Frank's Mystery SIFI Theater," *The American
Spectator* (October 29, 2012), at: http://spectator.org/archives/2012/10/29
/dodd-franks-mystery-sifi-theat.

5. Tom Schoenberg and Carter Dougherty, "Oklahoma, South Carolina,
Michigan Join Dodd-Frank Attack," *Bloomberg Businessweek* (September
21, 2012), at: http://www.businessweek.com/news/2012-09-20/oklahoma
-south-carolina-michigan-join-dodd-frank-attack.

6. For details, see Michael Greve, "Kill Dodd-Frank, and Save the
Constitution (I)," Library of Law and Liberty (October 5, 2012), at:
http://www.libertylawsite.org/2012/10/05/kill-dodd-frank-and-save-the
-constitution-i/.

7. Robert Barnes and Steven Mufson, "Court Says Obama Exceeded
Authority in Making Appointments," *Washington Post* (January 25, 2013),
at: http://articles.washingtonpost.com/2013-01-25/politics/36541588_1
_recess-appointments-richard-cordray-president-obama.

8. Michael S. Greve, "Kill Dodd-Frank (II)," Library of Law and Liberty
(October 6, 2012), at: http://www.libertylawsite.org/2012/10/06/kill
-dodd-frank-ii/. The suit is known to lawyers as *Schechter Poultry Corp. v.
United States*.

9. The classic treatment of this subject is Charles Murray, *Losing Ground:
American Social Policy: 1950–1980*, tenth anniversary edition (New York:
Basic Books, 1994). See also his recent book *Coming Apart: The State of
White America, 1950–2010* (New York: Crown Forum, reprint, 2013).

10. Danielle Kurtzleben, "National Debt Interest Payments Dwarf Other
Government Spending," *U.S. News and World Report* (November 19,
2012), at: http://www.usnews.com/news/articles/2012/11/19/how-the
-nations-interest-spending-stacks-up.

11. John Kitchen and Menzie David Chinn, "Financing U.S. Debt: Is There
Enough Money in the World—and at What Cost?" La Follette School of
Public Affairs Working Paper No. 2010-015 (August 12, 2010), at: http://
ssrn.com/abstract=1658543.

12. If you like the feeling of heart palpitations, you can watch U.S. debt grow in real time, at: http://www.usdebtclock.org/.

13. Jeff Cox, "Bill Gross: US Addicted to 'Budgetary Crystal Meth,'" CNBC (October 2, 2012), at: http://finance.yahoo.com/news/bill-gross-us -addicted-budgetary-145551532.html.

14. These estimates seem to get worse over time. This number is from summer 2011. Dennis Cauchon, "Government's Mountain of Debt," *USA Today* (June 7, 2011), at: http://www.usatoday.com/news/washington/2011-06 -06-us-debt-chart-medicare-social-security_n.htm.

15. Chris Cox and Bill Archer, "Why $16 Trillion Only Hints at the True U.S. Debt," *Wall Street Journal* (November 26, 2012), at: http://professional .wsj.com/article/SB10001424127887323353204578127374039087636 .html.

16. See John Hinderaker, "The National Debt, in One Chart," *Power Line* (blog, October 7, 2012), at: http://www.powerlineblog.com/archives /2012/10/the-national-debt-in-one-chart.php.

17. *Mandatory* spending came to $2.194 trillion in 2011, while total federal receipts from taxes were $2.174 trillion. From an Office of Management and Budget estimate in early 2011. See Jeffrey Anderson, "A Deficit Without Defense," *Weekly Standard* (March 15, 2011), at: http://www.weekly standard.com/blogs/deficit-without-defense_554150.html.

18. Jeffrey Anderson, "Mandatory Spending to Exceed all Federal Revenues—50 Years Ahead of Schedule," *Weekly Standard* (March 16, 2011), at: http://www.weeklystandard.com/blogs/mandatory-spending -exceed-all-federal-revenues-fiscal-year-2011_554659.html.

19. In 2011, the debt equaled the total annual output of our economy. Stephen Dinan, "Federal Deficit on Track for a Record This Fiscal Year: Government Debt to Exceed U.S. Economy," *Washington Times* (February 14, 2011), at: http://www.washingtontimes.com/news/2011/feb/14/debt -now-equals-total-us-economy/.

20. Robert Samuelson, "We've Promised More than We Can Deliver," *Newsweek* (April 11, 2011).

21. Strictly speaking, the Fed increases the money supply, and the U.S. Treasury mints coins. But this doesn't change anything significant in our discussion.

22. See Adam Fergusson, *When Money Dies: The Nightmare of Deficit Spending, Devaluation, and Hyperinflation in Weimar Germany* (New York: PublicAffairs, 2010).

23. John Maynard Keynes, *The Economic Consequences of the Peace*, pp. 235–248. Quoted in John Tamny, "Book Review: Adam Fergusson's *When Money Dies*," *RealClearMarkets* (May 12, 2011), at: http://www.realclearmarkets .com/articles/2011/05/12/book_review_adam_fergussons_when_money _dies_99016.html.

24. Alexis de Tocqueville, "What Sort of Despotism Democratic Nations Have to Fear" (Section 4, Chapter 6), *Democracy in America*. The entire text is available online, at: http://xroads.virginia.edu/~Hyper/DETOC /toc_indx.html.

ADDITIONAL RESOURCES

1. MoneySKILL (American Financial Services Association), at: http://www .afsaonline.org/financial_literacy/moneyskill.cfm.
2. *Common Sense Economics*, by James D. Gwartney, Richard L. Stroup, Dwight R. Lee, and Tawni H. Ferrarini (New York: St. Martin's Press, 2010).
3. Jay W. Richards, *Money, Greed, and God: Why Capitalism Is the Solution and Not the Problem* (San Francisco: HarperOne, 2009).
4. Henry Hazlitt, *Economics in One Lesson, 50th Anniversary Edition* (Birmingham, AL: Laissez Faire Books, 2008).
5. Arthur C. Brooks, *The Road to Freedom; How to Win the Fight for Free Enterprise* (New York: Basic Books, 2012).
6. Rev. Robert Sirico, *Defending the Free Market: The Moral Case for a Free Economy* (Washington, DC: Regnery, 2012).
7. George Gilder, *Wealth and Poverty, 30th Anniversary Edition* (Washington, DC: Regnery, 2012).
8. George Gilder, *Knowledge and Power: The Information Theory of Capitalism and How It Is Revolutionizing Our World* (Washington, DC: Regnery, 2013).
9. Peter J. Wallison, *Bad History, Worse Policy: How a False Narrative About the Financial Crisis Led to the Dodd-Frank Act* (Lanham, MD: Rowman & Littlefield/AEI Press, 2013).
10. Adam Fergusson, *When Money Dies: The Nightmare of Deficit Spending, Devaluation, and Hyperinflation in Weimar Germany* (New York: PublicAffairs, 2010).

ACKNOWLEDGMENTS
AND SOURCES

There were many people who provided valuable help for this book, some of them as keen editors, some as research assistants, and some as valuable sources of nonpublic information. I am grateful to all of them. I would especially like to thank my friend Jonathan Witt for editorial help with rough drafts, and Louisa Gilder and George Gilder, who provided excellent editorial help on the full manuscript. Thanks also to Bruce Chapman and Scott Powell, who provided valuable insights, and to Dr. Harold Black, for his careful reading of certain sections on finance. Finally, a special thanks to my wife, Ginny, who tolerated conversations about such spine-tingling subjects as mortgage-backed securities and option ARM loans.

Unfortunately, because of the sensitive nature of this book, many of those who have helped me have asked to remain anonymous. The value of their assistance has been profound. I have interviewed and had access to individuals with firsthand knowledge of the actions of the Consumer Financial Protection Bureau, the Center for Responsible Lending, and various activist meetings and campaigns. Whenever possible, I have provided public references in the endnotes to substantiate my claims. In some cases, however, the sources must remain confidential.

With a book like this, which is full of facts and figures, some unintentional errors and glitches may remain, for which I take full responsibility. Please check InfiltratedtheBook.com for any corrections after publication.

INDEX

ABOUT THE AUTHOR

Jay W. Richards, PhD, is coauthor of the *New York Times* bestseller *Indivisible* and author of *Money, Greed, and God*, which won a Templeton Enterprise Award. He is the Distinguished Fellow at the Institute for Faith, Work & Economics, and a Senior Fellow at the Discovery Institute.

He is also executive producer of several television documentaries, including *The Call of the Entrepreneur* and *The Birth of Freedom*.

Richards's articles and essays have been published in the *Harvard Business Review, Washington Post, Wall Street Journal, Investor's Business Daily, National Review, Washington Times, Philadelphia Inquirer, Huffington Post, American Spectator*, and a wide variety of other publications.

His work has been covered in the *New York Times, Washington Post, Wall Street Journal, Washington Times, Nature, Science, Astronomy, Physics Today, Chronicle of Higher Education, American Enterprise, Congressional Quarterly Researcher*, and *American Spectator*.

Dr. Richards has lectured at academic conferences and universities in the U.S., Europe, and Asia; at numerous public policy meetings; and to members of the U.S. Congress and congressional staff.

Dr. Richards has a PhD, with honors, in Philosophy and Theology from Princeton Theological Seminary. He also has an MDiv (Master of Divinity) and a ThM (Master of Theology).

He recently moved with his wife and children to northern Virginia.